ENVIRONMENTAL LAW FOR NON-LAWYERS

ENVIRONMENTAL LAW FOR NON-LAWYERS

by

DAVID B. FIRESTONE, ESQ.
Professor of Law
Vermont Law School

DR. FRANK C. REED
Lecturer
Botany Department
University of Vermont

ANN ARBOR SCIENCE
THE BUTTERWORTH GROUP

PREFACE

A few years ago, I became interested in communicating an understanding of the law to people who are not lawyers but whose professional work involves substantial contact with certain areas of the law. It is my belief that there is no need for law to be a mystery understood only by lawyers, and that an understanding of the law by non-lawyers would provide a healthier climate for critical analysis of the law. Sound critical analysis and an understanding of the objectives of the law would hopefully lead to meaningful changes where the law is not doing a good job, as well as less resistance to compliance with the law where it is doing a good job. These beliefs have led me to participate in various educational activities for non-lawyers during the last few years.

My primary teaching area, as a law school professor and as a teacher of non-lawyers, has been environmental law. I have presented numerous seminars and lectures to non-lawyers from industry and government whose jobs involve environmental law. The feedback from these people has indicated that they have benefited greatly from being exposed to environmental law in language that non-lawyers can easily understand. I hope this book will further my goal of providing an understanding of environmental law to those who administer it or live under it. Although Frank and I believe this book will also be useful to lawyers who do not specialize in the practice of environmental law and who want an overview of the area, our primary addressees are those people who have not had formal legal training. The book will therefore provide the reader with a basic discussion of some general legal concepts as well as environmental law topics. These concepts will be discussed in the context of specific environmental subject areas, e.g., solid waste disposal; however, the reader should be aware that a legal concept discussed in a solid waste context may also be applicable to other subject areas, such as noise pollution or control of radiation hazards.

Before beginning, let me note what we will not be doing in this work. Our role will be that of teachers rather than of advocates. We do not

v

view our job as an effort to convince the reader of what is the right or wrong position on any environmental issue. Our job will be to present arguments for the alternative positions, and, although it is inevitable that our biases will make themselves known, we do not crusade for a particular point of view.

David B. Firestone

A long time ago, I used to go and play in the woods near our house. Today, those woods are covered by tract homes, and the forest floor is now lawn. Every time I pass by this area, I wonder why my childhood playground had to be developed. Then I remember that there are more people on earth now than there were back then, and people do have to live someplace. But, I wonder when this growth will level off so some forest playgrounds will remain.

Later in my life (1969), while visiting Buffalo, New York, I stopped to buy some gasoline. The "rotten egg" odor of hydrogen sulfide was at once recognizable in the air, so I asked the gas station attendant how he could stand the smell, and he said, "What smell?" This encounter, along with numerous other experiences, left me aware of the fact that environmental problems do exist and that something ought to be done to control or eliminate them.

Over the years, I came to understand what could be done about such problems. The "answer" appeared to lie in environmental law coupled with environmental awareness. What is presented here is an attempt to pass along to you the awareness of, and the reasoning behind, the current regulation of perceived environmental problems. It is hoped that this effort will give you a perspective on the issues.

Frank C. Reed

ACKNOWLEDGMENTS

The authors wish to express their thanks to Vermont Law School for its cooperation and assistance in the preparation of this book. Special thanks go to Professor Les Peat, Librarian at Vermont Law School, to Rubina Benson, Sue Burns and Ruth Ford for their highly competent work on the manuscript, and to Barbara Harvey for her assistance with the drawings.

Firestone   **Reed**

David B. Firestone is Professor of Law at Vermont Law School, where he has been specializing in the field of Environmental Law for eight years. Prior to teaching law, he was an attorney with the United States Department of Housing and Urban Development. He was also an engineer with the Ford Motor Company and Douglas Aircraft. Mr. Firestone has presented numerous seminars and lectures before industry and professional groups and is thus experienced in providing knowledge of law to non-lawyers. He is a member of the Vermont and Massachusetts Bars and received his JD from Harvard Law School and a BS in Mechanical Engineering from Wayne State University.

Frank C. Reed received his BS from the State University of New York at Oswego. He then taught high school biology, chemistry, earth science, genetics and geometry in Central Square, New York. Subsequently, he received an MS in Biology and a PhD in Botany from Michigan State University. Dr. Reed has authored numerous papers in ecological journals and has recently authored papers concerning acid precipitation and clean air. He is currently a lecturer in the Botany Department at the University of Vermont and is also an environmental consultant. Dr. Reed is doing field experimental work on acid precipitation at the University of Vermont.

To our parents for the
environment they provided.

CONTENTS

CHAPTER 1

ENVIRONMENTAL LAW – To What Does It Apply? Do We Need It? Where It Comes From. How To Find the Law.

A. TO WHAT DOES IT APPLY?

Everyone knows what the environment is and that it should be protected, right? Not necessarily. Most people would be hard pressed to define what the environment is. In a theoretical sense, the environment could be said to be the occupation of space through time by definables. Or, the environment could be defined as that which is around us throughout our lifetime. The environment includes air, water, land, buildings, flowers, snakes, snails and even puppy dog tails. The environment is everything. The question which really needs addressing is how the environment is organized, since that must be examined prior to taking any steps to control or influence the environment.

For our purposes, let us consider the individual of a species as the least complex unit of organization. This is like saying that the person sitting next to you is an individual of the species called man. All the individuals of the species called man taken collectively constitute a unit called the species population. The aggregate of all species populations is called the community, while the community with the attendant abiotic factors (things that aren't alive) is called the ecosystem. This scheme is presented diagrammatically in Figure 1. Also, at this point, it might be helpful to realize that as the complexity of any system increases, the ability to define cause-effect relationships decreases. For example, with respect to the economy and the issue of acid rain, it is easier to define the economic cause-effect relationship between acid rain and an individual farmer raising a specified crop than the economic cause-effect relationship between acid rain and all farmers raising all crops. In the first case, the

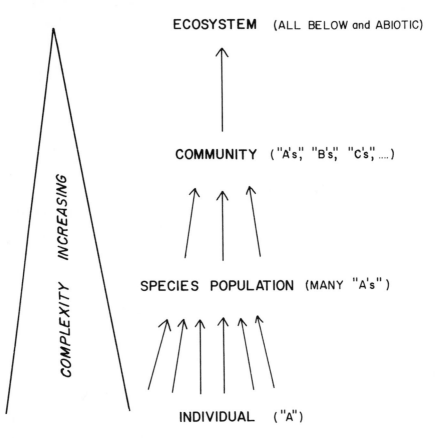

Figure 1.   A scheme to help understand one view of how the environment is put together.

question of cause-effect is at the individual level, while the second cause-effect relationship is sought at the species population level. In addition, it would be easier to define the cause-effect relationship between acid rain and farming than to define the cause-effect relationship between acid rain and all business enterprises which would include not only farming, but also steel production, fishing and automobile manufacturing. The greater the diversity of any system, the more difficult it becomes to define ultimate cause-effect relationships that may be detrimental, since what may cause a negative effect on one population may cause a positive effect on another. Furthermore, the effect that is being investigated will often greatly influence any policy decision being made. In other words, if we want to know the effects of acid rain on the economy, the answer may be much different from the effects of acid rain on human health and survivorship and, therefore, any decisions for action will probably be different depending on what effect is being investigated.

At this point, an example of what one might consider the environment to be is in order. To illustrate this, consider Figure 2, along with the following narrative. Suppose you are A, alone (notion 1), and you generate a waste to an external environment, rather than "your" environment. If there are not too many A's, then no one will notice or it will be someone else's problem. Now suppose that all the A's together (species population) collectively send a waste to an external environment (notion 2). If there are not too many A's, the "problem" will go unnoticed by the A's until there are a lot of A's. If the A's together with all the species populations (community) produce a common waste, the waste could still

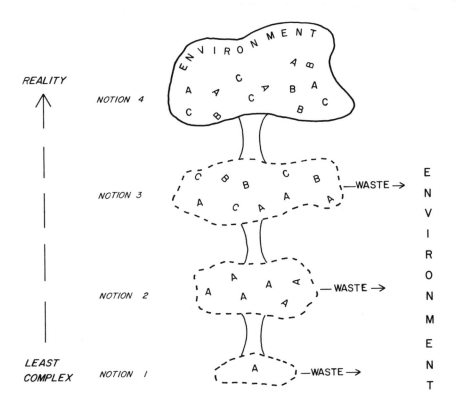

Figure 2. Waste Disposal? You can't always put everything someplace else.

go to an external environment and not be a "problem" (notion 3) if a large enough external environment exists; however, if we take into account all the species populations, it is highly unlikely that there can be an external environment. The A's, B's and all the other species are no longer able to find an external environment and consequently are putting a common waste directly into the environment of which they are a part — the ecosystem (notion 4). It is in this sense, the ecosystem as a whole, that the definition of environment and the questions of whether or not to control or influence it must ultimately be considered.

B. DO WE NEED IT?

The growth of environmental law has been phenomenal in recent years. The degree of governmental regulation with respect to the environment has multiplied many times and has expanded to cover many, many subject areas. This portion of the chapter will consider why there has been this tremendous surge of interest in environmental matters and whether the massive network of governmental regulation which has resulted is justified. We will then continue by setting aside, in part, the question of what the involvement of the law should be with respect to the environment, and devote the bulk of this book to an analysis of what the law is and what it means to business, to industry, to people who work for governmental bodies, and to individuals in their everyday lives.

Our analysis of what the law is will include both private law and public law control mechanisms. The private law mechanism usually consists of the bringing of lawsuits by individuals or corporations. These suits ask a court for relief without the request for relief being based on any action of a legislative body. For example, property owners might ask a court to prohibit a factory from polluting the air in their neighborhood because such pollution constitutes a nuisance which a court will act against even in the absence of federal or state air pollution control statutes. The public law mechanism, on the other hand, operates when a governmental body takes some form of initiative, such as enacting legislation. The spectrum of governmental initiatives includes actions such as prohibitions, permit requirements and educational efforts. Examples include: Congress prohibiting the manufacturing of a chemical; a state legislature requiring that a permit be obtained before a factory may discharge a pollutant into a river; or a city council establishing a publicity campaign to educate the public to voluntarily conserve gasoline.

Having noted some types of environmental control mechanisms which are available for use, let's begin by moving back a step and considering one series of arguments for and against strict governmental control of the environment in an attempt to see how people have reached different conclusions when answering the question: Do we need environmental controls at all and, if so, to what degree?

In 1972, a study called *The Limits to Growth* was published by a group of researchers from MIT.[1] Using the discipline of system dynamics and employing computer technology, they attempted to determine what future patterns of growth might look like, what limits there might be on such growth, and what the results of various patterns of growth might mean to mankind. Concerning patterns of growth, the study found that parameters such as population and industrial production exhibit the characteristic of exponential growth, i.e., growth which increases at a constant percentage rate and therefore increases numerically faster and faster (Figure 3). As one example, consider the meaning of Figure 3, assuming a 10% growth rate and an initial quantity at the beginning of Year 1 of 1000 units:

End of Year 1	$1000 + 10\%$ of 1000	=	1100
(Year 1 Growth = 100)			
End of Year 2	$1100 + 10\%$ of 1100	=	1210
(Year 2 Growth = 110)			
End of Year 3	$1210 + 10\%$ of 1210	=	1331
(Year 3 Growth = 121)			
* * *	* * *		* * *
End of Year 7	$1771 + 10\%$ of 1771	=	1948
(Year 7 Growth = 177)			

Thus, in seven years, 1000 units has become nearly 2000 units and, in another seven years (the doubling period for a 10% growth rate), we end up with nearly 4000 units. If the growth rate were reduced to 4%, the doubling period would be increased to eighteen years.

The second part of the "Limits to Growth" thesis is that some necessary resources are finite, for example, arable land or pollution absorption ability. When those finite resources (limits) are imposed on an exponential growth pattern, the "Limits to Growth" model predicts that the actual behavior of the growth parameters would be in the nature of catastrophic decline. Thus, to use population as an example, when exponential population growth reaches the finite limit of arable land, the result is famine and a massive population decrease (Figure 4). If catas-

---

1. Meadows, D. H., et al. *The Limits to Growth* (New York: Signet, 1972).

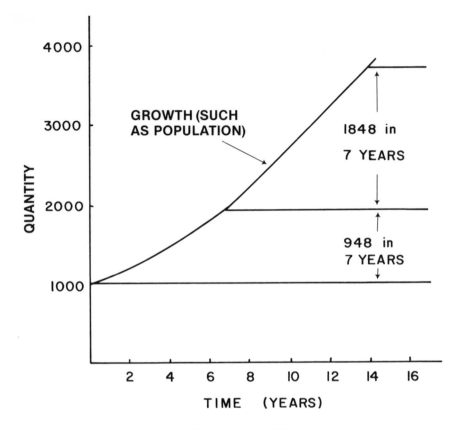

Figure 3.   Exponential growth at a 10% annual growth rate.

trophe is the result of reaching the finite limit rapidly (exponentially), what remedy is prescribed by those who agree with the "Limits" study? The remedy is to have strict control of variables such as population, pollution, and use of natural resources, and, since growth is taking place very quickly (exponentially), strict controls must be implemented very quickly.

The need for early action to avert catastrophe is best illustrated by a children's riddle: A lily plant grows in a pond and the plant doubles in size every day. If allowed to grow freely, it would completely cover the pond in 30 days, killing off all other forms of life. You decide not to worry about checking its growth until it covers half the pond. On what day will that be?[2] With the answer being the twenty-ninth day, there is

2. Ibid., p. 37.

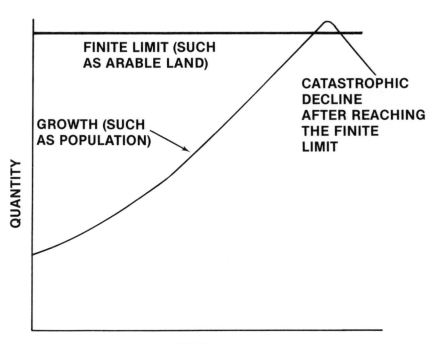

FINITE LIMIT (SUCH
AS ARABLE LAND)

CATASTROPHIC
DECLINE
AFTER REACHING
THE FINITE
LIMIT

GROWTH (SUCH
AS POPULATION)

QUANTITY

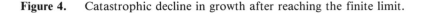

TIME

Figure 4.   Catastrophic decline in growth after reaching the finite limit.

only one day left for action to avert disaster. Maybe one could effectively control the lily plant in one day, but could population growth or pollution or petroleum use be effectively brought under control in a short time period? And, even if last minute control were possible, the drastic nature of the measures which would be necessary to achieve control, and the consequences of such measures, would be unpalatable and would argue in favor of taking less drastic action at an earlier time.

We should note in passing that the above discussion isolated variables like population and pollution; however, the "Limits" model does consider interrelationships of variables in great detail. Among the dozens of parameters built into the model are land yields, nonrenewable resources, industrial capital availability, pollution generation, and pollution absorption rates. As an example of the effects of the interrelationships of variables, consider population and pollution together. Increasing population might cause increasing pollution, but increasing pollution may cause a decrease in the rate of population growth due to possible deaths or shortened life spans from pollution-related diseases. The "Limits" model attempts to account for the interrelationships among variables and to present a "net behavior pattern" for each parameter evaluated.

Based on their evaluations, the proponents of the "Limits to Growth" hypothesis conclude that with current growth trends, the limits on growth will be reached within one hundred years and the likely result of reaching these limits will be a sudden, uncontrollable decline in population and industrial capacity. Furthermore, to return to our lily plant analogy, the point of no return (control possible without needing to use extremely drastic control measures) may be only one generation away. Those who accept the "Limits of Growth" type of reasoning would argue in favor of strict governmental controls with respect to the environment and would contend that implementation of those controls should not be delayed.

Having considered one theory with conclusions favoring strict environmental control, let's give equal time to those who are not convinced of the need for governmental regulation of our environment by presenting some of the arguments which characterize the "Limits" advocates as "prophets of doom."[3]

One challenge to the "Limits" theory attacks the concept of finite limits. For example, it may be argued that arable land is not finite in amount since technology can increase not only the number of arable acres (by methods such as irrigation), but also technology can increase productivity through means such as the use of new fertilizers or new varieties of plants. Similarly, technology can increase the availability of resources — petroleum from oil shale; freshwater from seawater. The concept of finite limits may thus be said to be illusory.

The "Limits" proponents might contend that while technology can indeed increase the magnitude of the limits, there still are finite limits, just at a higher level. The result is merely a brief delay in reaching the crisis point (Figure 5). The critics' response might be that if the growth parameters increase exponentially, technology can also make the limiting parameters increase exponentially. If a "limiting" parameter increases at a rate faster than growth demands, the result is divergence between the limiting parameter and the growth parameter such that no crisis point is ever reached (Figure 6). If the limiting variable increases more slowly than growth demands, then convergence occurs and there is a crisis; however, the crisis point would only be reached when the curves converge, which may be in the very distant future and beyond the level of reliability of our tools of prediction (Figure 7). Thus, those who do not accept a "Limits to Growth" type of reasoning would contend that there is no coming environmental catastrophe to worry about, and, while

---

3. Kaysen, C. "The Computer That Printed Out W*O*L*F," *Foreign Affairs,* 50:660–668 (1972).

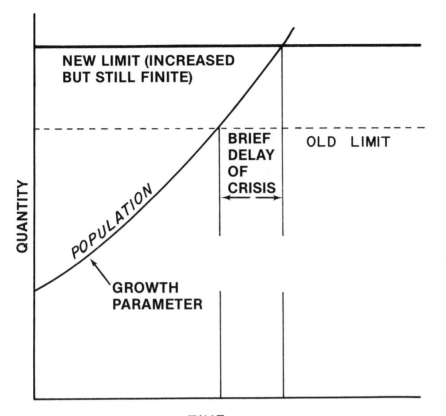

Figure 5.   Brief delay of crisis.

environmental concerns and the effects of growth should be considered, there is no need for strict governmental controls in areas such as pollution, use of natural resources, or population.

A second challenge to the "Limits" theory might be to attack the concept of catastrophe itself. If may be argued that there are social mechanisms which work in a manner such that as the "limit" is approached, natural decreases in the growth rate take place to keep the system below the limit. For example, as the use of a particular metal grows toward the limit of its availability (i.e., less and less is available due to past use), the price of the metal will rise and the use will taper off with either the introduction of substitutes, or with the less important or inefficient uses being abandoned (Figure 8). The result of the operation of these natural social mechanisms is that growth will not continue to a catastrophic collision

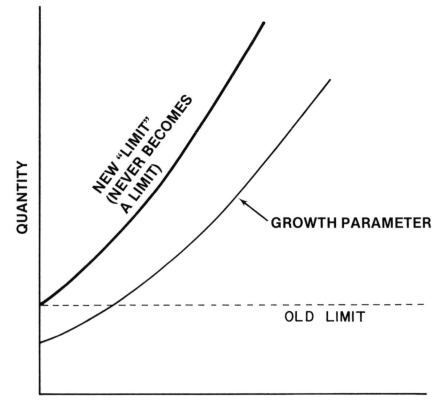

Figure 6.   Scenario of never reaching a crisis.

with a limit to growth, and thus, while limited environmental controls to improve day-to-day living might be justified, there is no need for immediate, strict governmental curtailment of economic growth to avert catastrophe.

The issue of whether one believes in the prophecy of the "Limits to Growth" thesis or dismisses the thesis based on arguments such as those noted above is relevant to one's belief concerning the role of government with respect to environmental issues. Should government take no action at all on behalf of environmental protection; should it take mild action such as educating the public toward voluntary conservation of resources; should it take firm action such as imposing actual limits on the amounts of a pollutant in the air; or should it take drastic measures to stop industrial growth?

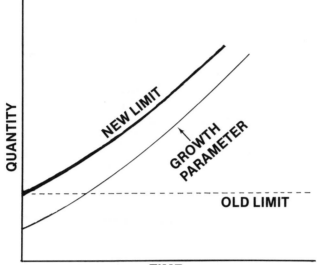

Figure 7.   Scenario of long delay in reaching a crisis.

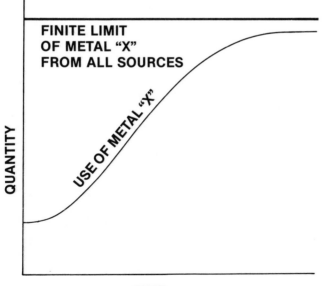

Figure 8.   Leveling off of growth as the finite limit of growth is approached.

Having considered the issue of whether legislative environmental controls are needed, let's briefly note two contrasting points of view on how to regulate various types of activities affecting the environment. Consider the hypothetical "pure economist" vs. the hypothetical "pure ecologist." While both are concerned with the environment, the economist would tend to balance environmental concerns with the economic benefits to be derived from an activity and allow environmental harm when it is outweighed by the economic benefits. On the other hand, the ecologist's tendency is to allow activities only if they are not detrimental to the environment: activities which are detrimental to the environment should be banned regardless of their economic benefit.[4] Diagrammatically, the resulting legislative alternatives would be:

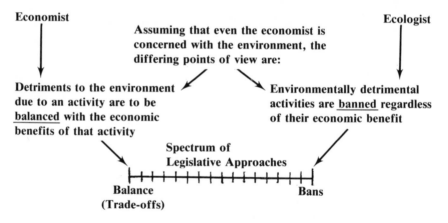

Of course, there is a spectrum between the legislative poles of always balancing benefits and detriments (allowing trade-offs), and of always banning detrimental activity. The type and magnitude of a particular environmental problem are relevant to where on that spectrum our legislatures should place themselves. Is the environmental problem one of physical health or mostly one of aesthetics? Is a health problem one which has proven, drastic consequences for large numbers of people or is the health problem speculative, relatively minor with respect to effects, or one involving very few people? Also quite relevant to where on the legislative spectrum a particular legislature will place itself is the degree of governmental control which is politically saleable. How many people would have favored a total shutdown of our automobile plants (with the

4. Heller, W., "Coming to Terms With Growth and the Environment," In *Energy, Economic Growth, and the Environment,* S. Schurr, Ed., 3:4–29 (1971).

resulting unemployment and economic decline) because the automakers could not meet the requirements of the Clean Air Act? The 1977 extension of the Clean Air Act deadlines on automakers was a trade-off clearly mandated by our political process. As we consider various pieces of environmental legislation, we will see that many are quite balance-oriented but some provisions are on the "ban" side of the spectrum.

With the above introduction, we will leave for the reader's determination the question of whether we need government-imposed environmental controls and, if so, where on the balance/ban spectrum of legislative approaches our government should be on any particular environmental issue. Regardless of our individual viewpoints on what should be the degree of involvement between government and the environment, we do have a substantial body of environmental law in existence at the federal, state, and local levels, and it is to the question of what the law is that we now turn our attention. Let us then begin to consider what the law is by first looking at the sources of power for governmental regulation of the environment.

C. WHERE IT COMES FROM

The basic source of federal power with respect to the environment is found in Article I, Section 8 of the United States Constitution (the Commerce Clause) which vests in Congress the power "to regulate Commerce. . .among the several States. . . ." Historically, this granting to the federal government of the power to regulate interstate commerce (as contrasted to intrastate commerce) was based largely on the idea of preventing states from enacting laws which, although they might be beneficial to one state, would have a detrimental effect on the economic system of the new nation. Actions which had been taken by individual states, such as discriminating against goods produced in other states, resulted in adverse economic effects on other states and on the nation as a whole. These types of actions contributed significantly to the weakness the country experienced under the Articles of Confederation. The new Constitution sought to remedy that weakness by giving Congress the authority to regulate interstate commerce.

Although the words have not changed, the past 200 years have seen massive expansion of the scope of the Commerce Clause from what was likely its originally contemplated function. That expansion, in the nature of broad powers claimed by Congress, has been found by the courts to be within Congress' power under the Constitution, and today, Congress' power is said to include not only the regulation of interstate commerce, but also activities carried on wholly within one state but which have effects on interstate commerce. Clearly, a natural gas pipeline from one state to others is a matter of interstate commerce and therefore, environmental regulation with respect to the pipeline is within the federal power, but what about local rubbish disposal? Consider the following chain of events: the disposal of rubbish at a local disposal site might lead to runoffs after rains; such runoffs might pollute a lake; polluted lake waters have fewer sport fish in them; fewer sport fish means fewer fishermen; fewer fishermen buy less gasoline and fishing equipment; gasoline and fishing equipment are items produced and marketed in interstate commerce. Thus a rubbish disposal activity which is wholly within one state may have an effect on interstate commerce. Since Congress has been found to have the authority under the Commerce Clause to regulate activities which affect interstate commerce, Congress has the authority, if it chooses to use it, to regulate local rubbish disposal.

One might contend that the effect on interstate commerce due to what happens at one local dump in rural New England is quite small and that Congress' control does not extend to this small dump. The United States Supreme Court answered that argument in the context of a farmer who was growing wheat for consumption on his own farm but in an amount in excess of his quota under federal legislation. The Court found that his excess production resulted in reduced demand for wheat in the marketplace and, while the farmer's "contribution to the demand for wheat may be trivial by itself...his contribution, taken together with that of many others similarly situated, is far from trivial."[5] The concept of Congress' power including activities which affect interstate commerce, together with the finding that small effects may be regulated since they are large when viewed cumulatively, indicates that the courts have given us a very broad interpretation of Congress' power under the Commerce Clause. Just as the one small farmer was found to be under Congress' control, so could the one small dump in rural New England be subject to environmental regulation by the federal government pursuant to the power of Congress under the Commerce Clause of the United States Constitution.

In addition to regulation at the federal level, there exists extensive environmental regulation at the state and local levels of government. The source of power for environmental regulation at these levels is the "police power," the power to protect the public health, public safety and the general welfare. The police power is inherent in the sovereign which is the

---

5. *Wickard v. Filburn,* 317 U.S. 111, 127 (1942).

state, and is also delegated by the states to the local governments which the states create. There are limits on the exercise of the state's police powers, such as state constitutional prohibitions against the taking of private property without just compensation. It would be fair to say, however, that the police power gives quite broad authority to state and local governments to regulate with respect to environmental matters.

D. HOW TO FIND THE LAW

The law on a given question is sometimes unclear. For example, the language in a statute may be subject to more than one reasonable interpretation or there may be a conflict between two regulations which purport to control the same activity. In most situations, however, the law is quite clear if one can find it. Finding the law is largely a matter of understanding what the sources of the law are, being familiar with a few rather simple systems for gaining access to these sources, and going to a law library or other library which has basic legal materials. Table I is a shorthand version of the narrative description for finding the law which follows. Although this description may appear complex, if one proceeds a step at a time through the process while in the library, the complexity will rapidly disappear.

One major distinction to be made when considering the sources of law is that between the so-called common law and law by legislation. Law by legislation is law which has been enacted through the legislative process of any level of government. Congress' National Environmental Policy Act (NEPA), the Freshwater Wetlands Act of the State of New York, and the zoning ordinance of the Town of Barnard, Vermont are all examples of legislation. In contrast to legislation, the common law has often been referred to as judge-made law because courts have determined that the facts of a situation are such that they should provide a remedy even though there has been no legislative enactment. One example of common law action which is often used in environmental matters is the "nuisance" action. An activity of X which causes a substantial and unreasonable interference with Y's use and enjoyment of Y's land will constitute a common law nuisance and a court will provide a remedy for Y even though no legislation prohibits X's activity or provides Y with a remedy. Both the common law and legislative law exist at the state and federal levels. In Chapter 3, using aircraft noise as an example, we will consider what happens when there is a conflict between state or local law and federal law. A less complicated situation exists where there is a conflict

Table I. Where to Look for the Law (Primary Sources)

Level of Government	Location of Legislative Law	Location of Administrative Law (Regulations)	Location of Common Law and Interpretations of Legislative and Administrative Law
Federal	United States Code United States Code Annotated United States Statutes at Large United States Code Service	Code of Federal Regulations Federal Register	aUnited States Reports (U.S.) Supreme Court Reports—Lawyers' Edition Supreme Court Reporter (S. Ct.) bFederal Reporter (F. or F.2d) cFederal Supplement (F.Supp.) Federal Administrative Agency decisions in publications such as the Public Utilities Reports.
State	(Name of State) Statutes	State Administrative Codes and State Administrative Regulations	dRegional Reporters State Reporters State Administrative Agency decisions in widely varying types of publications
Local	(Name of Municipality) Ordinances	Local Administrative Regulations	Local Administrative agency decisions in widely varying types of publications

aUnited States Supreme Court.
bU.S. Circuit Courts of Appeals.
cU.S. District Courts.
dRegional Reporters report cases from many states in the region.

between legislation and the common law at the same level of government. In such a situation, the common law is overridden by the will of the legislative process.

Federal legislative law (also known as "statutory law") is enacted by the Congress. At the end of each session, all of the legislation enacted in that session is compiled and published in chronological order in the *United States Statutes at Large.* While these volumes have subject indexes, they are not cumulative, and it would therefore be necessary to search through many volumes to find all of the statutes relating to a given topic. The federal statutes have therefore been codified, which means that they are arranged in a subject-oriented manner under fifty broad topics called titles. The official codification, which is called the United States Code (U.S.C.), is revised every six years and is updated between revisions by annual hardbound supplements. The two major lawbook publishers, West Publishing Company and Lawyers' Cooperative Publishing Company, publish unofficial versions known as United States Code Annotated (U.S.C.A.) and United States Code Service (U.S.C.S.), respectively. Both of these sets are updated by the issuance of annual "pocket parts"—supplemental pamphlets which fit into pockets at the back of the hardbound volumes. U.S.C.A. and U.S.C.S. are more useful than the official codification because, in addition to the statutory language, they contain references to court decisions and other valuable research aids. If one wanted to find the provisions of NEPA, the National Environmental Policy Act of 1969, one might look in the "Popular Name Table" of U.S.C.A. and find that NEPA is PL 91–190, Jan. 1, 1970, 83 Stat. 852 (Title 42, §§ 4321, 4331–4335, 4341–4347). NEPA is thus Public Law 91–190 which appears at volume 83 of the *United States Statutes at Large,* beginning on page 852. The provisions of NEPA also appear in Title 42 of the U.S.C., U.S.C.A. and U.S.C.S. in sections 4321, 4331–4335 and 4341–4347. Other access methods are possible depending on what you know and what you are seeking. For example, if the popular name were unknown but the subject matter were known, one might look in the index of U.S.C.A. under "Environmental Policy" in order to find provisions concerning the subject matter. Once the above-mentioned books are picked up and inspected, finding federal statutory law is quite simple; however, care must be taken to be sure that the law you find is up to date. This is done by checking the supplement volume of U.S.C. or the "pocket part" updates which are found in the backs of the volumes of U.S.C.A. and U.S.C.S.

State statutes may be found using similar tools in the state statute books which are published individually by each state and are once again readily obtainable in the libraries. Local legislative law is usually available at libraries in the local geographic area or through the local government unit itself.

When we come to finding the common law, the locating system is not much different from that used in finding legislative law. The basic structure and relationship of the federal and state court systems are shown in Figure 9. At both the federal and state level, court decisions are arranged and cited on a chronological basis by volume and page number in a "reporter" which contains the decisions of a particular court. United States Supreme Court decisions may be found in the United States Reports (U.S.), the Supreme Court Reporter (S.Ct.), or the Lawyers' edition of the Supreme Court Reports (Law. Ed.). Lower federal court decisions are found in the Federal Reporter (Fed. or F. and F. 2d for the later second series of the Federal Reporter) if they are United States Circuit Court of Appeals cases and in the Federal Supplement (F.Supp.) if they are United States District Court cases. State court decisions appear in regional reporters such as the North Eastern Reporter (N.E.) and the Pacific Reporter (P.) as well as in official State Reporters such as the Vermont Reports. It should be noted that while legislation is enacted through the legislative process and the common law is made by courts without action by the legislature, courts become involved with legislation

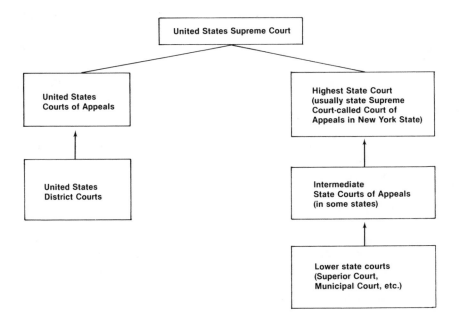

Figure 9.   The court structure.

by virtue of their role as interpreters of legislation. Thus, the fourth column of Table I shows the location of both the court decisions involving the common law and those decisions which provide interpretations of legislative law. Court decisions which contribute to the body of common law and those which interpret legislative law are all reported together and are all cited in the same manner. As examples, the common law nuisance case of *Boomer v. Atlantic Cement Co.* is 257 N.E.2d 870, and *Calvert Cliffs Coordinating Committee v. Atomic Energy Commission,* a case which interprets NEPA, is 449 F.2d 1109. This means that the *Boomer* decision appears in volume 257 of the second series of the North Eastern Reporter and begins on page 870.

If one knows the citation of a case, finding the case is a one-step process. If one knows only the name of the case or if one does not know of a particular case but wishes to find cases about a given topic, the additional step of consulting a reference tool such as a digest or legal encyclopedia must be added. There is a *Federal Practice Digest* and there are other digests arranged by region (the *Pacific Digest*), by state (the *Vermont Digest*), and chronologically (the *Decennial* and *General Digests*). These digests provide brief abstracts of cases, as well as case names and citations, under numerous subject matter headings. An example of a digest abstract is shown in Figure 10. In addition, the digests contain tables of cases listed alphabetically. Therefore, if one knows the name of a specific case but not its citation, the citation can be found in these alphabetical tables. Legal encyclopedias such as *American Jurisprudence 2d* and *Corpus Juris Secundum* can provide one with general discussions of many topics and case citations relevant to those topics. By using these reference tools and their various indices, cases which discuss the topic of one's interest may be located. Figure 11 shows an encyclopedia entry.

Just as we noted with respect to legislation, care must be taken when reading court decisions to be sure to determine whether those decisions are still "good law" or whether they have been overruled or narrowed in applicability by later cases. The analogue to checking the "pocket parts" and supplements in the statute books is to check the cases you have read in the volume of *Shepard's Citations* that applies to the court that wrote the decision. *Shepard's* is organized by listing cases by volume and by the page number on which they begin. Under each case citation, all other cases which have cited the case being checked are listed by their volume and page numbers. Abbreviations are used to indicate whether the subsequent cases merely mention the case being checked, follow the case being checked as the controlling case (f), or whether the subsequent cases took other action such as reversing a lower court's decision when the case was appealed (r) or overruling the case in a subsequent case involving another

25.5   HEALTH & ENVIRONMENT   44 FPD 2d – 240

For later cases see same Topic and Key Number in Pocket Part

mented 337 F.Supp. 167, motion denied 458 F.2d 827, 148 U.S.App.D.C. 5.

Final Impact Statement must discuss any existing alternatives. National Environmental Policy Act of 1969, § 102(2)(C), 42 U.S.C.A. § 4332(2)(C).
 Natural Resources Defense Council, Inc. v. Morton, 337 F.Supp. 165, supplemented 337 F.Supp. 167, motion denied 458 F.2d 827, 148 U.S.App.D.C. 5.

25.5(1). Regulations in general.

U.S.Dist.Col.   1975. National Environmental Policy Act creates discreet procedural obligation on government agencies to give written consideration of environmental issues in connection with certain major federal actions and right of action in adversely affected parties to enforce that obligation. National Environmental Policy Act of 1969, § 102, 42 U.S.C.A. § 4332.
 Aberdeen & Rockfish R. Co. v. Students Challenging Regulatory Agency Procedures (S.C.R.A.P.), 95 S.Ct. 2336, 422 U.S. 289, 45 L.Ed.2d 191.

---

ronmental Policy Act of 1969, § 101(a), 42 U.S.C.A. § 4331(a).
 Sierra Club v. Morton, 514 F.2d 856, 169 U.S.App.D.C. 20, certiorari dismissed American Elec. Power System v. Sierra Club, 96 S.Ct. 1091, 424 U.S. 901, 47 L.Ed.2d 105, reversed Kleppe v. Sierra Club, 96 S.Ct. 2718; 427 U.S. 390, 49 L.Ed.2d 576.

"Federal action" within National Environmental Policy Act includes not only action undertaken by federal agency itself, but also any action permitted or approved by the agency. National Environmental Policy Act of 1969, §§ 101, 102, 42 U.S.C.A. §§ 4331, 4332.
 Sierra Club v. Morton, 514 F.2d 856, 169 U.S.App.D.C. 20, certiorari dismissed American Elec. Power System v. Sierra Club, 96 S.Ct. 1091, 424 U.S. 901, 47 L.Ed.2d 105, reversed Kleppe v. Sierra Club, 96 S.Ct. 2718, 427 U.S. 390, 49 L.Ed.2d 576.

C.A.D.C.   1975. National Environmental Policy Act's requirement that an agency consider alternatives to its actions which would

Figure 10.   Digest abstract sample.

§ 77   POLLUTION CONTROL   61A Am Jur 2d

§ 77. – Federal aid to highways.

Laws concerning federal aid in construction of highways[25] require full consideration of possible adverse environmental effects including air pollution and are required to be consistent with any approved plan for the implementation of any ambient air quality standard.[26] But highway construction cannot be nullified on the basis of inconsistency with such plans, where there is no approved implementation plan.[27]

Figure 11.   Encyclopedia entry.

situation (o). By "Shepardizing" the cases you read, you will be able to determine the current importance of that case as "the law" as well as find additional later cases which may discuss the topic in which you are interested. The *Shephard's* entries for the case abstract shown in Figure 10 (422 U.S. 289) are listed in the highlighted portion of Figure 12.

Having considered how to find the law as enacted through the legislative process and the common law as made by the courts, we should next consider a second major distinction in sources of law—the distinction between legislation and regulation. Legislation is the product of the legislative process and it is binding unless it is violative of a constitutional provision. Regulations are usually the product of the administrative agencies, and they have the force of law if there is legislation which authorizes the creation of the regulation and the regulation is consistent with what the legislation mandates. Just as legislation exists at various levels of government, regulations can also be developed at the federal, state and local levels. At the state and local levels there are different systems for publishing regulations depending on your location, and librarian assistance should be obtained. The system for finding federal regulations is easily described.

The permanent home of a federal regulation is in the Code of Federal Regulations (CFR). CFR is organized and cited by title and section numbers. Title 40 is Protection of Environment. Title 10 is Energy. 40 CFR § 39.100-39.150 sets forth the EPA's administrative implementation of the Federal Water Pollution Control Act with respect to loan guarantees for wastewater treatment works. CFR is completely revised once a year (one quarter of the titles are revised in each calendar quarter) and prior to finding its way into a revision of CFR, a new federal rule or regulation will appear in the Federal Register (Fed. Reg.) which publishes activities of the federal agencies on a chronological basis. The Federal Register is published each business day and the contents for the day are shown at the beginning of the issue. Cites to the Federal Register are by volume and page. For example, at 44 Fed. Reg. 26743, EPA established tolerance levels for some pesticides on barley and wheat. This May 7, 1979, Federal Register publication amended 40 CFR § 180.332 to include barley and wheat and their tolerance levels for the particular pesticide on the list of agricultural commodities contained in §180.332. Revisions of CFR which are published after May 7, 1979, will reflect the additions to the list; however, the tolerance levels contained in the Federal Register are effective even prior to their being incorporated into the next CFR revision. Administrative regulations may be interpreted by courts or by the agencies themselves. The various locations of interpretations of administrative law may be seen in column four of Table I.

In closing this section on how to find the law, brief mention should be made of some additional sources of information concerning environmental law. Most law schools publish law reviews either annually or more frequently. Articles and Notes in these periodicals usually provide in-depth analysis and commentary on various aspects of the law includ-

Vol. 422   UNITED STATES SUPREME COURT REPORTS

624F2d1376	d494FS[2]958	93McA738	Calif	477FS[1]600	d477FS[2]654	—391—	619F2d[1]1299
624F2d[2]1378	83FRD131	285M4486	164CaR536	q479FS86	d480FS[1]240	471FS[1]519	621F2d[1]547
d624F2d	f85FRD[2]632	285M4499	166CaR862	481FS[1]488	e481FS[2]1107		f622F2047
[¹1379	e1BRW[2]587	46NCA505	610P2d433	489FS1058	f481FS[1]1110	—395—	f622F2d275
e627F2d819	4BRW[2]303	118NH906	614P2d294	NY	f482FS[1]412	442US[1]93	622F2d[3]276
627F2d[2]946	362ICC88	49NY181	Fla	430S2d466	f482FS1687	j445US347	624F2d130
f470FS113	7411A1034	49NY189	382So2d692	FID§3.06	f482FS[2]687	j445US411	624F2d[1]144
f470FS155	42OrA294	Alk	Ind		484FS[2]296	j445US502	f624F2d[1]443
f470FS[1]1023	90Wis2d195	611P2d75	397NL585	—271—	f485FS[2]33	600F2d1236	624F2d[1]767
f470FS1039	Del	Calif	Kan	444US[1]242	486FS[2]38	605F2d1678	e624F2d1955
f470FS1259	412A2d346	160CaR918	608P2d956	612F2d[1]200	486FS[1]1124	606F2d1414	624F2d1266
f470FS[2]1261	Ill	162CaR138	Mich	e625F2d1680	487FS[2]1279	j607F2d[1]376	f625F2d934
471FS[1]889	393NL723	162CaR828	283NW863	472FS[1]674	490FS1289	616F2d[1]1001	625F2d[3]934
f471FS[1]910	Me	167CaR9	NJ	481FS488	9MJ76	620F2d1895	625F2d[5]943
f472FS[2]951	402A2d868	Colo	405A2d440	491FS[1]1223	100CA3d934	623F2d1116	f626F2d[4]662
e473FS[1]204	Mont	597P2d1037	Pa	AA§1.12	101CA3d304	627F2d1657	626F2d[1]1118
f473FS208	597P2d1153	Conn	414A2d53		25C3d328	472FS801	f626F2d1120
f473FS[2]375	Ore	418A2d919	65ABA923	—289—	26C3d867	472FS[1]1235	j626F2d1127
f473FS[2]697	600P2dd891	DC		442US[3]363	26C3d886	476FS[1]1016	627F2d[4]618
f474FS[2]454	W Va	404A2d530	—225—	442US[2]453	26C3d891	479FS489	470FS334
e474FS681	262SL760	407A2d577	439US[2]219	f442US[2]458	192Col474	480FS[1]802	470FS[1]1155
475FS[2]448	MFP§4.23	Ga	599F2d[3]509	598F2d119	194Col408	483FS550	470FS1284
f476FS278	FTCR§1.07	268SL397	599F2d1228	599F2d[5]1344	271Ind477	d483FS[1]555	471FS22
f477FS[2]892		Ill	601F2d[4]169	f599F2d[3]1345	91McA316	f486FS[1]191	f471FS686
477FS1032	—86—	394NL689	602F2d553	604F2d[1]1013	298NC476	493FS[1]1327	f471FS[4]698
f477FS[1]1167	603F2d[3]700	398NL599	604F2d801	604F2d[3]1090	83NJ306	83FRD[1]288	471FS[5]727
f477FS1254	604F2d[2]1148	408NL385	e605F2d[3]552	e606F2d[5]1056	486Pa503		f471FS[1]752
f477FS[2]1255	626F2d[2]554	La	f607F2d[4]320	607F2d[2]1229	Calif	—405—	471FS[2]752
f478FS[2]141	627F2d271	385So2d206	613F2d[4]1155	619F2d[3]241	158CaR378	440US[4]306	471FS[1]769

f478FS522	477FS1109	Md	619F2d[4]987	619F2d[5]1377	161CaR363	440US[4]587	472FS314
478FS671	93FTC816	403A2d1222	622F2d[4]936	625F2d[1]1074	161CaR567	j440US602	f472FS[4]1321
f480FS227	93FTC1017	404A2d268	j624F2d343	d626F2d1354	164CaR520	h441US[1]758	f474FS1259
f480FS893	93FTC1036	Mich	e624F2d654	626F2d[5]1358	164CaR532	j442US283	474FS[4]1332
f481FS[1]55	AA§3.14	287NW369	478FS374	471FS[3]144	164CaR535	442US[1]375	475FS[1]119
f481FS[2]56	FTCR§17.02	NM	484FS[4]1102	476FS[3]128	599P2d684	e443US[1]204	475FS[1]353
d481FS57	—151—	612P2d1314	d493FS[5]1336	476FS[2]129	610P2d417	j444US158	475FS[3]670
f482FS[2]396	441US19	NY	86FRD626	477FS[3]999	610P2d429	598F2d[1]437	475FS[1]1108
482FS[2]934	474FS[1]685	400NL347	7MJ564	d481FS[2]399	610P2d432	598F2d[2]437	f476FS[3]306
f482FS[2]1125	f480FS[1]432	400NL352	372Mas343	483FS[2]644	DC	598F2d1256	f477FS507
f482FS[2]1168	71FCC1026	424S2d407	94Nev148	485FS[3]834	403A2d310	599F2d334	f477FS[1]1080
e483FS[2]565	—171—	424S2d412	80NJ480	54FPC2329	Iowa	e600F2d[1]598	f477FS[2]1090
f485FS[2]68	600F2d[1]152	NC	80NJ486	352CC452	290NW341	e600F2d[2]599	477FS[1]1170
d485FS225	601F2d[1]932		Alk	352CC476	293NW579	600F2d759	477FS[3]1170
485FS[2]504	604F2d503	—184—	602P2d791	126MCC315	Mich	600F2d[1]1022	f478FS[1]460
f485FS875	609F2d[1]769	26C3d666	Ind	129MCC650	283NW736	600F2d[2]1022	478FS[3]996
f485FS997	610FSd[1]419	Calif	397NL1034	46NCA371	Mo	j600F2d1025	f478FS[1]1229
f485FS[2]1216	d613F2d[1]610	163CaR261	401NL338	94Wis2d275	603SW613	601F2d[1]1298	f479FS[4]35
f485FS[2]1295	615F2d[1]269	607P2d1285	403NL829	NC	NJ	602F2d[1]798	f479FS[1]112
e486FS[2]502	d618F2d	—205—	408NL1283	265SL905	416A2d386	603F2d[1]602	480FS545
487FS[4]19	[¹1211	601F2d[1]827	Iowa	Wis	NY	603F2d985	480FS[1]552
f487FS[2]305	618F2d[1]1240	607F2d1056	291NW348	288NW174	430S2d818	605F2d[1]459	480FS[1]683
487FS[2]577	622F2d[1]1100		Mass	—332—	NC	605F2d[1]1035	480FS1033
487FS[2]662			405NL980	439US443	259SL873	605F2d[1]1337	480FS1114
e487FS[2]1052			406NL710		Pa	606F2d804	f481FS[1]201

Figure 12.   Shepard's Citation entry example.

ing environmental law. Some law reviews have devoted themselves entirely to publication of articles relating to environmental matters. Law review articles are indexed in the *Index to Legal Periodicals* and in *Current Law Index* and may be found by author or by subject matter. For keeping up-to-date on changes in the law, numerous looseleaf services which provide information on environmental topics can be consulted. A few illustrative examples might be the *Environment Reporter* from the Bureau of National Affairs (BNA), *Energy Management* from the Commerce Clearing House (CCH), and the *Environmental Law Reporter* from the Environmental Law Institute (ELI). These contain material such as current developments in addition to statutory and regulatory material.

ADDITIONAL READINGS

Cohen, M. L. *Legal Research in a Nutshell* (St. Paul: West, 1978).

Council on Environmental Quality and Department of State. *The Global 2000 Report to the President* (Great Britain: Penguin Books, Ltd., 1982).

Fiebleman, J. K. "Theory of Integrative Levels," *Brit. J. Phil. Sci.,* 5:59–66 (1954).

Leopold, A. *A Sand Country Almanac* (New York: Ballantine Books Inc., 1949).

Meadows, D. H., D. L. Meadows, J. Randers and W. W. Behrens III. *The Limits to Growth* (New York: Signet Publishers, 1972).

Mesarovic, M. and E. Pestel. *Mankind at the Turning Point* (New York: Signet Publishers, 1974).

Odum, E. P. *Fundamentals of Ecology* (Philadelphia: W. B. Saunders Co., 1971).

Willson, M. F. "Ecology and Science," *Bull. Ecol. Soc.,* 62:4–12 (1981).

CHAPTER 2

NATIONAL ENVIRONMENTAL POLICY ACT (NEPA)

A. SUBSTANTIVE POLICIES, PROCEDURAL REQUIREMENTS AND THE EIS

Although NEPA[1] contains provisions which create the Council on Environmental Quality (CEQ) and require an annual Environmental Quality Report from the President to Congress, the most well known, most litigated, most harmful or most beneficial (depending on one's point of view), but clearly the most important single aspect of NEPA is the environmental impact statement (EIS) requirement. In contrast to other federal statutes which we will consider later, the primary addressees of this operative mechanism of NEPA are the agencies of the federal government — not individuals, not corporations and not states. We will see that these other entities may be greatly affected by NEPA because of relationships which they may have with the federal government; however, it is only "all agencies of the Federal Government" who are directed to include as part of their "major Federal actions significantly affecting the quality of the human environment, a detailed statement by the responsible official on — (i) the environmental impact of the proposed action. . . ."[2] Since NEPA applies to "all agencies of the Federal Government," an EIS may be required not only for activities like the Department of Transportation funding highway construction, but also when the Comptroller of the Currency considers the chartering of a bank.

NEPA's EIS requirement is a specific procedural step which federal

---

1. 42 U.S.C.A. § 4321 et seq.; PL 91–190, Jan 1, 1970, 83 Stat. 852.
2. PL 91–190, § 102.

agencies are directed to take. NEPA also makes some broad declarations, somewhat lacking in specificity, concerning the nation's environmental policy and goals and the federal government's responsibility for promoting and attaining them. The analysis of the distinction between NEPA's procedural requirements and its statements of substantive policy was presented in *Calvert Cliffs' Coordinating Committee v. Atomic Energy Commission.*[3] The distinction serves to define the role of the court system in the NEPA process—a process which is directed at the administrative agencies.

The substantive policies and goals of NEPA are found in § 101 of the Act and are broadly worded declarations such as Congress' desire to "promote the general welfare, to create and maintain conditions under which man and nature can exist in productive harmony..." and Congress' direction that the federal government act so that the nation may "fulfill the responsibilities of each generation as trustee of the environment for succeeding generations" and "assure for all Americans safe, healthful, productive, and aesthetically and culturally pleasing surroundings...."[4] The court, in *Calvert Cliffs',* noted that Congress directed that these substantive goals and policies be pursued by the federal government using "all practicable means." In contrast, Congress directed that the procedural requirement of an EIS, found in § 102 of the Act, was to be followed "to the fullest extent possible." Based on this difference in the language used by Congress in the two sections of the Act, the court found that the substantive aspects of the Act were directives to the agencies which allowed for flexibility and agency discretion and thus provided only a very limited role for the courts. With respect to the § 101 substantive aspects of NEPA, courts could only interfere with an agency decision when its decision was "arbitrary or clearly gave insufficient weight to environmental values." With respect to the § 102 procedural requirements, however, the court found that the language "to the fullest extent possible" was not highly flexible and that the language made the courts responsible to reverse agency decisions which were reached procedurally without the required consideration and balancing of environmental factors. Thus, if an agency failed to do an EIS where one was required, or did not do a legally sufficient EIS, or in some other way violated NEPA's relatively inflexible procedural directives to the federal agencies, the courts would reverse the agency's decision.

Even the very limited role for the courts that the *Calvert Cliffs'* case

---

3. 449 F.2d 1109 (1971).

4. PL 91–190, § 101.

recognized with respect to the substantive aspects of NEPA may be in some doubt. In the United States Supreme Court case of *Strycker's Bay Neighborhood Council v. Karlen,*[5] the dissenting opinion of Justice Marshall pointed out that earlier Supreme Court cases did not stand for the proposition that court review of agency action under NEPA is limited solely to determining whether the agency procedurally considered environmental consequences. Marshall said an agency decision must be set aside by the court if it is substantively arbitrary. The majority opinion in *Strycker's Bay* said in a footnote, however, that if the agency had acted arbitrarily, the court *might* agree that plenary review is warranted. The use of the word "might" can be interpreted to be less than a full commitment by the majority of the court to the position that arbitrary substantive decisions of agencies are to be set aside by the courts even if the agency has complied with NEPA's procedures. With respect to the procedural requirements of NEPA, however, it does seem quite clear that the courts have a significant reviewing role to play.

We should note carefully that while the procedural requirements of NEPA, including the preparation of an EIS, are not highly flexible, this does not mean that NEPA is requiring that environmental values not be sacrificed. Environmental values may be sacrificed under NEPA; all that NEPA requires is that environmental values be considered in the balance of the agency decision-making process. The substantive environmental concerns of § 101 are not exclusive goals of an agency and those concerns may, on balance, lose out. That is allowed under the flexible language of § 101, but the environmental concerns must be given consideration—that is inflexible. Viewed with respect to the balance/ban legislative approaches we referred to in Chapter 1, NEPA is a balance statute—no activity is banned, but environmental values must be balanced with the economic benefits of a proposed agency action. The EIS is the mechanism for reporting on the balancing process and it is the main procedural requirement of NEPA.

We have determined that the basic operative mechanism of NEPA is the EIS. Does this mechanism work? How does requiring a detailed statement of the environmental impact of a proposed action serve the purpose of fostering proper consideration for environmental values? First, the agency itself will have environmental concerns and information before it for the purpose of writing the EIS. This information will hopefully be considered by the agency, whereas prior to NEPA and the need to write an EIS, environmental information was often never even com-

---

5. 100 S. Ct. 497 (1980).

piled. Second, the EIS requirement seeks to bring the public and other agencies, in addition to the agency proposing to act, into the picture by informing them of environmental consequences and giving them an opportunity to comment on them and possibly come up with alternatives to the proposed action. Third, if others outside the agency are able to see the agency's statement of the justification for its decision spelled out in the EIS, an informal pressure is placed on an agency to make a rational decision and to include environmental considerations in that decision. The theory is that better decisions are made when "someone is watching."

The above logic supports Congress' decision to use the EIS mechanism as the procedural tool to implement its substantive policies involving environmental protection; however, there are many who contend that the procedural requirement of an EIS has little or no positive effect on the environment and is just another "red tape/legal technicalities/bureaucratic nightmare" standing in the way of those who seek to have government work to serve the interests of society. The basis of this position is that the preparation of an EIS is a time-consuming chore which adds large amounts of lead time and other economic costs to any project. Also, the EIS requirement allows a small number of people to tie up a project for long periods of time in a complex litigation process. These arguments might be made by people who would label themselves as being in favor of progress, economic growth, and development rather than being "environmentalists," but many "environmentalists" would join them in attacking the EIS process as undesirable. Some environmentalists claim that as agencies become accustomed to the EIS procedure and to what the courts require for compliance with that procedure, an agency can make any decision look reasonable on paper regardless of whether it is a good balance between the agency's program goals and NEPA's environmental goals. It is the opinion of these environmentalists that the only way for the § 101 substantive goals of NEPA to really be taken into account is for the courts, being independent bodies without any agency program goals, to be willing to take a close look at the substantive correctness of an agency decision rather than looking only at whether the § 102 procedures were followed. What is needed is for the courts to look more closely at whether an agency decision is right or wrong with respect to the environment rather than to only inquire whether the agency decision was "arbitrary or clearly gave insufficient weight to environmental values."[6] It is for you to determine whether you believe that the EIS is a sound mechanism for environmental protection, or that the EIS severely handicaps

---

6. *Calvert Cliffs'* at 1115.

agencies' efforts to work toward a better society, or that the EIS can only work to attain NEPA's substantive environmental goals if the courts take a more active role in watchdogging agency actions which affect those goals. The status of the law is that the EIS requirement does exist but, if the agency complies with the § 102 procedural steps, the courts will, at most, evaluate the substance of an agency decision to make sure it is not arbitrary with respect to its consideration of the environment.[7]

Having now considered the basic structure of NEPA as established by Congress and as interpreted in the *Calvert Cliffs'* case, let us digress and see how, in *Calvert Cliffs',* the Atomic Energy Commission ran afoul of the EIS requirement. In *Calvert Cliffs',* the AEC's procedure for licensing energy-producing facilities was challenged. The AEC made some quite reasonable arguments concerning how NEPA was supposed to be inapplicable to the fact situation in that case. Acceptance of those arguments might have narrowed NEPA's overall applicability and effect, but the AEC's reasonable arguments were rejected by the court. One can only speculate concerning whether that rejection (and perhaps a resulting broader interpretation of NEPA's scope) was in any way influenced by the following and possibly not-so-reasonable argument which the AEC made.

Under Section 102, copies of the EIS must "accompany" a proposal through the agency review process. The AEC adopted a literal definition of the word "accompany." With respect to some license application situations, the AEC had the EIS physically "accompany" the application, but the AEC rules precluded the EIS from being considered in the decision-making process of the licensing hearings. The court found that Congress did not intend by use of the word "accompany" to create a situation requiring physical proximity of the EIS without any requirement that it be considered by the decision-maker and that "the Commission's crabbed interpretation of NEPA makes a mockery of the Act."[8] The court was clearly outraged by the AEC's approach to its NEPA responsibilities. One may wish to consider what contribution, if any, has been made to the general proliferation of environmental controls and litigation by a few instances of agency or industry recalcitrance or lack of good faith in complying with existing environmental regulations. How much influence have the worst cases of lack of good faith had on the overall scheme of environmental controls?

---

7. *Environmental Defense Fund v. Corps of Engineers,* 470 F.2d 289, 298–300 (1972).

8. *Calvert Cliffs'* at 1117.

B. APPLICABILITY OF THE EIS REQUIREMENT – MAJOR FEDERAL ACTIONS

NEPA applies to all federal agencies; however, an EIS is not required every time an agency undertakes to do something. NEPA requires an EIS only for recommendations or reports on proposals for legislation and other "major Federal actions significantly affecting the quality of the human environment."[9] What are "major" actions and what actions are not major? What actions significantly affect the environment and what actions have insignificant effects? Let's begin with the words "significantly affecting." Different federal courts in different parts of the country have used different interpretations of these words, but, in general, the words have been interpreted broadly. For example, courts have decided that if a project "may cause a significant degradation"[10] or "could have a significant effect"[11] or "arguably will have an adverse environmental impact"[12] or has a "potentially significant adverse effect,"[13] an EIS is required.

The word "major" has also been given a broad interpretation by the courts and, in general, one could say that in close cases, courts have tended to find that NEPA applies and an EIS is required. Numerous different parameters, such as the amount of money to be spent, the geographical size of the area to be covered, and whether the project effects are long- or short-term, have been used to determine whether an action is major. The facts of a particular case are extremely important since they will determine the types of parameters which will be applied. The answer to the question of whether an action is major will depend on which parameters are used. Perhaps the best way to see what are and what are not major actions with significant effects is to list and compare some decided cases. No case would be needed to decide if NEPA's EIS provision applied to the trans-Alaskan pipeline, but an EIS was also required by the courts in the following less clear situations:

1. adoption of Department of Transportation regulations to increase accessibility of the handicapped to mass transportation;[14]

---

9. PL 91–190, § 102.

10. *Save Our Ten Acres v. Kreger,* 472 F.2d 463, 467 (1973).

11. *Minnesota Public Interest Research Group v. Butz,* 498 F.2d 1314, 1320 (1974).

12. *SCRAP v. U.S.,* 346 F.Supp. 189, 201 (1972).

13. *Hanly v. Kleindienst,* 471 F.2d 823, 831 (1972).

14. *American Public Transit Association v. Goldschmidt,* 485 F.Supp. 811 (1980).

2. a Department of Housing and Urban Development (HUD) loan of $3.5 million to construct a high-rise apartment building in an area containing no other high-rise buildings in Portland, Oregon;[15]
3. the promulgation of standards by the Department of Labor under the Occupational Health and Safety Act;[16]
4. participation of the United States in Mexican herbicide spraying of marijuana and poppy plants.[17]

In contrast, NEPA was found not to apply to:

1. an action by the Secretary of Transportation approving the crossing of an interstate highway by a huge strip-mining shovel;[18]
2. a HUD-insured loan of $3.7 million to construct a 272-unit apartment complex on 15 acres in Houston, Texas;[19]
3. a soil conservation service project deepening a natural drainage channel for 11 miles at a cost of $295,000.[20]

Let's compare the two HUD examples and analyze why the results with respect to the need for an EIS might have been different in the two cases. First, consider some possible explanations which are largely independent of the substance of the HUD cases. The two HUD cases were decided in different jurisdictions. Issues of interpretation of a statute like NEPA are usually decided by the Federal District Courts or the Federal Circuit Courts of Appeal. There are different courts in different areas of the country and they sometimes have different ideas on what the law is. Some, but not all, of these differences are resolved by the United States Supreme Court or by Congress. In the absence of a resolution of the conflict by one of these bodies, each lower court opinion is the law within the jurisdiction of that lower court even though the law may thus be different in different parts of the country. It is possible that even if the two HUD cases had had identical rather than similar facts, the U.S. District Court in Oregon may have interpreted the "major Federal action" test more broadly than the U.S. Fifth Circuit Court of Appeals in Texas and an EIS could have been required in Oregon but not in Texas.

Another possible explanation of differing results in similar cases might

---

15. *Goose Hollow Foothills League v. Romney,* 334 F.Supp. 877 (1971).

16. *Dry Color v. Dept. of Labor,* 486 F.2d 98 (1973).

17. *NORML v. Dept. of State,* 452 F.Supp. 1226 (1978).

18. *Citizens Organized to Protect the Environment v. Volpe,* 353 F.Supp. 520 (1972).

19. *Hiram Clarke Civic Club v. Lynn,* 476, F.2d 421 (1973).

20. *Simmans v. Grant,* 370 F.Supp. 5 (1974).

be that the cases were decided at different times. The country's mood on environmental protection changes and the mood of the courts also shifts with time. While the HUD cases do not represent time periods with great disparity in the nation's level of environmental concern (they were 1971 and 1973 cases), it would not be surprising to find an air pollution case with a given set of facts which was decided against industry in the early 1970s and a case with similar facts being decided in favor of industry in the energy shortage years of the 1980s.

Besides explanations based on different jurisdictions or different time periods, the results in the HUD cases can be reconciled because their facts are distinguishable. The dollar amounts in the two cases were nearly the same, but one was a HUD loan and thus involved dollars coming out of the federal treasury. The other case was a HUD-insured loan where the funds would come from private sources and the only time money would leave the federal treasury would be if the borrower defaulted in repaying the loan. This second situation arguably involves less in the way of direct federal action and thus might not be a major federal action. Another factual explanation might be that the case in Oregon which required an EIS was dealing with a high rise in an area with no other high rise buildings. Even though the case which did not require an EIS was a proposal to build 272 units on 15 acres, the site was in Houston, Texas, which is a city that has much in the way of land use inconsistency and little in the way of land use controls. What actions are major actions requiring an EIS and what actions are not major is often an "I know it when I see it" situation; however, the courts have tended to resolve the doubtful cases in favor of requiring an EIS.

Let's next turn to another part of the "major Federal action..." test and consider the word "human." Clearly the human environment involves things such as air pollution, water pollution and toxic chemicals in our food, but it has also been interpreted to include subjects such as housing, unemployment and crime.[21] Thus, the courts have again given a broad interpretation to the words used by Congress when they have considered the phrase "human environment." Nevertheless, NEPA does say "human" and an agency action which might have a severe effect on something in nature might not be covered by NEPA unless a substantial link to humans and their needs could be shown.[22] Opinions may differ

---

21. 471 F.2d 823.

22. Section 43.21C.030 of the Revised Code of Washington, Annotated.*

* The Washington State Environmental Policy Act, which is nearly a carbon copy of NEPA with words like "Federal" changed to "State," does not contain the word "human" but says "major actions significantly affecting the quality of the environment."

about whether the destruction of a unique habitat for a type of plant or fish is really a significant effect on the human environment, but we should recognize that, in NEPA, Congress' concern was not for the plant or the fish. While the plant or fish and its unique habitat may be protected under another statute such as the Endangered Species Act, if the habitat's destruction were not demonstrably connected to the human environment, NEPA might not apply and an EIS might not be necessary.

We have now considered the types of actions to which the NEPA substantive policies and the NEPA procedures apply — major actions significantly affecting the quality of the human environment — but only if they are major "Federal" actions. What then is a federal action? In answering this question, we will see that although NEPA is addressed to the agencies of the federal government and they are the ones from whom an EIS is required, the private sector and state and local governments may also be greatly affected by NEPA.

What are NEPA's effects on nonfederal entities? Certainly there are the economic costs of the EIS process and those costs are borne by all segments of society. Also, the EIS process may result in a substantial delay before a private company receives a license or permit which it needs to conduct its business or before a state or local government receives a federal grant. A less obvious effect of NEPA on nonfederal entities arises when action which is largely that of private business becomes "federal" because of the business' contact with the federal government and the private company is precluded from proceeding with its activity until a federal agency prepares its EIS. An example of this situation was a private developer of housing who had a HUD mortgage guarantee and interest grant. HUD could not provide its assistance until an EIS was filed, but the court also found the private developer could be enjoined from going forward with construction on his own property without HUD aid while HUD prepared its EIS. The court's theory for halting the private developer's action was that HUD's initial commitment to the developer made them partners in the undertaking, and, even though he was still only a potential recipient of HUD assistance, the developer had enough contact with HUD so that his action without HUD assistance could be stopped pending a HUD EIS.[23]

Yet another step down the road of far-reaching effects of NEPA can be seen by noting that certain business organizations must register with the Securities and Exchange Commission (SEC). The SEC has the authority to require these companies to disclose information to their investors. As part of the NEPA process (to which the SEC is subject since it is

---

23. *Silva v. Romney,* 473 F.2d 287 (1973).

a federal agency), the SEC was required to consider adopting environmental disclosure requirements for business organizations registering with the SEC.[24] Improper disclosure may mean a company is violating the securities law. Proper disclosure will possibly publicize some of a company's more controversial operations and have adverse effects on the company's image or even on its ability to sell its products or to raise capital. Thus, NEPA, which is addressed to federal agencies, can affect the private sector and nonfederal governmental bodies in numerous ways.

It should be noted that NEPA has had a substantial carryover effect on state efforts at environmental regulation. Many states require environmental impact statements by state agencies when those state agencies undertake a state project that will significantly affect the quality of the environment. While the applicability and comprehensiveness of the state requirements vary among states, some states require at the state level just what is required by NEPA for a federal project.

In summary, if a proposal is for a major federal action significantly affecting the quality of the human environment, NEPA requires the responsible federal agency to prepare an environmental impact statement prior to commencing action under that proposal. Although NEPA requires an EIS from the *federal government* in situations of major *federal* action, the private sector and nonfederal governmental entities are very much affected by the EIS requirement. It should, however, be clearly understood that NEPA is not a statute which prohibits any specific activities by the federal government. What it does is require that environmental factors be taken into account in the decision-making process of whether or not to go forward with a project. We will now look at how those factors are taken into account by considering questions involving the content of an EIS.

C.   CONTENT OF ENVIRONMENTAL IMPACT STATEMENTS

Within the EIS is supposed to be a consideration of the effect of a proposed action on the human environment through use of the mechanism of a detailed report by the responsible official on:

1.   the environmental impact of the proposed action;

---

24. *Natural Resources Defense Council v. S.E.C.,* 432 F.Supp. 1190, 1196 (1977).

2. any adverse environmental effects which cannot be avoided should the proposal be implemented;
3. alternatives to the proposed action;
4. the relationship between local short-term uses of man's environment and the maintenance and enhancement of long-term productivity; and
5. any irreversible and irretrievable commitments of resources which would be involved in the proposed action should it be implemented.[25]

To accomplish the above task, an EIS is supposed to clearly present the environmental impacts of the proposed action and the alternatives to the proposed action with the purpose of sharply defining the issues and providing a clear basis for choice among the options by the decision-maker and the public.* Within the alternatives section, the EIS should explore *all reasonable* alternatives including the no action alternative and should identify the agency's preferred alternative. The EIS must describe the affected area concisely using summarized data indicating the impact. The environmental consequences shall be scientifically examined in a comparative manner as stated above and the scientific analysis and discussion should include accounts of governmental conflicts in plans, policies or controls. Also included should be energy requirements, conservation potentials, and requirements for natural or depletable resources by the project and by the alternatives. Probably, the most important consideration here is the direct and indirect effects caused by any proposed action or alternative. Such effects might include ecological, economic, historical, aesthetic or social aspects. Indirect effects relate principally to population-induced changes and resultant uses of land, air and water.

An environmental impact statement will evaluate the proposed action by considering the environmental consequences of the proposed action and alternatives to that proposed action. A cost-benefit analysis, which includes environmental costs and benefits as well as other costs and benefits, is used to provide a comprehensive evaluation of the desirability of following the proposed course of action. For example, if flood control could be accomplished to varying degrees depending on which of five alternative dam configurations were selected, one would want to consider the initial construction cost of each configuration, the operation and

---

25. PL 91–190, § 102(2)(c).

*For a complete description of the Council of Environmental Quality guidelines for an EIS, see Appendix A. An example of the content of an EIS may be seen in Appendix B, which contains the Table of Contents and Summary and Conclusions sections of an actual EIS.

maintenance cost for each, and the dollar amount of flood damage which each configuration would be expected to prevent. In addition, NEPA mandates that effects such as the destruction of wildlife and losses in commercial and recreational fishing for each alternative be made a part of the decision-making process. These costs must be put into the decision-making balance just as one would add the cost of cement. Also, some dam configurations might provide increased recreational opportunities such as boating. These benefits are a part of the decision-making process just as are the benefits of avoiding flood damage. NEPA asks that the federal decision-maker incorporate all the costs and all the benefits in his evaluation of a proposal, including those costs and benefits which are environmental in nature. Of course, not all elements of decision-making can be expressed in terms of dollars. What is the dollar cost of destroying 500 raccoons, 50 deer, or 10,000 starlings? What is the dollar benefit of saving 10 human lives every 50 years? Would saving those lives be worth an extra expenditure of $500, $500,000 or $500,000,000? An administrator's decision-making process, the evidence of which is the EIS, must consider these less quantifiable aspects of our environment as well as those which are more simply expressable in monetary terms.

Besides dealing with the questions of which parameters should be evaluated in the decision-making process and how these parameters should be evaluated, issues arise concerning the required scope of an environmental impact statement. If a federal agency is proposing a program to lease federal lands for energy production, is an EIS required for the leasing of each individual site, for each geographic leasing area, or only for the establishing of the overall leasing program with its rules and regulations? The Council on Environmental Quality has encouraged the use of overall "umbrella" statements for general programs. They believe that "umbrella" statements foster the desirable end of comprehensive planning and evaluation of long-term environmental goals and effects. The CEQ recognizes, however, that an overall program statement without a particularized statement on, for example, the leasing of site XYZ, may reduce or eliminate consideration of particular environmental problems of special significance at site XYZ. Thus, they have said that individualized statements should also be prepared, in addition to the overall program statement, when the individual actions will have significant impacts not adequately evaluated under the "umbrella" statement for the whole program. Repetitive discussion of the same issues for the specific project as were discussed in the general program statement is avoided by "tiering" of environmental impact statements. Tiering says that the EIS for the specific project only needs to summarize any issues which were already discussed in the overall program statement[26]

A related issue with respect to the required coverage of an EIS is often referred to as "segmentation." Suppose that an agency's long-range planning contemplates a reasonable possibility of a 200-mile highway being constructed over the next 10 years, but current construction and funding is being proposed for only a 20-mile stretch. Should the entire 200-mile corridor be the subject of the EIS or just the 20 miles currently proposed? It would be extremely costly and time-consuming to do the EIS for the whole 200 miles and, besides, if construction is never funded beyond the 20 miles, the EIS work on the rest is wasted. In addition, an EIS done today might be of questionable value with respect to work not to be undertaken for eight more years. It could thus be argued that the EIS should be limited in scope to the 20-mile segment currently under consideration. The danger of allowing this segmented approach to fulfilling the EIS requirement is that segmenting may undermine objective consideration of environmental issues by unfairly loading the EIS balance in favor of construction. In the diagram below, no significant environmental problems exist in proposed highway segments AB or CD, but a major environmental drawback to superhighway construction exists at point X. If the scope of today's EIS were limited to AB, no environ-

mental problems are present to argue against construction. Once AB is built, the next likely segment to be undertaken by a dedicated superhighway builder is CD, and again, no environmental problems present themselves to inhibit construction of CD. Concerning the construction of BC, an objective evaluation of segment BC by itself might result in a "no construction" decision because, on balance, the costs (including environmental costs) outweigh the benefits of construction; however, if that balance is struck with the added factor of already constructed superhighways AB and CD emptying onto winding country road BC and the resulting traffic problems which may now exist in BC because of AB and

---

26. 40 CFR 1502.4, 1502.20, 1508.28.

CD, a "yes construction" decision may be hard to avoid. The segmenting of the EIS into three parts has undermined the ability to fairly consider the environmental detriment of a superhighway through point X. If an EIS for the whole route, ABCD, had been done prior to construction of the first segment, the problem at point X might have been considered important enough to mandate a different route such as AMND as shown below.

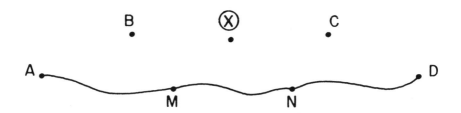

The courts have attempted to resolve the conflicting policies of, on one hand, not wanting to waste time and money on an over-encompassing EIS and, on the other hand, not wanting to allow the objectivity of the EIS balancing process to be jeopardized. The courts have said that if construction of one part of a potentially larger project has independent "local utility" and will thus not involve an irreversible or irretrieveable commitment of government funds, the EIS may be limited in scope to that one part of the project.[27] Even if no further action were taken beyond the part of the project currently being funded for construction, if construction of that part alone would still be a sound decision, the EIS does not need to go beyond that segment of what might someday become a larger project. In this way, the courts have tried to mitigate the argument of "now that we have AB and CD, we need BC to relieve the traffic problems those other segments have caused." AB and CD can only be built if they can stand as sound projects on their own without causing detriments which could only be overcome by constructing BC regardless of the environmental costs of building BC.

D. WHY AN EIS HAS PROBLEMS

To this point, we have considered, in terms of an EIS, the substantive policies, the procedural requirements, the major federal action prereq-

---

27. *Conservation Society of So. Vt. v. Sec. of Transportation,* 531 F.2d 637, 640 (1976).

uisite, and the content of the EIS. We have apparently concluded that if an EIS is properly prepared and the judgment is favorable, the project will get a green light from the government. It therefore seems apparent that we should examine some objections, problems and possible pitfalls in the NEPA process with respect to the EIS requirement and its use. One major overall objection to the preparation of an EIS is the amount of paper consumed in generating an end product which, in turn, is so cumbersome, detailed and interdisciplinary that no one person could possibly read and/or understand the whole thing. If any citizen were to simply lift the EIS for the Dickey-Lincoln Dam Project in Maine, the futility of the "common man" examining and commenting on the draft statement would become apparent. Therefore, one objection is the length of the EIS. To help alleviate this problem, an EIS has a summary attached that supposedly condenses the project's environmental impact to the information necessary before a required permit is issued. Since most preparers of the summary are usually members of the agency wishing to complete the project, the summary may not necessarily reflect all controversial environmental impacts of the proposal, nor adequately examine all alternatives, including the alternative of withdrawing the proposal.

Specifically, let's examine some problems that might arise as each of Congress' mandates is addressed in light of the CEQ guidelines in Appendix A. First, we will consider the EIS and a hypothetical situation and then a real life situation, not one that has happened but rather one that is currently happening, and where the EIS is in preparation. The hypothetical situation goes like this: Some federal agency is contemplating building a dam to control flooding of a number of towns downstream from area A. The dam will be located between area A and the towns. These towns were built many years ago before very much logging and building took place upstream in area A. That was back in the days when floods were few and far between. Recently, flooding has become a problem because of lack of upstream water retention by vegetation and soil. As a result of this dam building, numerous acres of wildlife habitat and farmland will be seasonally flooded behind the dam, water flow downstream of area A will be controlled, and homes will be saved from the inevitable floods. This seems a rather simple undertaking since while some forests and farmlands will be flooded seasonally and some permanently, water-related recreation opportunities will increase and increased income may be realized from water-related recreational sales and services. Let's return to the NEPA mandates listed on pages 34–35 along with the CEQ guidelines. The following are some possible problems that might arise when an EIS is prepared involving our hypothetical situation. With respect to this hypothetical situation, let's focus on mandates **i, iii** and **iv.**

i. NEPA requires that the environmental impact be assessed. In this instance, the environment behind the dam will be altered from primarily terrestrial (forest and farms) to mainly aquatic. The natural use of this area will change. Suppose that deer use part of the area that will be flooded for winter yarding and this area will become permanently flooded if the project is implemented. Further, suppose that the total number of deer wintering yards in the area has reached a critical level and the elimination of this deer yard will reduce the deer herd size in the area in such a way that not enough reproduction will take place to effectively replenish the herd and local extinction is predicted. Remember, the scientists only assume that the critical level can be defined and only make a statement that if this level is reached, the deer population will *probably* be eliminated because reproduction does not replace deer as quickly as they are eliminated. On the other hand, if the dam is built and the inevitable flood is avoided on the downstream side of the dam, property values will probably increase, insurance rates decrease and more people move into the area because of the *certainty* of less risk of flooding. While each of these scenarios has impacts on the environment, the "answer" to implementation of the proposal is usually more a function of who is asking the environmental impact question, deer hunters or downstream homeowners. In terms of the cost-benefit ratio, one would certainly expect the dam to "win," but consider the number of hunting licenses bought, the number of guns and ammunition purchased, the gasoline purchased to get there, the overnight or longer-term accommodations provided for hunters and various other economic quantifiables that may build a financial case for continued hunting. Consider this in relation to no hunting at all.

iii. Alternatives to this plan may well be as costly both economically and with respect to economically unassessable factors as implementation of the plan itself. Withdrawal of the plan could be viewed as the most economical alternative and the one least impacting on the environment, but is this really certain? If no dam is built, the downstream town may be vacated by current homeowners as jobs disappear in the area because of uncertainty with respect to flooding. Or everyone may seek government aid because of flooding or welfare because of no jobs. Maybe the deer population will die out anyway even though the dam is not built and all that deer-related revenue will be lost regardless. Alternatives such as relocating the towns or reforesting and maintaining the upstream soil absorption capacity for water might also be examined. All of these alternatives might be effective but it is usually the one advanced by the responsible official that gets the green light. This is also usually the proposal with the "best" cost-benefit ratio.

iv. The relationship between the local short-term uses and the maintenance and enhancement of long-term productivity is a very difficult analysis to approach. The immediate result of the project would certainly be less risk of flooding while the deer population could provide a food source for the area over a long period of time. This latter proposition must consider the whole geographical area because if another deer yard nearby is lost for some other reason with the result of the deer dying even if this dam were built, then any argument advanced here about long-term deer management for food becomes a somewhat useless exercise. The loss of resources, deer populations, farmland, forests or some other resource by the implementation of this project will only be realized when one of these resources becomes scarce enough to indicate a critical level. Let's face it, if any project or many projects get implemented, then eventually something may become scarce enough to cause alarm. Perhaps many of the potential consequences of a course of action are too complex or too speculative in nature to make environmental evaluation meaningful.

While the above is definitely not a thorough examination of the environmental issues involved, what this hypothetical situation hopefully begins to bring to you is an awareness that there is no real "answer" to any situation such as the above regardless of whether an EIS is required or not. We are dealing with the balance/ban continuum and must consider these proposals based on that concept. Overall, the EIS produces a data set that creates a circumstance where data interpretation is necessary. All the possible interpretations are themselves only statements of statistical probability based upon the data taken. Therefore, if some questions were not asked and data not taken on that aspect, then the picture presented by the EIS may be somewhat unrealistic.

Although the above situation was hypothetical, many similar situations do exist. For our next illustration of problems with the EIS system, let's consider a real situation concerning a real project in which a federal agency is involved. So, keeping in mind the limited examination we made of the hypothetical, consider this real situation that exists today in the Green Mountains of Vermont.*

A major developer in the skiing industry, Sugarbush Valley, Inc., recently purchased another ski resort north of its Sugarbush Valley Ski Resort. Between these two ski resorts is a tract of mountainous land that currently is covered by forest. Much of this land lies within the boundaries of the Green Mountain National Forest, which is administered by

---

*This is the proposed Sugarbush expansion project as currently understood by the authors.

the U.S. Forest Service. The forested area steeply slopes into a valley drained by Slide Brook. The floor of the valley is mostly undeveloped, comprised of farmland and the population centers of Warren, Fayston and of Waitsfield. The population of Warren is approximately 883, of Fayston, 445, and Waitsfield, 1154. A two-lane highway (Rt. 100) passes through the area in a north to south direction. The current capacity of the two Sugarbush Valley ski areas is about 5,400 (the two ski areas are currently called Sugarbush South and Sugarbush North). Now comes before us Sugarbush Valley, Inc., with the following proposal.

Sugarbush Valley, Inc., would first like to more than double its skier capacity to 11,650 and second, eventually become a major destination ski resort. To accomplish the first endeavor, it is proposed that existing trails be widened, several lifts be replaced and several new trails and lifts be constructed in the Slide Brook area between Sugarbush South and Sugarbush North. To implement this proposal, Sugarbush Valley, Inc. must get a new permit from the U.S. Forest Service since this would be an expansion of the current leasehold and the issuance of a new leasehold. The new lifts and trails, as well as the old ones, are located on U.S. Forest Service land, and everyone agrees that an EIS is required.

As previously mentioned, Sugarbush Valley, Inc. also envisions creating a resort complex of some sort that will give housing and presumably other accoutrements to the numerous ski buffs who want to come to the Sugarbush area for extended periods of time. These other facilities will, of necessity, include restaurants, police protection, fire protection, transportation facilities, sewage facilities, and nighttime entertainment centers. All of these facilities will require their own service personnel in addition to other service personnel connected with an increased "resident" population. This means new school space, new dwellings, new roads, new traffic lights and new or increased problems associated with population growth. However, no one can agree if these considerations should be of concern in the EIS prepared by the Forest Service. In fact, the Forest Service maintains that there are only two questions it must address in terms of environmental impact. These two questions center on the size of the area impacted and the impact of increased use in the area. The area being considered is only the area of Forest Service land that will be impacted. The Forest Service does not believe it has any mandate to consider the overall project (ski trails and lifts as well as housing and services) but only that portion of the project on government land.

That this initial posture of the Forest Service creates problems for concerned citizens should be quite evident from reading the mandates and guidelines presented at the beginning of this chapter. A related problem may be that the Forest Service only considers the "project" to be ski trails and ski lifts and not the additional housing and services necessitated by increased use patterns. Maybe the question here is where to draw the line—what is the "project" anyway? A too narrow interpretation of what is the "project" will result in a failure to fully account for environmental issues involved with the development. A too broad interpretation may be more costly and time consuming than warranted and, of more significance, may not be the type of inquiry which Congress asked for in NEPA.

Another "problem" with this impact statement as with others is who prepares the studies before the EIS is written and who pays for it. In this case, Sugarbush Valley, Inc., is paying for the studies being conducted for the Forest Service. The studies are being completed for the Forest Service by a consulting firm hired by Sugarbush. While this may not necessarily create biased data, the developer-hired consultant approach leaves the whole process open to question. One issue raised is when is an EIS adequate and how can those who do not believe that all the data is present and unbiased get additional data and get that data reviewed by the federal decision-maker. Gathering data usually costs a substantial amount of money and private parties other than developers usually cannot afford the cost.

Even if this EIS as it is finally completed does consider the secondary effects of development on Forest Service land, there is no indication that the project will not go forward and it should be reemphasized that NEPA does not intend that projects which create environmental harm be rejected so long as the benefits of the project outweigh those harms. If the project does go forward, the application of NEPA should take into account the possibility of phasing in the development in such a way that the area's growth rate is controlled. The EIS should be used as a tool that allows for decisions in favor of the development of an area in a sensible manner by realizing that while the population must have space to use for various activities, doubling the resident population in a period of less than ten years may create more long-term problems than the short-term gains realized.

As a final comment concerning problems with the EIS process, we should note that although NEPA was instituted for the protection of people, it is apparently such a costly process to be involved in that it really excludes most people. Not only does it exclude most private citizens with environmentalist leanings, but also the costliness of the process may exclude all developers except those who are very large from becoming involved in a project which will require an EIS from the federal government. Also, the costly and cumbersome EIS process often fails to politically address the issues. Instead, it regularly polarizes various citizens or governmental groups into positions of making value judgments which would not be made but for the polarization created by the EIS process itself. The question must be raised as to whether the EIS balancing process itself is, on balance, a net benefit to society. While numerous questions have arisen and will continue to arise in the Sugarbush issue concerning principally water, human services and land use patterns, this brief inspection of a real situation should provide some insight into the practical problems of dealing with the EIS process.

E.   REMEDIES

To conclude our discussion of NEPA, let's consider the question of remedies for noncompliance by a federal agency with NEPA's EIS requirement. The general remedy is an injunction to maintain the *status quo* — the court orders that the project be halted until a proper EIS is prepared; however, a *status quo* injunction is not granted in all situations of inadequate environmental impact statements. If a delay in continuing the project might result in safety or health hazards or heavy economic losses and if the environmental harm is not very great, a court may refuse to hold the project in its *status quo* position. Instead, the court may issue a limited injunction which would prohibit certain activities (like site clearance) but allow other project activities to continue (like relocation of people from the site to be cleared). The likelihood of a *status quo* injunction with respect to the entire project would appear to be proportional to the seriousness of the environmental harm which the project threatens to create. Also, intentional noncompliance by an agency with NEPA may tend to induce a court to grant a broad injunction even though, in the absence of agency bad faith, the factual situation might have led the court to grant a limited injunction.

While in most situations, the remedy of a *status quo* injunction will be all the court involvement that is necessary, lurking in the background is the possibility that the court will tell an agency that it has violated NEPA and, since it should not have proceeded with its project, it must undo what has been done. This remedy is rather severe and is thus reserved for extreme situations. Again, agency good faith would not be irrelevant to a court's determination of whether to apply this severe remedy.

Another remedy which some people have claimed is available under NEPA is the right of private citizens to bring suit when estimates or predictions made in an environmental impact statement are not adhered to or do not prove to be true once the project is approved and undertaken. Citizens have contended that when NEPA has thus been violated, they have an "implied private right of action" under NEPA. The courts have found that Congress did not intend such a remedy to be available under NEPA and have dismissed lawsuits seeking to invoke such a remedy. The courts have said that if this private remedy were available, then decision-makers would receive and report distorted information which was "hedged" to ensure that information used as an estimate or prediction would in fact turn out to be true in practice. This would be inconsistent with the statutory purpose of NEPA which is to provide decision-makers with the best available information on which to base their decisions.[28] On the other hand, one may want to consider the argument that if representations made in the EIS as a basis for reaching the decision to proceed with a project are shown to not be coming true as the project is being implemented, should the agency not have to reevaluate whether the project should continue based on the new information now available. Such reevaluation might result in a different decision on the project or modifications to the project which would provide greater consistency with the substantive policies that Congress asked be pursued using "all practicable means."[29]

ADDITIONAL READINGS

Orloff, N. *The Environmental Impact Statement Process* (Washington, DC: Information Resources Press, 1978).
Orloff, N., and G. Brooks. *The National Environmental Policy Act* (Washington, DC: Bureau National Affairs, Inc., 1980).

---

28. *Noe v. MARTA,* 644 F.2d 434 (1981).
29. PL 91–190 § 101.

CHAPTER 3

POLLUTION

A. DEFINING THE PROBLEM

It is necessary, before we deal with specific pollution problems, to share some basic ideas on how the whole ecological system is put together so that we will better understand how pollution becomes a problem. In the simplest sense, all things are connected. We are sure you have heard the phrase before, but let us go a little further and examine what this simple phrase can mean.

We will begin by examining how the connections in the ecosystem are put together, using Figure 1 as a reference point. While not all parts of all ecosystems look like those shown in Figure 1, the parts we will designate are quite common in most localities. In the figure, A represents the surface of the earth, where various human activities take place. These activities include manufacturing, mining, electrical generation, silviculture (logging), agriculture, fishing and just plain living. In short, A represents the land and the activities we perform on the land. Designation B represents the air above the surface of the earth. For our purposes we will consider only the lower part of the troposphere, the layer of air closest to the earth. Generally, this air moves from west to east in the North Temperate Zone where most people live and most industrial processes take place. This air can and does carry various materials such as gases, metals and dust which originate from naturally occurring earth processes or from anthropogenic (man-made) sources. The distances these materials travel in the air and the form in which they return to earth will be discussed more thoroughly later. The letter C is used to represent a lake basin where water level is a function of E, the boundary between the saturated and unsaturated soil areas which will also be discussed later. The lake basin is like a teacup at the bottom of a funnel; it catches

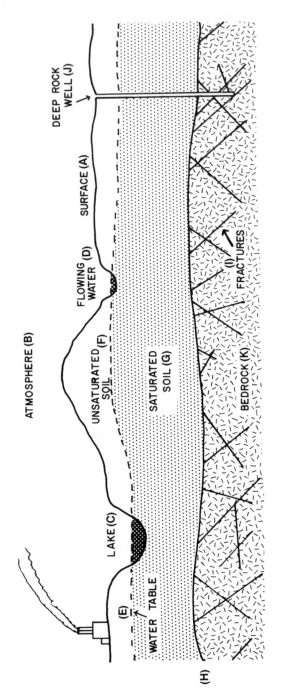

Figure 1.   A diagrammatic representation of how the ecosystem is put together.

all the water that runs over the land and down the hill and additionally gets some water or exchanges some water with water in the areas designated F and G. So, material from land activities, A, can get washed into the lake basin C. Lakes are large bodies of water and, therefore, the total amount of water in the lake takes a long time to be replaced, if ever. The letter D designates a river or stream. This body of water is the kind that runs downhill to a lake or some other larger body of water (sea, ocean). The rivers and streams carry with them materials that have run off from the land, fallen from the sky and entered from F and G. These watercourses try to fill the teacup through the funnel. Since the water in these bodies of water is always moving, replacement of water in any defined space is very rapid compared to replacement in C. The boundary between F and G is designated as E, where E represents the area between the unsaturated soil material F and the saturated soil material G. The distance below the soil surface (surface of the earth) of E is variable both spatially and temporally, depending on soil composition, the frequency and amplitude of rainfall (how often and how much), temperature, and ground level land use patterns. In other words, E is not fixed, but moves as conditions change. Therefore, lake levels vary and some streams dry up as E moves, since where E breaks the surface of the earth there is a body of water. In theory there is no real distinction between area F and G other than the degree of water saturation. Both F and G really contain groundwater. The differences are mainly that in area F there is unsaturated water flow (water flows downhill) while in area G there is a saturated flow (water usually moves laterally, if at all). The rate of flow in area F is very dependent on soil composition. The rate of flow in area G is also a function of soil composition and of some type of water drawdown (well) but is still very slow. As the movement of water in area G is very slow, so too is the movement of chemicals, although these movements are not necessarily the same. The letter H designates the boundary between soil and bedrock, K, while the letter I designates fractures (holes) in the bedrock that can accumulate water. When drained quickly, the area I will usually refill rather quickly. It is into the bedrock that many wells are drilled, but the depth and the composition of the deepest part of any well, J, is a function of the geographic location of the well. The letter J then is used to designate a deep rock well, one that crosses fractures in bedrock. These types of wells are drilled to a depth where recharge (water replacement) after drawdown (water pumped out) is sufficient to accommodate the use for which the well was drilled. Wells then, really get their water from the surface after it has permeated through soil and reached a layer of saturation (G) or an area of storage (I). Although subsurface conditions vary from one geographic location to another, we can safely say that where water goes, material that can be physically or chemically carried by water will be carried by water as it passes around the ecosystem. The connectedness in the ecosystem is then established as the flow of material, such as water, between and among the parts of the ecosystem.

As an example of connectedness more specific than the generality of Figure 1, let us look at a simplified version of the nitrogen cycle. Nitrogen is a needed nutrient, an important part of all protein. What we are concerned with here is the structural forms of nitrogen in nature and the direction of flow from one nitrogen form to another. If we start with nitrogen as organic nitrogen (protein nitrogen) we can follow nitrogen around the connections of the nitrogen cycle (Figure 2). We see that organic nitrogen in plants or animals upon their death is eventually transformed into ammonium. Ammonium is changed into atmospheric nitrogen or nitrate or is taken up by plants and made into organic nitrogen in plants. The shortest cycle is then organic nitrogen in plants converted to ammonium after plant death and then taken back up by other plants. If you follow some other pathways, the idea that materials (nitrogen here) go through cycles will become apparent. In fact, most materials we know about go around in cycles through processes that change their chemical makeup.

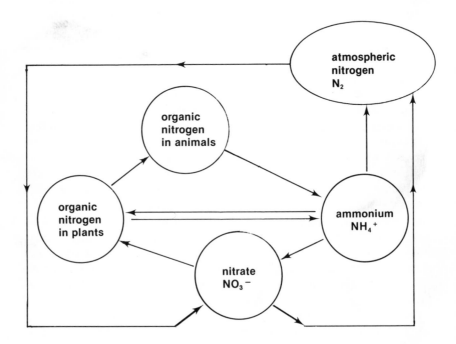

Figure 2.   A simplified view of the nitrogen cycle.

Having demonstrated the idea of how things are connected, we shall proceed to examine the concept of pollution and what kinds of problems seek a resolution. While we can relate to the whole ecosystem concept, society has broken the problem of pollution into two broad categories based, presumably, upon a policy decision. These two broad categories are water pollution and air pollution. Apparently, since in each category there is a transport of materials, and since in different geographic areas either air or water, but not necessarily both, were perceived to be of lower quality than the public health and welfare might tolerate, we elected to regulate them separately rather than collectively. While we may, in hindsight, criticize this decision, the fact remains that when society perceives a problem, it often tries to deal with that isolated problem. Therefore, to briefly outline the scope of the problem, we will consider water and air pollution separately after we examine the nature of pollution.

"Pollution" is defined by the federal government in one instance to mean the man-made or man-induced alteration of the chemical, physical, biological and radiological integrity of water.[1] A literal reading of this definition would make it appear that beneficial as well as detrimental effects are considered pollution. This definition seems to view man apart from nature with nature as the norm and anything done by man as being pollution. In point of fact, we will see that pollution control statutes concern themselves largely with adverse effects on man and to a much lesser degree with adverse effects on nature. Another attempt to cope with the concept of pollution is to define "pollutant." The federal government has defined "air pollutant"[2] as including any physical, chemical, biological or radioactive matter which enters the air. Again, this definition could encompass the effects of almost any event; however, we will see that in practice the application of this definition is not nearly so far-reaching.

1.   Water Pollution

Man-made delivery of pollutants to common waters (usually surface water) is accomplished by direct (point source) and indirect (nonpoint source) means. These respectively are the ones we know about and the ones we wish we knew more about. According to the Clean Water Act, a "point source" is a discernable, confined and discrete conveyance from which pollutants may be discharged. Since every public and private

---

1. 33 U.S.C. § 1251 et seq. at § 1362 (Clean Water Act).

2. 42 U.S.C. § 7401 et seq. at § 7602(g) (Clean Air Act).

facility that discharges any potential pollutant directly into waters of the United States is required to get a permit that describes discharge limitations for specific materials, we have presumably isolated and identified these point sources. Notable exceptions are single households that pipe wastewaters directly into bodies of water. By 1980, about 59,000 such permits had been issued, of which about 26% were for municipal sources, with the remainder being industrial permits. Industrial uses of water include refining gasoline from crude oil (10 gal water/gal gasoline), making steel (35 gal water/lb steel), refining synthetic fuel from coal (265 gal water/gal fuel), and automobile manufacturing (100,000 gal water/ automobile).[3] To look at it another way, about 1600 gal of water were used per person per day in the United States in 1980. What happens to this used water? A large portion of it is treated by various methods to remove identified pollutants, and is then discharged into our watercourses. The modern approach is either to treat industrial wastewater separately or to pretreat it before it flows to a municipal sewage treatment plant. Industrial treatment or pretreatment is used to recover (this is becoming more economical) metals such as silver and cadmium, and to remove toxic chemicals such as carbon tetrachloride, trichloroethylene, and other organic as well as inorganic chemicals before discharge. Most municipal sewage treatment plants are not geared to accomplish the above, and rarely test for the presence of pollutants other than those specified by law. Therefore, most municipal plants test for biochemical oxygen demand (BOD), suspended solids (SS), total coliform (TC), and fecal coliform (FC) as required by law, and many also test for phosphorous and nitrate, as well as pH (a measure of 6.0 to 9.0 is required[4]). Why do we test for these pollutants? Well, one reason is that we do not have all that much faith in our treatment plant technology, while another is a basic lack of faith in the operators of these treatment facilities who might be trying to save money. Probably the main reason we test is our concern for safe drinking water and water for recreation (swimming, fishing, etc.). The things we test for are good indicators of the level of pollution we wish to control. BOD is a measure of the oxygen demand of microorganisms in the water as they break down organic material. This demand for oxygen reduces the amount of oxygen available for fish and other water creatures. If the BOD is too high, the dissolved oxygen in the water will be too low to support fish such as trout, which require at least

---

3. Miller, G. T., Jr. *Living in the Environment* (Belmont, CA: Wadsworth Publishing Co., Inc., 1982).

4. 40 CFR § 133.

5 parts per million (ppm) of oxygen in water. SS is a measure of particles in the effluent discharge. If SS is high, aquatic life can be killed when breathing spaces are plugged. Also, sunlight is prevented from penetrating the water, plants die and increase the BOD as they decompose. TC and FC are monitored as indicators of human pollution in water and as a test for chlorination effectiveness in effluent from municipal treatment plants. Maximum levels are established to ensure that disease-causing bacteria are ineffective. The measurement of phosphorous and nitrate was added in many places when it became apparent that these two nutrients (assumed to be limiting) could stimulate aquatic plant growth to such an extent that few other organisms (fish) could survive at the low dissolved oxygen (DO) level caused by plant decay. Therefore, through monitoring and a permit system we have identified most point sources of possible water pollution, and may eventually have all facilities operating as outlined in the Clean Water Act. The real problem here will be spacing facilities along a watercourse such that the BOD never forces the water's dissolved oxygen to fall below a critical level for fish. The above briefly illustrates some of the problems with point source discharges into surface water.

The second major source of pollutants in our surface water and groundwater is from nonpoint sources of pollution. Nonpoint sources include agriculture, construction, silviculture, urban runoff, mining, livestock operations and home septic systems. The major pollutants from these sources are suspended solids from erosion and nutrients such as nitrogen and phosphorus. For example, agriculture loses about 4.8 billion tons of soil to erosion each year, of which 3.8 billion tons is eroded by water and 1.0 billion tons is blown away on the wind. About half of this eroded soil is deposited in watercourses. In Illinois, this amounts to about 2 bushels of soil per bushel of corn. In 1979, United States farmers used over 51 million tons of fertilizer that contributed 7.5 million tons of nitrogen and 0.6 million tons of phosphorus in runoff to our waterways. Construction is another major contributor of sediment from erosion. One bared acre of ground can contribute over 150 tons of sediment from erosion in one year. Silviculture may cause landslides, and certainly extensive erosion results from poor logging practices. Urban runoff (storm drains) carries metals (lead) and toxics as well as suspended solids into our watercourses. Mining operations—mainly strip mining for coal—have left over 400,000 acres of unreclaimed soil surface in Ohio alone. Water washing across this pyritic spoil turns acid before it enters watercourses. In Pennsylvania this has resulted in the destruction of many good trout streams. Pollution potential from livestock is enormous. Currently, about 1.2 billion tons of waste are produced each year by livestock, mostly from unconfined beasts (not feedlots). Most feedlot wastes are piled up and left to be washed out by rain, which carries many of the nutrients to waterways. These wastes (manure) cannot be directly used for fertilizer because of their high levels of antibiotics which kill the organisms in the soil that would ordinarily decay the manure. Over 19.5 million homes are serviced by septic tanks, presumably with leach fields. Many of these are poorly maintained and serviced only when a noticeable problem develops. That is usually long after soil water has been contaminated. What all of this means is that a lot of pollutants are not really controlled because no point source can be identified.

Now, consider these nonpoint sources together with sanitary landfills and secured landfills (hazardous waste) as well as with proposals for deep well injection of some wastes, and the entire problem becomes clearer. When water, polluted or not, comes in contact with any material it can physically or chemically carry, it will carry that material. Therefore, groundwater as well as surface water has the potential to become polluted. Furthermore, it is next to impossible to completely clean groundwater once it has become contaminated. There are now many major cities that have municipal wells contaminated with organic solvents, pesticides and other hazardous wastes and their breakdown products (such as DDE from DDT). Another problem with both surface water and groundwater is that pollutants in the air can reach this water even if the water itself is far removed from the pollution source. We thus have a very distinct connection between water pollution and air pollution.

2.   Air Pollution

Air pollution is a bit more difficult to deal with than water pollution. Water has organisms in it that can act to cleanse the watercourse, at least to a large degree. Air does not have these agents. It does not have an assimilative capacity like water. One way to view air pollution is to think of the atmosphere as a sewer in the sky. Like any sewer system, we dump material into the air and hope that the old saying "dilution is the solution to pollution" takes over. This is accomplished using tall smoke stacks, many of which occur upwind from areas currently complaining of acid rain (Table I).[5] At one time tall stacks were considered the "answer" to air pollution problems. What we did not adequately understand was that material placed into the air eventually gets washed out of the air when it

---

5. Council on Environmental Quality. *Environmental Quality* (Washington, DC: U.S. Government Printing Office, 1980).

Table I. Regional Distribution of Tall Stacks Built
by Electric Utilities, 1970–79

Region	Stack height (ft)				Total
	800	700–799	600–699	500–599	
New England	—	—	—	7	7
Middle Atlantic	2	7	7	5	21
East North Central	11	4	11	27	53
West North Central	1	5	7	5	18
South Atlantic	15	9	7	8	39
East South Central	8	6	7	8	29
West South Central	—	1	3	1	5
Mountain	—	—	3	4	7
Pacific	—	—	1	—	1
Total	37	33	46	70	186

Table II. National Ambient Air Quality Standards[6]

Pollutant	Averaging time	Primary standard levels, $\mu g/m^3$ [a]	Secondary standard levels, $\mu g/m^3$ [a]
Particulate matter	Annual (geometric mean)	75	60
	24 hr[c]	260	150
Sulfur oxides	Annual (arithmetic mean)	80 (0.03)	—
	24 hr[c]	365 (0.14)	—
	3 hr[c]	—	1300 (0.5)
Carbon monoxides	8 hr[c]	10 (9)	10 (9)
	1 hr[c]	40 (35)	40 (35)
Nitrogen dioxide	Annual (arithmetic mean)	100 (0.05)	100 (0.05)
Ozone	1 hr[c]	240 (0.12)	240 (0.12)
Hydrocarbons (nonmethane)[b]	3 hr (6 to 9 a.m.)	160 (0.24)	160 (0.24)
Lead	3 mo	1.5	1.5

[a]Numbers in parentheses represents parts per million.
[b]A nonhealth-related standard used as a guide for ozone control.
[c]Not to be exceeded more than once a year.

6. 40 CFR § 50.0 et seq.

rains, and enters watercourses or soil. We also found out that a material placed in the air (primary pollutant) could be chemically altered to produce a different pollutant (secondary pollutant) before it is washed out of the air. An interesting example of this is the production, in the atmosphere, of sulfuric acid (H_2SO_4) from sulfur dioxide (SO_2). As time passed, we began to discover many types of air pollutants. The situation that led to this discovery is outlined in Figure 2 of Chapter 1. As more and more sources of pollutants were placed in production (we built more utility plants, more industrial facilities, and more motor vehicles with high compression engines), more pollutants were discharged into the atmosphere. Thus, the overall quantity of pollutants in the air increased and eventually we began to notice them. We currently recognize seven air pollutants for which we have established primary and secondary ambient air quality standards (Table II). Primary standards are intended for protection of the public health; secondary standards are to protect the public welfare. Ambient air is the air around us as opposed to the air coming out of the point source. That air is called an emission and is also limited in certain categories by the federal government.[7] Probably the most familiar are limits for coal- and oil-fired electric generating plants on emissions of sulfur dioxide, nitrogen oxides, and particulate matter, but there are also emission limits for various air pollutants for incinerators, sulfuric acid plants and petroleum refineries. For coal-fired electric utilities built after 1971, the emission limit for sulfur dioxide is 1.2 lb of sulfur dioxide per one million Btu derived from the coal. That means that if 1 lb of coal contained 12,000 Btu of "heat," then for every 83 lb of coal burned, up to 1.2 lb of sulfur dioxide may be emitted (there are other qualifications such that home coal heating units and other facilities are not subject to these standards). That means that if all the sulfur in the coal is oxidized to sulfur dioxide (SO_2), the above coal could be about 3.0% sulfur (S). As the Btu rating per pound of coal decreases, the amount of coal burned to get the 1 billion Btu figure increases, while the level of sulfur allowed decreases. Rather unfortunately, the western coal that is so low in sulfur is also low in Btu content, while eastern strip-mined coal which is high in sulfur (some is over 6%) is also high in Btu content per pound. In the United States we emit over 25.0 metric tons (tonnes) of sulfur dioxide every year, mostly in the east north central region (see Table I). Other emission limitations, notably those for cars, are also geared to reduce our air pollutant problems. Data (Table III)

---

7. 40 CFR § 60.0.

Table III.   National Emissions Estimates, 1970–78
(million tonnes per year)[8]

Year	TSP	SO$_2$	NO$_2$	Volatile organic compounds	CO
1970	23.2	29.8	19.9	28.3	102.6
1971	22.0	28.2	20.6	27.8	103.1
1972	21.0	29.3	21.6	28.3	104.4
1973	20.3	30.4	22.4	28.4	103.5
1974	17.9	28.5	21.8	27.1	99.6
1975	14.6	26.2	20.9	25.3	97.2
1976	14.1	27.4	22.5	27.0	102.9
1977	13.6	27.2	23.4	27.1	102.4
1978	12.5	27.0	23.3	27.8	102.1
Percentage change, 1970–78	− 46.1	− 9.4	+ 17.1	− 1.8	− 0.5

1 million tonnes = approximately 1.1 million short tons.

Table IV.   Sources of Hazardous Pollutants with
Established Emissions Standards[9]

Pollutant	Source
Asbestos	Asbestos mills, road surfacing with asbestos tailings, manufacturers of asbestos-containing products (fireproofing, etc.), demolition of old buildings, spray insulation
Beryllium	Extraction plants, ceramic manufacturers, foundries, incinerators, rocket motor manufacturing operations
Mercury	Ore processing, chlor-alkalai manufacturing, sludge dryers and incinerators
Vinyl chloride	Ethylene dichloride manufacturers, vinyl chloride manufacturers, polyvinyl chloride manufacturers

indicate, however, that except for particulate material, the total amounts of emissions have not varied much over the last decade.

More recently, concern has surfaced concerning hazardous air pollutants and emission standards. Emission standards have been set for some

---

8. Council on Environmental Quality. *Environmental Quality*. (Washington, DC: U.S. Government Printing Office, 1980).
9. Council on Environmental Quality. *Environmental Quality*. (Washington, DC: U.S. Government Printing Office, 1980).

of these (Table IV). An ambient air quality standard has been established for lead (Pb), recognizing the potential harm this gasoline additive can produce; however, we are just beginning to recognize hazardous air pollutants, and setting emission standards for them is a difficult process.

Setting both ambient air quality standards and emission limitations is, by virtue of their natures, a very probability oriented venture. Consider the following argument. We know that we will emit mercury (Hg) to the air if we burn strip-mined coal from the west. We know there are control measures that can reduce or eliminate mercury emissions during the coal burning process. We know that mercury emitted to the air can fall back to earth, be combined to an organic molecule by bacteria and pass up the food chain. We know that high levels of mercury in the human system can cause nervous disorders. We *do not know* how mercury will disperse when emitted into the air. We *do not know* where this emitted mercury will land. We *do not know* how rapidly biological magnification will cause concentrations to reach levels in humans that cause nervous disorders. We *do not know* geographically which humans where will probably die. The installed equipment to remove this pollutant from emissions almost completely will cost about $14 billion 1981 dollars. That amounts to about $65 for every person in this country. Now, the problem is not only whether we put in the equipment to control emissions, but also when do we put in the equipment and who pays for it. These are not very easy decisions to make when there are economic interests (stockholders) to protect as well as environmental health interests. Consider what might happen when and if light and heat became air pollutants much like noise is today. These "pollutants" would probably be even more cumbersome to handle. Yet, to ignore them ignores such questions as what happens to an observatory's ability to function when housing developments, with their accompanying lighting, spring up all around it. Although light and heat do not currently present problems of the level of importance of other air pollutants, rational decisions must still be made with respect to whether these "minor" pollutants should be subject to control and, if so, to what form of control. Pollution is apparently a problem that resulted from a small population thinking that resources were limitless and that the by-products of consumption could simply be discarded with immunity from any future detriment. This is like notions 1 and 2 presented in Figure 2 of Chapter 1. Then population grew and the discarding of the by-products of consumption could no longer take place without accompanying detrimental effects. Pollution is a problem that will not disappear. If we remove the mercury from the emission, what do we do with it? Our former hazardous air pollutant is now a hazardous solid waste. How do you ask your neighbor (person next door, state, other country) to stop polluting your air and water, when you are either using products resulting from this pollution production or making similar pollutant contributions yourself? The number of pollution problems and the alternatives for dealing with those problems are perhaps limitless. The next sections will explore some of the mechanisms which have been put into effect to attempt to control pollution of one form or another.

B. PRIVATE LAW REMEDIES – NUISANCE AND NEGLIGENCE, INJUNCTIONS AND DAMAGES

One method of analytically describing and evaluating the legal system's mechanisms for pollution control is to separate them into private pollution control mechanisms and public pollution control mechanisms. Private control mechanisms might include lawsuits instituted by individuals (or other entities, such as corporations or states) against a polluter where the lawsuit is based on a common law wrong such as negligence by the polluter or the polluter maintaining a nuisance. Remedies for these common law wrongs can be provided by the judicial system, even though no legislature has prohibited any specific actions or provided remedies for wrongful actions. By contrast, public pollution control is based on the enactment of legislation — federal or state statutes or local ordinances. This section will focus on private controls; the public mechanisms will be discussed subsequently.

1. Nuisance

Consider this example: Assume that a cement plant is located near where you live and it is discharging dirt and smoke into the air. You want to stop the pollution, so what might you do? You might hope for a statute or administrative regulation which would prohibit the pollution and bring with it a governmental enforcement scheme or at least provide you with the opportunity to bring a citizen's suit to enforce the prohibition. In the absence of such a statutory or administrative prohibition, you might initiate a private lawsuit against the cement company and ask the court for an injunction ordering the cement company to stop polluting and/or to order payment of damages for the harm they have done to you. Your case would be a tort case claiming "nuisance." This action basically claims that the cement company has a duty not to interfere with your peaceful enjoyment of your land, that it is so interfering and that it is thus a nuisance. The common law (judge-made law from previous court cases) recognizes this tort of nuisance and allows judges to enjoin the action causing the nuisance and to provide compensation for harm. This private control mechanism also works on a deterrence principle — e.g., manufacturers who cause damage by polluting and are held liable for payment for that damage may be deterred from polluting.

This cement company situation is similar to the New York case of *Boomer v. Atlantic Cement Company.*[10] In *Boomer,* the plaintiffs were successful in establishing that there was a nuisance. The question that was raised for the appeals court concerned the appropriate remedy to be given to the plaintiffs. The alternative remedies considered by the court were: (1) to issue an injunction prohibiting the cement company from maintaining the nuisance (stop polluting or close down) with a postponement of the injunction for eighteen months to allow the company an opportunity for technical advances to eliminate the nuisance, or (2) to in effect allow the company to continue operating as it had been on the condition that it pay permanent damages to the plaintiffs which would compensate them for the total existing and future economic loss to their property caused by the cement company.

In deciding between these two potential remedies, the court considered that the plaintiffs' economic harm was relatively small compared to the consequences of an injunction. An injunction could have resulted in the closing of a $45,000,000 plant with over 300 employees. In addition to the magnitude of the economic harm to the company and the community, the court was influenced by the fact that the company was up to date in air pollution control technology and eighteen months would not result in meaningful technical advances. Furthermore, the court believed that the making of technical advances should be an industry responsibility rather than the responsibility of the defendant company. As for the deterrence of pollution, the court believed that the risk of being required to pay permanent damages would be a sufficient incentive for research by cement plant owners for improved techniques to minimize pollution. The court thus opted for permanent compensatory damages. Plaintiffs would be paid off for past and future harm but the pollution would be allowed to continue.

A dissenting opinion was filed in *Boomer.* The dissenting judge contended that by letting the cement company pollute if it paid damages, the court was licensing a continuing wrong. The company could do what the law said was wrong so long as it paid a fee. Perhaps the court could be accused of supporting or helping establish a societal norm of accepting polluted air because it has placed an official stamp of approval on pollution-causing activity so long as the polluter pays a price. The

---

10. 309 N.Y.S. 2d 312, 257 N.E. 2d 870 (1970).

reader should consider which side he would favor given the factual circumstances—to stop the pollution or just make the company pay for the harm. Maybe if the cement company pays for 100% of the harm, then it is not really "polluting" since the benefits from the cement plant outweigh the detriments because there are no detriments due to the fact that those suffering have been fully compensated for their loss. Full compensation results in no harm and without harm perhaps there can be no such thing as "pollution." Regardless of the reader's position, the difference between the philosophies of the majority of the New York high court and the dissenting judge should be carefully noted since it is basic to the continuing environmental debate—should an activity which does cause harm be stopped or can it continue if it pays its way? It can be argued that if the company can produce the cement, pay for the pollution damage, and still make a profit by asking and getting a high enough price for the cement to cover the damages it has to pay, then the utility to society of the cement outweighs the harm which its manufacture creates.

While the court in *Boomer* chose compensatory damages over enjoining the nuisance, other cases have resulted in the issuance of an injunction. It is possible that these different results are due to the fact that states vary with respect to what their body of common law contains; however, an attempt at explaining differing results based on factual differences rather than jurisdictional differences is worthwhile. First, we should note that *Boomer* may have been an example of "good guys or bad guys" law. What was in fact the proper remedy in *Boomer* may be said to be a close or at least reasonably debatable question. In close cases the court may tend to give the benefit of the doubt to a defendant with a good track record. Perhaps the result in *Boomer* might have been different if it had not been found that the most modern dust control devices available had been installed in the defendant's plant and that it was unlikely that the defendant itself could develop improvements in the near future. Second, we should consider what factual situations have led other courts, as opposed to the *Boomer* court, to enjoin the operation of facilities that were causing nuisances by polluting.

One case in which an injunction prohibiting the operation of a polluting facility was issued was *Spur Industries, Inc. v. Del E. Webb Development Co.*[11] That case involved a cattle feedlot which had been operating lawfully but became a nuisance when nearby land was developed for residential purposes (Del Webb's Sun City in Arizona). The odor and flies from the feedlot were at the least annoying and perhaps also unhealthy for the nearby residents. Del Webb's request for an injunction

---

11. 108 Ariz. 178, 494 P. 2d 700 (1972).

against Spur's operation was granted by the court. The court raised some factors which, if present in a given situation, may lead courts to be willing to grant an injunction. If a large number of people or an entire neighborhood were affected by the nuisance rather than a small number of persons, a court might be more likely to enjoin the nuisance rather than provide damages as a remedy. In *Spur* the court also emphasized the type of injury as a factor in its decision. A breeding ground for flies which are capable of transmitting disease had been declared dangerous to the public health by the Arizona legislature. Another factor possibly supporting the granting of the injunction may have been the harshness of the injury to the developer, Del Webb. Its parcels of land were difficult if not impossible to sell. Factors such as those discussed here have led courts to find that the nuisance is a "public nuisance" rather than a "private nuisance" and to be more willing to enjoin it. Yet a remedy based on a finding of "public nuisance" is still within the realm of private pollution control since it is a court-made remedy which does not need to be based on legislation.

In the *Spur Industries* case, Spur's operation of a feedlot was found to be a nuisance and, for the above reasons, the operation was enjoined; however, Spur did not come away from court as a total loser. The court recognized that at the time Spur established its feedlot there was no indication that a new city would spring up alongside it in what had been a rural, agricultural area. The court said that Spur was enjoined not because of any wrongdoing on its part but because of the court's regard for the rights of the public. The court also found that Del Webb was not blameless with respect to the problem. It had taken advantage of the lower land values and the availability of large tracts of rural land. The court thus required Del Webb to indemnify Spur Industries for damages to Spur occasioned by the injunction requiring Spur to cease operation or move its feedlot.

The court itself noted that the result in *Spur* "may appear novel," and the court also carefully limited its decision to cases where a developer has, with foreseeability, necessitated the granting of an injunction against a lawful business by coming into a previously agricultural or industrial area. This novel decision raises some interesting questions. The court clearly finds that the polluting nuisance must be stopped, but it also acknowledges that when one who is engaged in lawful activity is stopped from continuing that activity because of changes in circumstances, perhaps consideration should be given to the idea of not requiring that the heretofore lawful enterprise also bear the losses brought about by the changed circumstances. If United States Steel has been operating in a lawful manner for years and the public decides that air pollution problems require stricter emission standards and hence installation of pollution control equipment by United States Steel, should not the public compensate the company for its costs brought about by the public's new demands rather than leaving those costs to be borne by the shareholders or customers of the company? One response to this argument might be that although United States Steel has been using the public's air in the past when the new emission standards were not in effect, that prior use does not give the company any interest which should be financially protected with respect to its continued use of the air without meeting the new restrictions. An effort to reconcile this response with the *Spur Industries* case runs into problems. In the operation of its feedlot Spur was not confining itself to its own land and the air above it. Odor and flies appeared on or above land owned by others. For a period of years no one complained, but when interests of the public required that the odor and flies be halted, the court appears to have found that Spur's prior use was relevant to giving it an interest which was to be financially protected when its continued use of the surrounding air was inconsistent with the public interest.

A question related to the above discussion is: if Del Webb was simply asking that its land and property rights not be interfered with by others in a way which is prohibited by the common law of nuisance, then why should it have to pay to have that prohibited interference stopped? If Spur is the one causing the pollution, it would appear that Spur should bear the costs of stopping the pollution rather than the cost being placed on Del Webb, which was merely making sound business use of land which it owned. Perhaps the "novel" *Spur Industries* case is an example of the legal system working at its best and reaching a compromise solution to a problem which may be the fault of no one and the costs of which are better shared than placed on one party. Yet, what would the court have done if those many residents surrounding the feedlot had bought and built there individually rather than buying from a land developer? Would the court have required them to indemnify Spur for Spur's losses due to the injunction, or would the court have refused to issue an injunction? Should the result in the case have depended on the fact that Del Webb was a convenient corporate treasury which was both allowed and required to buy an injunction?

2. Other Private Law Mechanisms

In addition to nuisance actions, there are other legal mechanisms not based on pollution control statutes which parties have sought to utilize for pollution control purposes or to obtain compensation for harms which may have come to them due to the conduct of a polluter. Since these private law mechanisms are applicable to fewer pollution situations and/or have met with less success than the tool of a nuisance suit, some but not all of them will be noted here, and our consideration of them will be relatively brief.

If your drinking water supply became polluted because of the unintentional but careless discharge of a toxic water pollutant, you might bring a negligence suit against the discharger of the pollutant and seek monetary compensation for the harm done. This suit is like a negligence suit brought against a driver who struck your car in the rear because he was following you too closely. Negligence suits may be contrasted to nuisance suits by noting that negligent conduct can generally be described as a "one-shot deal" rather than the continuing conduct and continuing harm which forms the basis of a nuisance suit. Thus monetary compensation for harm is the appropriate remedy, since there is not continuing wrongful conduct to enjoin. Although a negligence suit does not stop the polluting event from taking place (it has already happened), negligence suits can be mechanisms for pollution control in addition to providing compensation for pollution's harms. At least in theory, the potential liability of a polluter for his negligence will result in greater care being taken by people so as not to be negligent, causing a deterrence of negligent conduct and thus a reduction in pollution. The practical effect of this deterrence mechanism is dependent on factors such as the added costs to the potential polluter of greater care compared to the costs of paying for damages caused by negligent conduct. Furthermore, the utility of negligence suits as a pollution control tool is attenuated by factors such as the cost and bother for a victim to bring a lawsuit when harm has been done but either its magnitude is not worth the effort of the suit or the victim's insurance covers the loss. Additional discussion of the theory of negligence suits and the difficulties which a victim may face with respect to winning such a suit may be found in Chapter 6.

Some of the other approaches to private pollution control may be illustrated by the examples of suits based on the federal antitrust laws and provisions of the federal constitution. While these suits are not common law actions, they are discussed here as private pollution control since the statutes or constitutional provisions being invoked were not specifically directed at pollution problems.

One attempt to invoke the antitrust laws to combat pollution involved a suit wherein plaintiffs alleged that automobile manufacturers had conspired to eliminate competition among themselves with respect to the development, manufacture and installation of automotive air pollution control devices.[12] The plaintiffs asked the court to find that there was such a conspiracy, that the conspiracy was a violation of the Clayton Act which prohibited conspiracies that restrained competition, and to order the automobile companies to retrofit with effective air pollution control devices those automobiles which they had manufactured and sold to the public without such devices. The court found that while "the invitation to provide an innovative solution to it [smog] is tempting," the only purpose of the antitrust laws is to prohibit restraints on competition in order to guarantee a free marketplace in which an unsophisticated consumer can be assured of the best possible product for the least possible expense. Even assuming that there was a conspiracy, the court found that retrofitting automobiles with pollution control devices would not further the purpose of the antitrust laws and that the antitrust laws do not provide a remedy for pollution.

An attempt to bring provisions of the United States Constitution to bear directly on pollution problems without resorting to statutory or common law remedies was made in *Tanner v. Armco Steel Corp.*[13] Among other contentions, the plaintiffs claimed a right to a healthy and clean environment pursuant to the Ninth Amendment of the United States Constitution. The Ninth Amendment states: "The enumeration in the Constitution of certain rights, shall not be construed to deny or disparage others retained by the people." The court determined that this residual retention of rights by the people would not be interpreted to embody a legally assertable right to a healthful environment. While neither the antitrust approach to pollution control nor the attempt to use the Ninth Amendment were successful, they are noted here to raise the question of whether, if the facts of a case were compelling enough and if resort to some nonenvironmental body of law were necessary to provide a remedy for a wrong, might a court accept an invitation to provide an innovative solution to an environmental problem.

Perhaps there may be better potential at the state level for success in bringing constitutional provisions to bear on the environment without resorting to statutory mechanisms. Some state constitutions have provisions which speak expressly of environmental concerns. For example, Article 1, Section 27 of the Pennsylvania Constitution states: "The people have a right to clean air, pure water, and to the preservation of the natural, scenic, historic and esthetic values of the environment...."

---

12. *In re Multidistrict Vehicle Air Pollution*, 481 F. 2d 122 (1973), 367 F. Supp. 1298 (1973).

13. 340 F. Supp. 532 (1972).

In an appropriate case, a court may be disposed to invoke such a state constitutional provision, in and of itself, as the basis for a remedy. Since these state constitutional provisions deal specifically with the environment and are not a part of the common law, from the point of view of the organization of this chapter they are really a part of our next section— Public Pollution Control.

C. PUBLIC POLLUTION CONTROL— STATUTES AND REGULATIONS: FEDERAL, STATE AND LOCAL

As an introduction to our discussion of pollution control mechanisms which are established through legislation, we should note that the legislation addresses various subject areas, such as pollution of the air and water and pollution by noise, heat, and even light. These subject areas are often interconnected with respect to how they pollute and are polluted. The legislative enactments have usually separated these subject areas and treated them individually. While for purposes of analysis this section will also tend to treat these subjects individually, we should not completely forget their interrelationships. In addition, the reader should be aware that issues that will be discussed here in one context, such as air pollution, are often relevant to other pollution subject areas such as water or noise. The discussion of similar issues will not be repeated for different subject areas; however, the reader is encouraged to consider how an issue raised under water pollution might apply to air pollution.

1. Air Pollution—Control Mechanisms, Prevention of Significant Deterioration of Air Quality, Emission Reduction vs Dispersion Techniques, Accounting for the Costs of Control

The main tools for air pollution control are created by the Clean Air Act.[14] The Clean Air Act vests the EPA Administrator (the head of the federal Environmental Protection Agency) with information gathering, research, and planning functions, but of more significance to us are the direct operative control mechanisms that the statute establishes. The act segregates automobiles and aircraft as "moving sources" of air pollution

---

14. 42 U.S.C. § 7401 et seq.

and requires administrative establishment and enforcement of emission standards for these sources. Also segregated for special treatment in the way of research and regulation are potential problems relating to ozone in the stratosphere. While these topics are certainly of great importance, our discussion will emphasize the parts of the statute that establish quality standards for the air around us (ambient air quality standards) and emission limitations for nonmoving or "stationary" sources.

Leaving the moving sources and ozone sections aside, the Clean Air Act can be thought of as having three focuses: (1) the medium (air), (2) the sources and (3) the pollutants. With respect to the medium, the act provides for establishment of and compliance with ambient air quality standards for various pollutants. This mechanism states that regardless of where the pollutants come from, there may only be certain levels of them present in the air. With respect to sources of pollution, the act says that regardless of whether the air around us is clean or dirty, there is no justification for allowing stationary sources of pollution (like factories or power plants) to emit higher levels of pollutants than necessary so long as we take into account available control technology and the cost of such technology. Thus emission standards are established for stationary sources. With respect to the focus on the pollutants themselves, Congress has decided that some air pollutants are so hazardous that high costs and the unavailability of technology cannot be allowed to justify emissions of those pollutants beyond the level which provides an ample margin of safety to protect the public health from such hazardous air pollutants. The act thus provides a different control mechanism for pollutants which cause, contribute to, or may reasonably be anticipated to result in an increase in mortality or serious irreversible or incapacitating reversible illness. The Administrator of EPA establishes emissions standards for those hazardous air pollutants to provide an ample margin of safety to protect the public health regardless of costs or unavailability of technology. Those standards may not be exceeded except by an exemption from the President based on national security reasons or for a limited time to allow installation of controls if the source is an "existing" as opposed to a "new" stationary source. An example of an emission standard for a hazardous air pollutant (mercury) is:

(a) Emissions to the atmosphere from mercury ore processing facilities and mercury cell chlor-alkali plants shall not exceed 2300 grams of mercury per 24-hour period.

(b) Emissions to the atmosphere from sludge incineration plants, sludge drying plants, or a combination of these that process wastewater treatment plant sludges shall not exceed 3200 grams of mercury per 24-hour period.[15]

Having outlined the "pollutant" focus of the Clean Air Act (the approach used to control hazardous air pollutants), let's next consider the control mechanism that focuses on the medium (the air) — the ambient air quality standards. Congress has said that the quality of our air should be protected and enhanced to promote the public health and welfare. The Administrator is thus directed to study the effects of pollutants having negative impacts on the public health and welfare and to establish national primary and secondary ambient air quality standards based on that study. The national primary ambient air quality standards are those the attainment and maintenance of which are requisite to protect the "public health." The national secondary ambient air quality standards are those the attainment and maintenance of which are requisite to protect the "public welfare" from known or anticipated adverse effects.

Because of the use of the words primary/health vs. secondary/welfare, one might conclude that the primary standard is the more restrictive ambient air quality standard. In fact, just the opposite is true (see Table II). This is because of the Clean Air Act's definition of effects on welfare. Effects on welfare are said to include, but not be limited to, effects on items such as soils, waters, crops, animals, climate, property damage and personal comfort. The list is very broad, but even if one could think of something adversely affected that is not on the list, the "but is not limited to" clause would allow its inclusion. With this extremely broad range of what is "welfare," it is likely that the standard needed to protect some item of the public welfare is more restrictive than needed to protect the public health. Although the secondary standard may turn out to be numerically more restrictive than the primary standard, Congress clearly attached higher priority to the primary or public health standard. The primary standard is supposed to be attained "as expeditiously as practicable" and no later than three years from an established time, while the secondary standard is to be attained within a much more open-ended "reasonable time."

The setting of the ambient air quality standards is done at the federal level. Congress determined that there should be federally set air quality standards. The attainment or implementation phase of the ambient air quality standards mechanism is a good illustration of the fact that many environmental statutes are political compromises between those who favor state control and those who favor federal control, either because of

---

15. 40 CFR § 61.52.

differing beliefs about which level of government can best peform a task or about which level should be in control of local geographic areas. The air quality standards are set by the federal government, but each state has the opportunity to implement the standards and to choose its own methods of doing so. Thus one state may choose to implement the standards by being more restrictive with respect to automobiles, while another may choose instead to emphasize limiting industrial growth. The states submit their state implementation plans to EPA, which may approve or disapprove a plan or any portion thereof depending on whether it meets requirements listed in the statute. Those requirements include items such as having monitoring and enforcement programs, showing the capability of attaining the air quality standards within the time frames set by the statute, and containing provisions to prohibit any stationary source within the state from emitting pollutants which will prevent another state from attaining the ambient air quality standards. If a state does not adopt an approvable state implementation plan, then EPA is authorized to establish an implementation plan for the state and to impose it.

The last operative mechanism of the Clean Air Act that we will consider focuses on the sources of pollution. We have noted that the act uses separate approaches for dealing with moving vs. stationary sources and we will here discuss the stationary source standards. As we noted earlier, the stationary source standards mechanism of the act is based on the premise that stationary sources of pollution like oil refineries, power plants and cement plants should only be allowed to emit levels of pollutants that they cannot prevent with available control technology. Even if the ambient air meets the federal standards, stationary sources should control their emissions. The key point of contrast between the stationary source emission standards and the hazardous air pollutants emission standards is that while high costs are not an excuse for emitting hazardous air pollutants, in the setting of standards for performance of stationary sources EPA is required to take into consideration the cost of achieving emission reductions. The stationary source emission standards are thus a product of a "balancing" of environmental and economic factors, while the hazardous air pollutants emission standards are a "banning" of harmful amounts of pollutants because the harms are such that Congress decided that a balance with economic factors was inappropriate. One may want to consider the question of why hazardous air pollutants are to be controlled without balancing the economic costs of doing so. Is it simply because they create mortality and illness? Society certainly balances mortality with economic factors when it decides to build skyscrapers which will statistically cause greater mortality than low level buildings. One should consider the characteristics which should be present if an environmental harm is to be used to support a "ban" of an activity without considering economic costs rather than have that environmental harm balanced with economic costs.

As a final point in our description of stationary source standards, we should note that while existing stationary sources may become subject to emission limitations, the main thrust of the stationary source emission standards is on new stationary sources. Standards of performance for existing stationary sources may be less restrictive than for new sources and may take into account the remaining useful life of the existing source. Perhaps the justification for treating existing sources differently from new sources can be analogized to the court's requirement in the *Spur Industries* case (Section B) that the preexisting polluter be indemnified for its losses when it was ordered to stop its polluting activity.

With the above explanation of the operative mechanisms of the Clean Air Act as a base, let's next look at some of the issues of policy and interpretation which have arisen concerning this statute, how those issues were handled in the courts, and how subsequent amendments to the statute addressed questions which were raised in some of the court cases.

One issue that has been raised in connection with the stationary source standards required under section 111 is whether it is unfair discrimination to have different stationary source standards for different industries — e.g., one set of standards for cement plants, and less strict standards for power plants. One way of supporting the position that different standards are unfair discrimination is to argue that if the level of emission control is based on the available technology, then those industries that developed technology voluntarily prior to the statutory requirements would be punished for their good faith efforts in the past. They are saddled with a higher standard because the technology is available to them, while those industries that were the "bad guys" and never developed control technology willingly are rewarded with looser standards since technology is not available to them. When this issue was presented in court, the court's response was that Congress intended to clean up the air in whatever ways available technology would allow, and that no uniformity of standards for all industries was required.[16] Furthermore, it can be said that comparisons between industries should not matter since, as long as the standard is the same for all competitors within one industry, none are disadvantaged. The only time that comparisons between industries should be relevant is when the industries produce substitute or alternative products. In those situations, failure to at least take the interindustry competitiveness into account would be a

---

16. *Portland Cement Association v. Ruckelshaus,* 486 F. 2d 375 (1973).

failure to take into account the economic costs of achieving the section 111 standards, and the words of section 111 require that for emission reduction standards there must be a "taking into account the cost of achieving such reduction." The need for interindustry comparisons in such competitive situations was recognized by the court in the case noted above.

With respect to the section 109 ambient air quality standards, an issue that has generated longstanding and widespread debate is known as the question of "prevention of significant deterioration." This issue was litigated in the courts with a rather unsatisfying result (as will be discussed) and was subsequently addressed by Congress in its 1977 amendments to the Clean Air Act. The issue is whether air that is cleaner than the secondary ambient air quality standard (the stricter standard) should be allowed to be degraded to the level of the secondary standard or should this cleaner than secondary standard air be kept at or near its existing level of cleanliness.

In favor of allowing the air quality to deteriorate to the secondary level is the argument that having air that is cleaner than the secondary standard serves no purpose. The secondary standard is the level of air quality that is requisite to protect the public welfare from any known or anticipated adverse effects. That is a broad protection in and of itself but is further broadened by the Clean Air Act's definition of welfare as including but not being limited to effects on "soils, water, crops, vegetation, manmade materials, animals, wildlife, weather, visibility, and climate, damage to and deterioration of property, and hazards to transportation, as well as effects on economic values and on personal comfort and well-being."[17] These listed parameters appear to include everything imaginable, but the definition is made even broader by the words that say welfare includes but is not limited to even this comprehensive list. The argument thus says that the secondary standard protects everything and there is no reason to preserve air that is cleaner than the secondary standard if allowing deterioration will serve some function such as enabling more industry to locate in an area and bring with it jobs and a potentially better standard of living. Unindustrialized sectors of the country would argue that it is unfair to require them to keep their air cleaner than the all-inclusive secondary standard even if that is not their wish. To do so would impose on them the risk of losing out on industry, jobs, and a better standard of living. They would contend that just because they did not industrialize before the enactment of the Clean Air Act as other parts

---

17. 42 U.S.C.S. § 7602(h).

of the country did, they should not forever be precluded from industrializing. Also, they should not be required to forever be America's "clean air paradise" dependent on tourism revenues from those who live in more economically prosperous locations.

In favor of requiring that air that is cleaner than the secondary standard be kept substantially at that cleaner level is the argument that the secondary standard, while it appears to provide 100% protection, is really the product of both factual and political compromises. Factually, different scientific experts will disagree on what numerical standard of air quality is necessary to protect the public welfare. The secondary standard is likely to be a compromise between those who are very worried (or overworried) about the adverse effects of air pollution and those who are less concerned (or unconcerned). From the political perspective, people will disagree about matters such as what are the "known or anticipated adverse effects" which the secondary standard is required to protect against. This political disagreement among those involved in the decision-making process of setting the secondary standard may well result in a compromise on the numerical level that is set as the standard. Those who favor not allowing air that is cleaner than the secondary standard to be degraded down to the secondary standard say that since the standard is a product of compromise, society is better off to err on the side of caution and keep clean air at its existing level of cleanliness.

The issue of prevention of significant deterioration of cleaner than secondary standard air was presented to the courts in *Sierra Club v. Ruckelshaus*.[18] The United States District Court looked at one of the stated purposes of the Clean Air Act, which is to "protect and enhance the quality of the Nation's air resources" and concluded that the words "protect and enhance" evidenced Congress' intent to improve air quality and prevent deterioration rather than allowing deterioration. The court further noted that Congress had used the words protect and enhance in earlier air pollution legislation and that those words had been administratively interpreted as not allowing significant deterioration. Congress then used the same words in the Clean Air Act and thus the court said it must have intended that the same interpretation be adopted. Also of importance to the court was the legislative history of the Clean Air Act. The court cited a Senate Report, uncontradicted by the House, that said that air that was cleaner than the air quality goals should be maintained in its cleaner condition. The District Court's conclusion was that the EPA Administrator could not approve a state implementation plan that

18. 344 F. Supp. 253 (1972).

allowed areas with air quality cleaner than the secondary standard to have their air be degraded down to that standard. To do so would be contrary to Congress' policy of protecting the quality of the air. The District Court thus seemed to have resolved the deterioration issue in a straightforward way relying on the intent of Congress as manifested by its words, its actions, and the statute's legislative history. This "straightforward " decision was taken to the United States Supreme Court, which, one year later, voted 4 to 4 on the issue and did not issue an opinion.[19] Procedurally, an equally divided Supreme Court vote serves to affirm the lower court decision, but the 4 to 4 split underlines the legal and political division that existed on the issue. In an effort to remove the issue from the arena of statutory interpretation by the courts and to resolve it as a political matter to be decided by the people's representatives, Congress addressed the deterioration question in the 1977 amendments to the Clean Air Act.

In the 1977 amendments, Congress specifically required that state implementation plans must prevent "significant deterioration" of air quality in areas where the air is cleaner than the ambient air quality standards. Congress then went on to define what it meant by "significant deterioration." Its definitional mechanism is noteworthy because of its contrast to the usual relationship of statutes to administrative regulations. Usually Congress will leave the detailed numbers of an environmental standard to be established by the agency in its administrative regulations. This is what it has done with respect to setting the ambient air quality standards themselves. In the 1977 amendments, Congress itself established the numbers which would define when deterioration of air quality is significant deterioration and thus not allowable under a state implementation plan. These numbers were made part of the statute. The land areas of the United States were divided into three classes, with different maximum allowable increases in pollutants established for each land class. Any increase in a pollutant above the established maximum allowable increase is significant deterioration and unacceptable. For example, in class I areas (large national parks and wilderness areas) the maximum allowable increase in particulate matter is 5 $\mu g/m^3$ measured as an annual geometric mean. Class II areas are allowed 19 $\mu g/m^3$ as an increase and class III areas (where the most intensive development will be allowed) can have a maximum allowable increase of 37 $\mu g/m^3$. It should be emphasized that these increases are for areas where the air quality is cleaner than ambient air quality standards. These allowable increases do

---

19. 412 U.S. 541 (1973), with Mr. Justice Powell taking no part in the decision of the case.

not mean that the most restrictive ambient air quality standard can be exceeded.

The above is an example of how the courts and legislatures interact to resolve issues of interpretation which may arise when an administrative agency applies a statute that different interests feel should be interpreted in different ways. Another interpretation issue under the Clean Air Act which is closely related to the issue of prevention of significant deterioration involves the methods allowed for achieving the ambient air quality standards. Can a state implementation plan achieve its ambient air quality standards by allowing use of "dispersion techniques" such as tall smokestacks to disperse the pollutants over a wide area and thus bring localized concentrations within the ambient air quality standards, or must the standards be met by limiting emissions from the smokestacks? The use of dispersion techniques is related to the issue of prevention of significant deterioration, because if one location disperses its pollutants, when they go elsewhere they will degrade the quality of the air in the other location.

In the Fifth Circuit Court of Appeals case of *Natural Resources Defense Council, Inc. v. EPA,* [20] the question was whether a state implementation plan which allowed the use of tall stack dispersion techniques could be approved by EPA. The court found that tall stacks were acceptable as part of a state implementation plan only if: (1) emission limitations have been imposed to the extent they are feasible and those emissions limitations are not sufficient to meet the air quality standards or (2) emission limitations are, by themselves, sufficient to meet the air quality standards, and the state is employing dispersion techniques to make its air even cleaner than the standards. The United States Supreme Court heard this case but decided it based on issues other than the question of dispersion techniques vs. emission limitations. The Supreme Court did, however, indicate that it thought a state might be at liberty to choose to meet the ambient air quality standards by partial use of dispersion techniques even though emission controls could do the job. [21]

In the 1977 amendments to the Clean Air Act, Congress expressed its clear preference for emission control over dispersion techniques by limiting the amount of credit which the dispersion approach could generate toward the goal of meeting the air quality standards. Tall stacks can have only a very limited effect on the degree of emission limitation required. [22]

---

20. 489 F. 2d 390 (1974).

21. *Train v. Natural Resources Defense Council,* 421 U.S. 60 (1975).

22. *Alabama Power Co. v. Costle,* 606 F.2d 1068 (1979).

Congress did, however, allow states to use tall stacks for the purpose of providing air that is cleaner than the ambient air quality standards.

The reader may want to consider the question of whether tall stacks should be allowed to be used by a state to make the quality of the air in that state cleaner than that required by the ambient air quality standards. If emission limitations can and do result in air that meets the ambient air quality standards, why allow tall stack dispersion to be used to make the air cleaner still? While there may be nothing wrong with making the air cleaner than the federally set air quality standards, doing so by using dispersion results in the dispersed pollutants going somewhere and degrading the air quality in that other location. Under what circumstances, if any, should a state be allowed to have its industries use the tall stack dispersion approach? An analysis of this question would likely lead back to the points raised in our earlier discussion about preventing significant deterioration of air that is cleaner than the ambient air quality standards.

2. Water Pollution—Control Mechanisms, Federal Jurisdiction, Thermal Pollution

We have just concluded a detailed analysis of the Clean Air Act's mechanisms for air pollution control and some of the issues raised by those mechanisms which needed court interpretation or Congressional clarification. Rather than going through a similar discussion concerning water pollution and being quite repetitive at times, we will instead briefly summarize some of the similarities and differences between the Clean Air Act and the Clean Water Act.[23] We will then discuss two issues in the context of water pollution which could arise in an air pollution context just as issues similar to those we discussed in our air pollution section could arise with respect to water pollution.

The Clean Air Act's approach of addressing the medium being polluted, the sources of pollution and the nature of the pollutants themselves is also utilized in the Clean Water Act. Thus the ambient air quality standards (the medium focus) have their counterparts in the use of water quality standards and state implementation plans under the Clean Water Act. The counterpart of the stationary source standards for air pollution can be said to be the effluent limitations for point sources. The Clean Water Act also singles out toxic water pollutants for special control efforts following the Clean Air Act pattern of providing a separate control mechanism for hazardous air pollutants.

---

23. 33 U.S.C.S. § 1251 et seq.

Although similar in the above ways, the two statutes are significantly different in terms of the emphasis placed on the various control mechanisms. While the Clean Air Act made substantial use of the ambient air quality standards with state implementation plans to achieve them, the Clean Water Act leans very strongly toward pollution control by limiting the discharge of effluents from their sources. For different types of pollutants, different levels of technology are required to be used by specified dates to limit the amount of discharge of each type of pollutant. As examples, for "conventional" pollutants such as those classified as biochemical oxygen demanding (BOD) and suspended solids, effluent limitations must require application of the "best conventional pollutant control technology" (BCT) by July 1, 1984. For "toxic" pollutants, effluent limitations must require the use of the "best available technology" (BAT) economically achievable by July 1, 1984. BAT may be a higher level of technology than the BCT level. A lower level of technology, "best practicable control technology" (BPT) governs the effluent limitations for earlier years. Discharges of effluents are allowed only if they are in compliance with the effluent limitations, and only by obtaining a permit to discharge within those limits. Permits are issued federally, or by states if the state has an EPA-approved plan with limitations at least as strict as those of EPA. An example of some of the conditions which may be imposed on a discharger may be seen in Appendix D, which shows a portion of a Discharge Permit form used by the State of Vermont. A basic overall goal of the above mechanisms and of the entire Clean Water Act is the elimination of all discharges of pollutants into navigable waters by 1985.

With the above description of some of the federal methods used to control water pollution, and acknowledging that other significant control mechanisms have been omitted from our discussion (such as the massive federal grants made to finance municipal treatment works), let's consider in a water pollution context the issue of the extent of the federal government's power to deal with pollution matters. For this, we look at the case of *United States vs. Holland.*[24] The *Holland* case involved defendants who admitted that they were discharging pollutants into man-made mosquito canals and wetlands without a permit which the government said was required under the Water Pollution Control Act Amendments (now referred to as the Clean Water Act). The defendants claimed that they did not need a permit because they were discharging into waters which were not within the federal jurisdiction. Their argument had two

---

24. 373 F. Supp. 665 (1974).

distinct parts. One part was that Congress never intended that its statute be applicable to waters which were not navigable waters and, secondly, that even if Congress did want to assert jurisdiction or control over the waters at the point where defendants were discharging, it did not have the Constitutional authority to do so.

To answer the question of whether Congress intended to control the waters into which the defendants were discharging, the court looked at the statutory language that Congress had used which said that the statute applied to navigable waters. The court went on, however, to say that what was meant by "navigable waters" was not necessarily what it would mean in the technical sense or in average usage but rather what Congress intended it to mean. In the statute itself Congress had defined "navigable waters" to be "waters of the United States" and the legislative history of the statute from the House and Senate clearly indicated that Congress intended that the statute apply to "all waters of the United States." The court thus found that Congress had intended to control the waters into which the defendants were discharging even though they were wholly unsuited for navigation and even though the statute said it applied to "navigable waters." Thus an important lesson concerning the reading of statutes is that the words used do not necessarily mean what they appear to mean. At least in situations where a term is used in the statute and specifically defined in that statute, the term's meaning may not be its ordinary language meaning. Rather, the term will mean what the statutory definition says it will mean. In the Clean Water Act, "navigable waters" means "waters of the United States" and the legislative history adds the gloss of "all waters of the United States."

The second issue for our consideration in *Holland,* that of whether Congress has the constitutional authority to regulate pollution of non-navigable canals and wetlands, has more far-reaching implications and an interesting history that bears on the answer. As we noted in Chapter One, Congress' power to regulate concerning environmental matters comes from the Commerce Clause of the United States Constitution, which gives Congress the power "to regulate Commerce...among the several States...." We also noted that the scope of the Commerce Clause power has been interpreted to include the power for Congress to act with respect to matters which have an effect on interstate commerce. The court in *Holland* said that it is beyond question that water pollution has a serious effect on interstate commerce and Congress can thus regulate activities which cause pollution such as the dredging and filling in which the defendants were engaged. The court used the "effect on interstate commerce" approach to find that the pollution-causing activities at the defendant's site would have serious effects on interstate commerce. If it had not been able to use the "effect" approach, one can speculate that the court may well have taken the last remaining step in the historical expansion of Congress' power with respect to bodies of water. That expansion was detailed by the court as follows.

The court pointed out that since much of 19th century commerce was carried on the water, Congress' power "to regulate Commerce" had early been held to necessarily include the power over navigation.[25] If you are to effectively regulate navigation, you must have the power to keep navigable waters open and free, and Congress was found to have that power also.[26] Subsequent steps in the expansion of Congress' authority included the authority to regulate waters over which commerce is or *may be* carried on with other states;[27] waters capable of commercial use, not merely those in actual use;[28] waters with a history of commercial use;[29] and waterways which could be made navigable by reasonable improvements.[30] Few bodies of water could escape from the Congressional power under these expanded interpretations of what the Commerce Clause supposedly authorized Congress to control. If mosquito canals and wetlands could escape and if the "effect on interstate commerce" approach were not available to bring them within Congress' jurisdiction, it would not be difficult to imagine the court's taking the next step in the expansion to include those bodies of water also. The question to be left for the reader is whether, in light of the above-described scope of Congress' power under the Commerce Clause, is there any body of water (or land, or air, or mineral or . . .) over which Congress does not have the Constitutional power to act? Can Congress control what you do with a temporary puddle that forms in your backyard or basement after a rainstorm? Is it likely that the people who drafted the United States Constitution would have approved of such power being in the hands of the federal government?

As a final topic in our water pollution section, let's consider thermal pollution. Thermal pollution could be an air pollution problem as well as a water pollution problem, as anyone who has stood in heavy traffic on city pavement on a hot summer day can verify. Today's most significant thermal pollution problems are, however, water-related, and the Clean Water Act provides for thermal pollution control for bodies of water.

---

25. *Gibbons v. Ogden,* 22 U.S. 1 (1824).

26. *Gilman v. Philadelphia,* 70 U.S. 713 (1865).

27. *The Daniel Ball,* 77 U.S. 557 (1870).

28. *The Montello,* 87 U.S. 430 (1874).

29. *Economy Light and Power v. United States,* 256 U.S. 113 (1921).

30. *United States v. Appalachian Electric Power Co.,* 311 U.S. 377 (1940).

Thermal pollution problems result from the fact that even minor changes in water temperatures can affect the reproduction, migration and metabolism of cold-blooded heat-sensitive aquatic animals. Heat also causes adverse effects on aquatic plants and the death of a body of water could result due to heat-caused oxygen depletion.

A major cause of thermal pollution is the electric utility industry. Other sources include steel mills and pulp processing plants. In order to control thermal pollution problems, Congress has included "heat" within the definition of "pollutant" under the Clean Water Act, and thus water quality control measures like effluent limitations are to include thermal discharge standards. While Congress has recognized thermal pollution as a problem, it has also recognized that the characteristics of heat make its effects more temporary and localized than many other pollutants. With this in mind, the Clean Water Act provides that thermal discharges should not be subject to any limits more stringent than necessary to assure the protection and propagation of a balanced, indigenous population of shellfish, fish and wildlife in and on the relevant body of water. Some examples of mechanisms which have been used to control thermal pollution are allowing only limited rises in the temperature of a plant's outlet water over its inlet water, holding down the size of the water's "mixing zone" to prevent the formation of migratory barriers, and keeping the dissolved oxygen level sufficient to support local species.

Although heat is generally viewed as a pollutant of water and the law has sought to regulate it in at least a limited way, thermal discharges may have a positive side. Projects are underway which will explore the commercial possibilities of aquafarming of species like freshwater shrimp and rainbow trout using the heat from cooling water discharged by operations such as power plants. A pollutant could therefore become something from which a benefit could be derived and perhaps the better the control of the pollutant, the greater the enhancement of the benefit. That would be a highly desirable result for other pollutants as well as for heat.

3.   Acid Rain — A Hybrid Form of Pollution

Before discussing acidic metal-containing precipitation (acid rain) as a hybrid form of pollution, we will first examine what this phenomenon is and then proceed to discuss why the current approaches to regulation are seemingly inadequate.

Acidic metal-containing precipitation (acid rain) is, as far as we can determine, a phenomenon of recent origin. After World War II, the population of the United States indicated a dissatisfaction with the particulate emissions from industrial facilities that burned fossil fuels for various reasons. So, precipitators were installed at the facilities to remove most of the particulates (soot). While this provided a solution to one problem, it created another. Particulates had acted to neutralize sulfur dioxide emissions and essentially prevent the formation of atmospheric sulfuric acid that might eventually fall to earth. At the same time, we built a lot of tall smokestacks (Table I) to help remedy the local pollution situation by dispersing the pollutants over a wide area, an undertaking that has likely contributed to the regional problem we face today. Around 1950, the automobile industry introduced the high compression engine and with it a combustion product of much greater magnitude than previously experienced, nitrogen oxides. So, in our effort to be more efficient in one case (automobiles) and less polluting in another case (precipitators and tall stacks) we allowed two oxides into the air. The United States currently produces a lot of sulfur dioxide and nitrogen oxides (Table III). In the atmosphere, these oxides can be transported long distances and can be chemically altered to form sulfuric and nitric acids. These acids fall in rain and are apparently causing substantial harm in a number of areas of the United States. Currently, acidic rainfall in the northeastern United States is almost completely composed of dilute sulfuric and nitric acids in a ratio of 60:40 respectively. In addition to interacting with structures and thereby accelerating building deterioration, acid rain has been accused of causing or contributing to the decline of sport fisheries, the loss of tourism, the loss of profits from farming, increased respiratory disease in humans and the loss of forest productivity. The basic problem of causation is extremely difficult to assess. We do not know if the cause of harm is the two acids, one of the acids, the metals carried in the acid rain or those mobilized by rain falling on surfaces. We do know that something is happening; we do not know the exact cause-effect relationship.

With our limited scientific knowledge of what is taking place, now comes before us a potential "answer" to the problem, the Clean Air Act. The Clean Air Act approaches the problem of clean air in quite a straightforward fashion.[31] The Act recognizes what turns out to be the two main sources of acid rain — sulfur oxides and nitrogen oxides — with respect to both stationary sources and mobile sources, and sets emission limits on new sources for these oxides. Also, there are standards set for ambient air quality, including standards for sulfur dioxide and nitrogen oxides. These pollutants were originally selected for control for reasons other than their relationship to acid rain, e.g., health reasons. While this effort

---

31. 42 U.S.C. § 4701 et seq.

tried to balance concerns for clean air with concerns about not imposing extensive burdens on technology and costs on consumers, the problem of acid rain was not specifically addressed in the Act, probably due to a lack of awareness of the problem or its magnitude. Since the Clean Air Act did not specifically address the acid rain problem, but only by coincidence controlled the pollutants which cause it, additional control measures appear to be needed to properly deal with acid rain. In fact, acid rain may be thought of as not being an air pollution problem, but rather a water pollution problem. Let us examine this notion.

Sulfur oxides and nitrogen oxides are produced from stationary and mobile point sources when fossil fuels are burned. Our clean air purpose is to regulate these emissions (this model is applicable to other air pollutants) such that our air contains an amount of these pollutants less than or equal to the level indicated by the acceptable line in Figure 3. When the real level of air pollution goes above the acceptable level, we become concerned and seek some means to lower this real level or we increase the acceptable level, thereby bringing the real level back below the acceptable level. Acid rain results when these sulfur oxides and nitrogen oxides form sulfuric and nitric acid and fall to earth as rain (water). The damage that

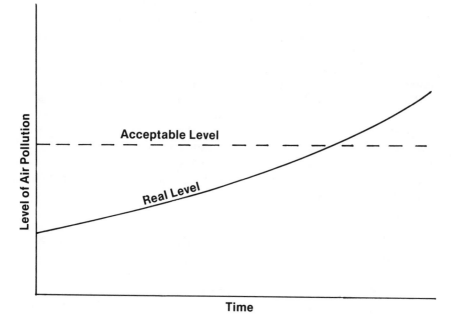

Figure 3. A simplified model of how we view air pollution.

is done is mainly in our lakes, rivers and soil solution. In reality, we have two gases emitted from point sources (these sources may all be complying with the law) that are further oxidized in the atmosphere to acids that fall to earth in a liquid form as rainwater. Therefore, these gases contaminate water in the air and this contaminated water falls to earth as a nonpoint source of pollution. The acidic properties of this water allow many materials to become soluble or remain soluble, a condition not considered normal in recent history. Even if *all* stationary and mobile sources of these two gaseous pollutants were to individually comply with current emission limits, acid rain would not disappear because of the cumulative effect of individual sources and atmospheric transformations.

Suppose we know that there are 500 stationary sources that each produce 100 tons of sulfur oxides every year. That means there are 50,000 tons of sulfur oxide released to the atmosphere. Suppose that this is an acceptable level for air pollution but acid rain is still polluting water. The problem is that even if we reduce emissions for these 500 sources, build 300 new sources and have the total loading from these 800 sources remain below the acceptable air pollution level, acid rain will not necessarily be curtailed because we do not know whether the amount of acid produced is a function of the amount of oxides emitted or a function of the atmosphere's potential to transform the oxides or both. Acid rain is like air cleaning: the rain washes the air but pollutes the water. And, as we build more stationary sources in a localized geographic area, the water pollution problem downwind from the air emissions may grow. Thus acid rain as a water pollution problem will not necessarily be curtailed by the issuance of more stringent air pollution limitations.

The problem of acid rain is really a water pollution problem downwind from emissions of air pollutants. Therefore, any resolution of this type of problem should specifically address the sources and the points of impact as they relate to acid rain. Existing legislation, while it coincidentally deals with those air pollutants which cause acid rain water pollution, does not address those air pollutants with the intent of controlling them as causes of acid rain.

4.   Noise Pollution — Control Mechanisms for Aircraft Noise and Nonaircraft Noise, Federation Preemption

We will conclude our discussion of public pollution control by considering what some people believe will soon become a major issue in the area of pollution control — noise pollution. While air pollution and water pollution problems have been coming under control to a large extent, noise pollution problems may be moving in the opposite direction. Some studies have indicated that the "ambient noise level" in urban communities is doubling every ten years and, should that pattern continue unchecked, noise could have direct lethal effects within thirty years. But without going to the extreme of noise being lethal in and of itself, noise is thought to be a possible contributing factor to disease such as heart disease, arthritis and diabetes, and to have adverse effects on unborn children. Some research has also indicated a possible relationship between noise levels and the human body's ability to handle toxic materials. Huge numbers of toxic substances are in common use in industry and business and there is some indication that the body's intake of substances such as toxic ozone from copying machines may be increased under the stress of high noise levels.

The above less well known, understood or accurate thoughts are, of course, in addition to the well documented hearing loss problems which are derivative of noise and the plain fact that noise is often unpleasant regardless of whether it also causes health problems. Job-related hearing loss is a problem which affects many, and excess noise in the workplace is said to have the potential of harming 16 million American workers. Regulations established pursuant to the federal Occupational Safety and Health Act (OSHA)[32] have sought to limit the permissible exposure of workers to noise. The question is not so much whether there should be permissible levels established, but rather what those levels should be. While prevention of overexposure to noise may be a sound goal, achieving noise control means accepting the costs inherent in control. The usual related questions are present. Is noise reduction to be achieved while taking into account the costs of achieving the reduction, or are the evils of noise sufficient in some circumstances to require reduction regardless of cost? Also, from a factual point of view, what is the noise level above which a certain type of harm will occur? As with most factual questions, opinions concerning the answer are often widely divergent. Our emphasis in the noise control area will be to consider the mechanisms for noise control established by or pursuant to the Noise Control Act of 1972 (as amended)[33] and then to discuss the question of whether state and local control of one type of noise, aircraft noise, is allowable or prohibited.

Just as we saw that there are mechanisms in the Clean Water Act that closely parallel those in the Clean Air Act, so too are there parallels between the Noise Control Act and the Clean Air Act. The Noise Control

32. 29 U.S.C. § 651 et seq.
33. 42 U.S.C.S. § 4901 et seq.

Act directs the EPA Administrator to establish levels of environmental noise the attainment and maintenance of which are requisite to protect the public health and welfare. This control mechanism (which might be called "ambient noise levels") could be thought of as analogous to the ambient air quality standards under the Clean Air Act since they seek to address the medium which is polluted without regard to the source of the pollutant. A critical difference exists, however, with respect to the utilization of those "ambient" standards or levels. The ambient air quality standards were required to be implemented by state implementation plans or by an EPA plan in the absence of an acceptable state plan. On the other hand, while the environmental noise levels are published for information and possible use in connection with other parts of the Noise Control Act or by other agencies or levels of government, there is no mandatory implementation of the noise levels which were found to be requisite to protect the public health and welfare.

A second parallel between the noise statute and the air statute is that both provide control mechanisms which focus on the source of pollution. The Clean Air Act has its stationary source standards, and various sections of the Noise Control Act are directed at major sources of noise such as certain products distributed in commerce (e.g. construction equipment, any motor or engine), railroads and motor carriers. For these products distributed in commerce to which the act is applicable, the Administrator publishes noise emission standards. These standards are to protect the public health and welfare and they take into account the magnitude and conditions of use of the products. Thus motors used for short periods of time in unenclosed spaces may be subjected to a less strict standard than those used continuously and in enclosed areas. The manufacturer of each applicable product warrants to the ultimate purchaser and subsequent purchasers that the product conforms to its noise emission standard at the time of sale. In addition, enforcement of the noise emission standards may take place through citizen suits, and willful or knowing violation of the emission standard regulations may result in criminal penalties. The noise emission standards are promulgated as a result of a balancing by the Administrator similar to the balancing which leads to new stationary source emission standards under the Clean Air Act. The noise emission limitations are to be set with a goal of protecting the public health and welfare by attaining the degree of noise reduction achievable by the best available technology but also by taking into account the cost of compliance.

Striving to achieve noise reduction through the use of the best available technology while recognizing economic reality and thus taking into account the cost of compliance is also the methodology of the sections of the act pertaining to railroad noise and motor carrier noise. Appendix C illustrates the typical statutory and administrative relationship for environmental matters, in this case regulating motor carrier noise. The statute imposes the duty on the Administrator to regulate motor carrier noise and provides general standards such as "best available technology," "taking into account the cost of compliance," and "assure appropriate consideration for safety." The Administrator must abide by the statutory direction and guidance; however, there is a substantial amount of administrative discretion allowed in the setting of the standards. The detailed standards, such as how much noise, at what speed, and measured how far from the vehicle, are contained in the administrative regulations. The reader is encouraged to study Appendix C not necessarily for its substantive content but to become acquainted with the relationship between statutes and regulations.

In addition to the mandatory control mechanism that applies to certain noise-emitting products (the noise emission limitations), a control mechanism of consumer education is also provided by the act. Products which emit noise capable of adversely affecting the public health or welfare, or which are sold on the basis of effectiveness in reducing noise, are required to give notice to the prospective user by labeling the product with information on the level of noise the product emits or its effectiveness in reducing noise. Thus even without mandatory controls, purchasers should be able to factor noise levels into their decision-making process regarding which of competing products should be purchased.

Another nonmandatory approach to noise control which Congress has utilized in the Noise Control Act is to encourage development of "low-noise-emission" products. A low-noise-emission product is one which emits noise in amounts significantly below the levels specified in the noise emission standards discussed earlier. Such products are eligible to be certified as low-noise-emission products. That certification may, by itself, provide a competitive advantage in the marketplace sufficient to encourage the development of low-noise-emission products; however, Congress has made the incentive even greater. The statute requires that the federal government purchase certified low-noise-emission products in preference to other products of its type so long as its retail price is no more than 125% of the least expensive product for which it is a substitute. A producer that develops a low-noise-emission product will thus have preferred access to a very large-volume buyer. Congress has established this incentive mechanism with a hoped-for result of quieter products which, once the products have been developed, will become available for purchase by the general public as well as by the government.

An area of federal noise control which has seen greater federal regulation than the subject areas covered in our above discussion of the Noise Control Act is that of aircraft noise. Under the Federal Aviation Act of 1958 and amendments thereto,[34] the Federal Aviation Administration has had the authority to provide for control and abatement of aircraft noise and sonic boom. Our inquiry in the area of aircraft noise will involve the nonfederal roles, if any, that exist in aircraft noise regulation, and our starting point will be the United States Supreme Court case of *Burbank v. Lockheed Air Terminal.*[35]

In the *Burbank* case, the City of Burbank had enacted an ordinance which made it unlawful for jet aircraft to take off from the Hollywood-Burbank Airport during certain hours (11 p.m.–7 a.m.). The validity of the ordinance was challenged based on the Supremacy Clause of the United States Constitution. The Supremacy Clause, found in Article VI of the United States Constitution, says that the "Constitution, and the Laws of the United States...shall be the supreme Law of the Land;... any Thing in the Constitution or Laws of any State to the Contrary notwithstanding." Two theories which might possibly invalidate a state or local law are derived from the Supremacy Clause. The first is where state or local law and federal law are in conflict because they address the same subject matter and are structured such that they cannot stand side by side. If, for example, state law required an aircraft to have blue lights and federal law said no lights other than red lights are allowed, one could not possibly comply with both state and federal law. There is a conflict and the state law is invalid pursuant to the Supremacy Clause. The Supreme Court did not address the conflict theory in *Burbank* but based its decision on the second theory derived from the Supremacy Clause— that of federal preemption.

If federal law set a 95 decibel (dB) maximum noise level for aircraft and local law set a 90 dB maximum level, there would be no conflict since one could comply with both laws. Operation at 90 dB or anything less would satisfy both laws. The preemption theory says that even though both laws could stand side by side since they create no direct conflict, if Congress intended to fully take over or "preempt" the field of regulation of certain subject matter, then the nonfederal law concerning that subject matter is invalid. Sometimes Congress will expressly indicate in its legislation that it is preempting a field of control. No express preemption existed with respect to aircraft noise control; however the Supreme Court found that Congress' intent to preempt the field of control was evidenced

---

34. 49 U.S.C.A. § 1431.

35. 411 U.S. 624 (1973).

by the pervasive nature of the scheme of federal regulation of aircraft noise. The Court said that the pervasive control vested by Congress in federal agencies left no room for local curfews or other local controls. The Court further pointed out that if local ordinances such as Burbank's were allowed and other localities followed suit, the federal government's flexibility in controlling air traffic would be severely limited with potential problems such as increased air traffic congestion resulting in decreased safety and possibly increased noise levels. The Burbank ordinance was thus invalidated as having been preempted.

In 1977 the Concorde arrived on the scene and the New York Port Authority sought to prevent its flight into New York due to noise (*British Airways v. Port Authority*).[36] Was that then a clear case of federal preemption and the Port Authority could not act? The answer is that the federal preemption finding in *Burbank* did not apply to the Port Authority because the *Burbank* case involved an ordinance of a government unit (a city) and the Supreme Court specifically stated in *Burbank* that it was not addressing the issue of the power of a proprietor of an airport to regulate aircraft noise. Although the Port Authority was a government unit, it was also the proprietor of the airport, whereas the City of Burbank was not the proprietor. The Second Circuit Court of Appeals decided that, as the proprietor of the airport, the Port Authority was fully within its power to regulate aircraft noise. The reasoning behind what might appear to be a strange distinction (allowing regulation by a proprietor but invalidating regulation by a local government) was: (1) that Congress never intended to preempt aircraft noise control by proprietors—this statement of "intent" came from the legislative history in the form of House and Senate Reports, and (2) that proprietors of airports are liable for harm to others which may result from noise of aircraft using the proprietor's facility. Thus the proprietor must have the right to protect against this liability by restricting the use of his airport. The "proprietor" exception to the *Burbank* preemption rule resulted in the Port Authority having the power to regulate aircraft noise.

Two notes in closing: First, if the Port Authority was found to have the power to regulate noise, and since it clearly wanted to limit access by the Concorde, why did the Concorde avoid being controlled? The answer is that while proprietors may regulate their airports, such regulation must be reasonable and nondiscriminatory. The Port Authority never found a way to exclude the Concorde in a reasonable and nondiscriminatory way and it did not want to exclude other aircraft as well. Second, the viability

---

36. 558 F. 2d 75 (1977).

of the position that airport proprietors are liable for aircraft noise was reinforced in 1979 in *Greater Westchester Homeowners Association v. City of Los Angeles.*[37] The California Supreme Court in fact expanded the proprietor's liability in that nuisance case to include not only the traditional liability for property damage but also liability for injury to the person. Although public law with respect to pollution has relegated private law to a secondary status in recent years, the *Greater Westchester* case indicates that private law remedies in the pollution area continue to be available and even adaptable to current needs.

D.   ENVIRONMENTAL MEDIATION

We have previously discussed two ways which we use to resolve environmental disputes. The first was private law remedies (the adversarial process) which creates the feeling of a winner and a loser. The second way was through the legislative process which, because of the large number of interests to which it must respond, often results in a cumbersome mechanism that tries to serve everyone responsibly while clearly considering economics as the overriding variable.[38] Although the former appears an acceptable means of dispute resolution in situations such as automobile accidents, falling ceilings in theaters, manure odor from beef feedlots and even smokestack emissions from a single industrial site, this process was not really designed to address large-scale environmental issues. These issues do not need a winner and a loser, nor a court that fashions contorted legal remedies. These issues may need resolution in a forum that addresses the central issue and seeks a resolution acceptable to everyone involved. The legislative approach also has its shortcomings with respect to resolving environmental disputes, because the economic position is often viewed as paramount. Legislative resolution may come, but only if there is an economically sound, which usually means cheap, solution. There might be another way!

One suggested method of resolving environmental disputes is the process of mediation. This process attempts to bring together all parties involved in a dispute to try to reach a solution that is legally supportable by and fundamentally acceptable to all parties. This type of undertaking requires trust among all parties, truthfulness and openness, and a commitment to abiding by the result of the collective process. Professional

---

37. 603 P. 2d 1329 (1979).

38. Wolin, S. S. "The New Public Philosophy," *Democracy.* 1(4):23–36 (1981).

mediators will be needed in such instances. This type of forum is receiving some attention, as evidenced by a recent conference on the concept of the use of mediation in environmental disputes.[39] Central to the idea of using mediation is the necessity of compromise and an issue that is capable of resolution by compromise. What mediation also provides is a less costly means of "solving" a problem. What mediation does not provide is a winner, nor does this process really create a binding result. There is always still the recourse to the courts or, theoretically, the legislative arena where new law could greatly alter the result which the parties have reached through mediation.

Another approach to the resolution of environmental issues where scientific uncertainty is at question is the use of a science court.[40] While the use of a science court is geared, and should be geared, to ascertaining only what we can scientifically agree on, it is a step in the resolution process. The possibility of coupling a science court for making factual scientific determinations with the process of mediation for resolving conflicts once the facts have been determined presents a potentially powerful tool for the resolution of environmental disputes.

ADDITIONAL READINGS

Cushman, R. M., S. B. Gough, M. S. Moran and R. B. Craig. *Sourcebook of Hydrologic and Ecological Features* (Ann Arbor, MI: Ann Arbor Science Publishers, Inc., 1980).

Environmental Protection Agency. *Acid Rain* Environmental Protection Agency, EPA-600/9-79-036 (Washington, DC: ORD, 1980).

Miller, G. T., Jr. *Living in the Environment* (Belmont, CA: Wadsorth Publishing Co., Inc., 1982).

Smith, W. H. *Air Pollution and Forests* (New York: Springer-Verlag New York, Inc., 1981).

Wetstone, G. (Ed.) *Water Pollution: Law and Legislation in the United States* (revised annually) (Washington, DC: Environmental Law Institute, 1979).

Williamson, S. J. *Fundamentals of Air Pollution* (Reading, MA: Addison-Wesley Publishing Co., Inc., 1973).

---

39. Conference on Environmental/Developmental Mediation. Vermont Law School. November 1981.

40. Kantrowitz, A. 1976. "The Science Court Experiment: An Interim Report," *Science* 193:653–56.

CHAPTER 4

LAND USE

A. CONTROL VS. NONCONTROL

1. What Is Land?

On the surface land could be measured in terms of area, but land is really three-dimensional. Scientifically, land is a mixture of particles of various sizes. Larger particles are called gravel and what is usually called soil consists of sand, silt and clay. These are differentiated by size (Table I). The greater amount of sand in a soil, the more porous the soil, and therefore water and other liquids will move through it faster. Conversely, as the amount of clay increases, the less porous the soil and the more slowly liquids move through it. This is the reason that ponds and some landfills and waste disposal sites are often lined with clay. The belief is that "pure" clay is so impermeable that leakage is not a problem. Soils are classified throughout the world based on the above properties as well as other characteristics such as depth prior to reaching bedrock, water holding capacity, organic matter content, color, iron content and aluminum content. An example of one very large-scale classification of soil is given in Figure 1.

In addition to the makeup of the soil itself, other important properties are latitude, altitude, slope of the land and the amount and seasonal distribution of rainfall. These factors are important not only in classification of soil but also in the use of such land.

2. Land Classification

Various methods have been used to classify land, resulting in numerous maps with definitions of land classifications based on the current uses of

Table I.   Sizes of Soil Particles as Currently Used by the United States Soil Conservation Service

Soil Particle	Diameter (mm)
Sand	2.0–0.02
Silt	0.02–0.005
Clay	≤0.005

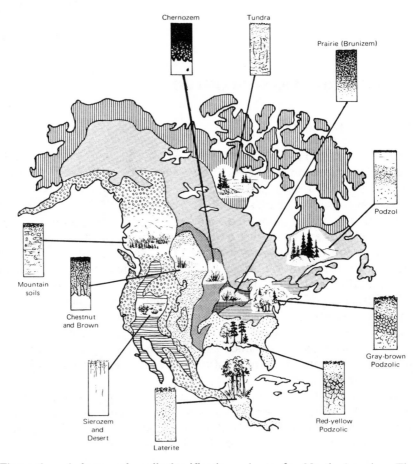

Figure 1.   A large-scale soil classification scheme for North America. The system considers soil in great groups.[1]

---

1. Smith, R. L. *Ecology and Field Biology.* (2nd ed.). (New York: Harper & Row, Publishers, Inc., 1974).

the land, the potential uses of the land or simply the soil types grouped together into general use categories that may describe both the current and potential uses. These maps and classifications are usually prepared by or for some governmental agency for use in assessing, allocating or controlling land use patterns.

Let us look at two examples of land classification: one by the Fish and Wildlife Service of the United States Department of the Interior, and the other, the ongoing effort of the Soil Conservation Service of the United States Department of Agriculture. In 1974, the Fish and Wildlife Service assigned its Biological Services Office the task of making an inventory of the wetlands of the United States. To accomplish this task the office decided to first define the limits of wetland as a natural ecosystem with the eventual objective of inventory, evaluation and management of such areas. Realizing that no definition adopted by them could withstand scrutiny in all cases, the drafters decided on the following definition:

> Wetlands are lands transitional between terrestrial and aquatic systems where the water table is usually at or near the surface or the land is covered by shallow water. For purposes of this classification wetlands must have one or more of the following three attributes: (1) at least periodically, the land supports predominantly hydrophytes, (2) the substrate is predominantly undrained hydric soil, and (3) the substrate is nonsoil and is saturated with water or covered by shallow water at some time during the growing season of each year.[2]

Hydrophytes are plants that either tolerate or enjoy being extremely wet. Hydric soils have their pores totally filled with water during at least some time during a typical year. Most commonly, one considers bogs, marshes, swamps or rocky shores as wetlands. The above definition and its characterization eventually led the Fish and Wildlife Service to identify the systems shown in Figure 2 as either wetlands or deepwater (permanently flooded) habitats. What is classified as a wetland is of major land use significance since local, state and federal restrictions often prevent wetlands from being used as building sites.

The Soil Conservation Service has classified the soil of most counties in most states. While the process is continually being updated as better mapping information is required or as new information or techniques become available, and thus the information may be presented in different formats, the classifications all attempt to evaluate the soil in a particular location with respect to possible uses for that soil. Examples of

---

2. Department of the Interior. *Classification of Wetlands and Deepwater Habitats of the United States.* (Washington, DC: U.S. Government Printing Office, 1979).

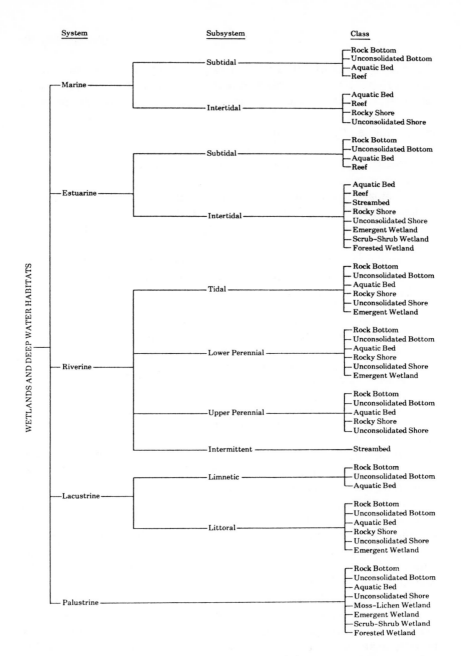

Figure 2. Classification hierarchy of wetlands and deepwater habitats, showing systems, subsystems and classes. The Palustrine System does not include deepwater habitats.[3]

---

3. Ibid.

evaluations of soils are given in Figures 3 and 4. Though these soils are in different parts of the United States and were evaluated at different times, one can see that the same basic considerations are included in each report.

3. The Uses of Land

The major uses of land in the United States and the approximate numbers of acres allocated to each use are indicated in Figure 5. As one can see from the figure, the amount of cropland and specialized land use has increased, while the acres of marsh, desert and tundra, as well as those of forest and grassland, have decreased. Let us take a closer look at each of these land uses and examine not only the uses but some consequences of the uses.

Cropland is a resource used to produce not only much of the food consumed either directly or secondarily in the United States, but also as a food resource for other parts of the world. Currently, the United States contains in excess of 400 million acres of agricultural land, or about 6,250 square miles. Reportedly, each year about 3 million of these acres are converted to development while an additional 2 million acres become nonproductive after isolation by development. If this rate of reduction were to continue, there would be no agricultural land left in 80 years. Obviously, the demand for food and the realization of the need for agricultural land will eventually act to preserve such lands. The questions are what role, if any, should government play concerning agricultural land preservation, and when should it act. Conversion and isolation are but two mechanisms by which cropland is lost. Two other mechanisms are erosion and loss of fertility. Current estimates indicate that about 3 million acres of cropland are lost annually to erosion. Loss of fertility is a rather newly recognized form of cropland conversion. Since the discovery of the Haber process, it has been possible to make synthetic fertilizer containing nitrogen at a low cost. Having an inexpensive source of fertilizer made from various synthetic chemicals has allowed farmers to dispense with green manuring or animal manure as a source of nutrients for crops. These synthetic chemicals have proven both effective and reliable for farmers in terms of dependable production. However, the application of these chemicals also enhances the breakdown of organic matter in soil and consequently alters soil structure, making the soil more susceptible to flooding and water erosion as well as wind erosion. Additionally, the soil's binding ability for nutrients and water is decreased. Thus, the fertility of the soil itself is being lost and much agricultural soil has become merely a holdfast for crops while they are fed nutrients so

Soil Series: Matherton

Area _____ Michigan

Date: August, 1965

Advance Copy - SUBJECT TO CHANGE

ENGINEERING INTERPRETATIONS

Somewhat poorly drained soils with loamy surface layer over sandy clay loam or clay loam. Calcareous, stratified gravel and sand at a depth ranging from 24 to 42 inches. Outwash plains and moraines. Water table fluctuates between 2 and 10 feet.

ESTIMATED PHYSICAL AND CHEMICAL PROPERTIES

General Soil Profile	Classification			% of material passing sieve			Permeability		Available water capacity in./in.	Soil reaction pH	Shrink-swell potential
	USDA Texture	Unified	AASHO	No. 4 4.7 mm.	No. 10 2.0 mm.	No. 200 0.074 mm.	Inches per hour	Minutes per inch			
Sandy loam		SM	A-2 or A-4	95-100	25-45	25-45	2.5-5.0	12-24	0.14	5.5-7.0	Low
12" Sandy clay, loam and clay loam		SC or CL	A-6	95-100	85-95	35-65	0.8-2.5	24-62	0.16	5.5-6.5	Moderate to high
24" / 36" / 48" Stratified gravel and sand		GP or SP	A-1	40-80	35-70	0-5	over 10	less than 6	0.02	7.5-8.0 calcareous	Low
60"											

SUITABILITY OF SOIL AS RESOURCE MATERIAL

RESOURCE MATERIAL	SUITABILITY
Topsoil	Fair for sandy loam, good for loam - medium content of organic matter, gravel and cobble on surface in some areas, seasonal high water table.
Sand	Good - stratified sand and gravel, excess wetness hinders excavation.

Gravel	Good - stratified sand and gravel, excess wetness hinders excavation.
Borrow for highway fills	Fair to poor in upper 24 to 42 inches.- moderate volume change, fair to poor bearing capacity. Good in sand and gravel - low volume change, good subgrade material.
Impermeable material for dams and levees	Good in upper 24 to 42 inches - fair workability and compaction. Not suitable in sand and gravel - rapid permeability, subject to piping.

FACTORS AFFECTING USE

USE	FACTORS
Highway construction	Seasonal high water table. Wet conditions may exist and hinder construction. Substratum has fair to good bearing capacity.
Winter grading	High moisture content may exist and hinder operations.
Foundations for low buildings	Seasonal high water table, fair to good bearing capacity, low volume change on wetting or drying, low compressibility, high shear strength.
Pond reservoir areas	Medium seepage rate in subsoil, seal blanket required when porous sand and gravel substratum is exposed.
Dams, dikes, and levees	Upper 24 to 42 inches has fair to good stability and compaction properties, slow seepage rate; substratum has fair stability and compaction properties; rapid seepage rate.
Septic tank disposal field	Seasonal high water table, rapid percolation of effluent may pollute shallow water supplies. Need on-site investigation.
Sanitary land fill	Seasonal high water table, upper 24 to 42 inches has fair compaction and workability, fair to poor bearing capacity, and rapid seepage rate. Sand and gravel has good workability, good bearing capacity, and rapid seepage rate.
Artificial drainage	Drainage usually needed. Seasonal high water table. Moderate permeability above 36 inches, rapid below. Special blinding required for tile.
Irrigation	Medium to low water holding capacity, rapid water intake rate, moderate depth to sand and gravel.
Corrosion hazard	Metal conduits: Moderate Concrete conduits: Low

UNITED STATES DEPARTMENT OF AGRICULTURE   National Cooperative Soil Survey - USA
SOIL CONSERVATION SERVICE in cooperation with
MICHIGAN AGRICULTURAL EXPERIMENT STATION

DEGREE OF LIMITATION OF SOIL FOR VARIOUS USES [1]

URBAN USE

USE	LIMITATION AND QUALIFICATION
Residential development with public sewer	Moderate - seasonal high water table; wet depressions in some areas; fair to good bearing capacity; material flows when wet; low volume change; driveways and streets subject to cracking and frost heave; wet basements are a problem during wet periods.
Residential development without public sewer	Moderate - seasonal high water table; wet depressions in some areas; fair to good bearing capacity; material flows when wet; low volume change; driveways and streets subject to cracking and frost heave; wet basements are a problem during wet periods; severe limitations for septic tank filter fields because of wet conditions; filter fields are saturated during wet periods.
Buildings for light industrial and commercial use	Moderate - seasonal high water table; wet depressions in some areas; fair to good bearing capacity; low volume change; construction difficult during wet periods; filling and grading required in many areas.
Highways and streets	Moderate - seasonal high water table; wet depressions in some areas; fills required in wet areas; construction difficult during wet periods; fair to good bearing capacity; low volume change; moderate frost heave problem.

RECREATION

USE	LIMITATION AND QUALIFICATION
Cottages and utility buildings	Moderate - seasonal high water table; wet depressions in some areas; fair to good bearing capacity; low volume change; dries out slowly in spring and after rain.
Intensive camp sites	Moderate - seasonal high water table; wet depressions in some areas; fair to poor bearing capacity for vehicles and foot traffic when wet; dries out slowly in spring and after rain; soft and muddy when wet; good strength for tent stakes.
Picnic areas	Moderate - seasonal high water table; wet depressions in some areas; soft and muddy when wet; dries out slowly in spring and after rain; fair to poor bearing capacity for foot traffic when wet; turf easily maintained.
Intensive play areas	Moderate - seasonal high water table; wet depressions in some areas; soft and muddy when wet; fair to poor bearing capacity for foot traffic when wet; dries out slowly in spring and after rain; turf easily maintained.

Paths and trails	Moderate - seasonal high water table; wet depressions in some areas; surface layer muddy and soft when wet; dries out slowly in spring and after rain; fair to poor bearing capacity for foot traffic when wet.
Golf fairways	Moderate - seasonal high water table; wet depressions in some areas; dries out slowly in spring and after rain; fair to poor bearing capacity for foot traffic and motorized carts; turf easily maintained.

AGRICULTURE AND OTHER VEGETATION

USE	LIMITATION AND QUALIFICATION
Land capability class and soil management group	Class II. Class III in northern zone if undrained. If not drainable, soil is Class V, VI, or VII, depending on degree of wetness. Group 3b.
Farm crops	Slight - seasonal high water table; artificial drainage required for optimum crop yields; sandy material below 18 to 42 inches is unstable when wet and caves in readily; wet depressions in some areas; wide crop adaptability; fair to poor bearing capacity for farm machinery during wet periods; moderate to severe limitations if drainage cannot be obtained.
Trees	Severe - low to medium production for both hardwoods and conifers; seasonal high water table limits root development; severe windthrow hazard; drainage required before planting.
Lawns and shrubs	Moderate - seasonal high water table; water-tolerant shrubs required in undrained areas; dries out slowly in spring and after rain; difficult to establish lawns during wet periods.

1/ The soil is evaluated only to a depth of 5 feet or less. Soils are rated on the basis of four classes of soil limitations: Slight - relatively free of limitations or limitations are easily overcome; Moderate - limitations need to be recognized, but can be overcome with good management and careful design; Severe - limitations are severe enough to make use questionable; Very Severe - extreme measures are needed to overcome the limitations and usage generally is unsound or not practical.

Figure 3. Sample soil interpretation sheet for Matherton soil in Michigan.

SOIL INTERPRETATIONS RECORD

HADLEY SERIES

LRA(S): 142, 144, 145, 146
SEPTEMBER, 1979
YPIC UDIFLUVENTS, COARSE-SILTY, MIXED, NONACID, MESIC

THE HADLEY SERIES CONSISTS OF DEEP WELL DRAINED SOILS ON FLOODPLAINS. THEY FORMED IN RECENT ALLUVIUM. TYPICALLY THESE SOILS HAVE A VERY DARK GRAYISH SILT LOAM SURFACE LAYER 11 INCHES THICK. THE SUBSTRATUM FROM 11 TO 68 INCHES IS OLIVE BROWN OR BROWN SILT LOAM AND FROM 68 TO 72 INCHES IS OLIVE BROWN LOAMY FINE SAND. SLOPES RANGE FROM 0 TO 3 PERCENT.

ESTIMATED SOIL PROPERTIES (A)

DEPTH (IN.)	USDA TEXTURE	UNIFIED	AASHTO	FRACT >3 IN (PCT)	PERCENT OF MATERIAL LESS THAN 3" PASSING SIEVE No.				LIQUID LIMIT	PLAS-TICITY INDEX
					4	10	40	200		
0-11	SIL, VFSL	ML, CL-ML	A-4	0	100	95-100	85-100	60-90	<30	NP-9
11-68	SIL, VFSL, VFS	ML, CL-ML	A-4	0	100	95-100	80-100	50-90	<30	NP-12
68-72	LFS, S	ML, CL-ML, SM, SP-SM	A-4, A-2	0	100	95-100	50-100	5-30	<30	NP-12

DEPTH (IN.)	CLAY (PCT) (<2MM)	MOIST BULK DENSITY (G/CM3)	PERMEA-BILITY (IN/HR)	AVAILABLE WATER CAPACITY (IN/IN)	SOIL REACTION (PH)	SALINITY (MMHOS/CM)	SHRINK-SWELL POTENTIAL	EROSION FACTORS		WIND EROD. GROUP	ORGANIC MATTER (PCT)	CORROSIVITY	
								K	T			STEEL	CONCRETE
0-11	4-10	1.20-1.50	0.6-2.0	0.15-0.25	4.5-7.3	—	LOW	.49	5	—	2-5	LOW	MODERAT
11-68	2-10	1.20-1.50	0.6-6.0	0.13-0.20	4.5-7.8	—	LOW	.49	5			LOW	MODERAT
68-72	1-8	1.20-1.50	0.6-6.0	0.10-0.20	5.1-7.8	—	LOW	.49				LOW	MODERAT

	FLOODING			HIGH WATER TABLE			CEMENTED PAN		BEDROCK		SUBSIDENCE		HYD POTENT FROST ACTION
	FREQUENCY	DURATION (MONTHS)	MONTHS	DEPTH (FT)	KIND	MONTHS	DEPTH (IN)	HARDNESS	DEPTH (IN)	HARDNESS	INIT. (IN)	TOTAL (IN)	GRP
	COMMON	BRIEF	FEB-APR	4.0-6.0	APPARENT	NOV-APR	—		>60		—	—	B	HIGH

CONSTRUCTION MATERIAL (B)

SANITARY FACILITIES (B)			ROADFILL	FAIR-LOW STRENGTH
SEPTIC TANK ABSORPTION FIELDS	SEVERE-FLOODS			
SEWAGE LAGOON AREAS	SEVERE-FLOODS, SEEPAGE		SAND	IMPROBABLE-EXCESS FINES
SANITARY LANDFILL (TRENCH)	SEVERE-FLOODS, SEEPAGE, WETNESS		GRAVEL	IMPROBABLE-EXCESS FINES

SANITARY LANDFILL (AREA)	SEVERE-FLOODS, SEEPAGE
DAILY COVER FOR LANDFILL	GOOD

BUILDING SITE DEVELOPMENT (B)

SHALLOW EXCAVATIONS	MODERATE-FLOODS
DWELLINGS WITHOUT BASEMENTS	SEVERE-FLOODS
DWELLINGS WITH BASEMENTS	SEVERE-FLOODS
SMALL COMMERCIAL BUILDINGS	SEVERE-FLOODS
LOCAL ROADS AND STREETS	SEVERE-FLOODS, FROST ACTION
LAWNS, LANDSCAPING AND GOLF FAIRWAYS	OCCAS: MODERATE-FLOODS FREQ: SEVERE-FLOODS

WATER MANAGEMENT (B)

TOPSOIL	GOOD
POND RESERVOIR AREA	SEVERE-SEEPAGE
EMBANKMENTS DIKES AND LEVEES	SEVERE-PIPING
EXCAVATED PONDS AQUIFER FED	MODERATE-DEEP TO WATER
DRAINAGE	DEEP TO WATER
IRRIGATION	FLOODS, ERODES EASILY
TERRACES AND DIVERSIONS	ERODES EASILY
GRASSED WATERWAYS	ERODES EASILY

REGIONAL INTERPRETATIONS

RECREATIONAL DEVELOPMENT (W)

CAMP AREAS	SEVERE-FLOODS		
		PICNIC AREAS	OCCAS: SLIGHT FREQ: MODERATE-FLOODS
	PLAYGROUNDS	OCCAS: SLIGHT FREQ: MODERATE-FLOODS	0-2% OCCAS: MODERATE-FLOODS 2-3% OCCAS: MODERATE-SLOPE,FLOODS FREQ: SEVERE-FLOODS
	PATHS AND TRAILS	SLIGHT	

CAPABILITY AND YIELDS PER ACRE OF CROPS AND PASTURE (HIGH LEVEL MANAGEMENT)

CLASS-DETERMINING PHASE	CAPA-BILITY	CORN SILAGE (TONS)	TOBACCO (LBS)	POTATOES, IRISH (CWT)	CORN, SWEET (TONS)	GRASS-LEGUME HAY (TONS)	ALFALFA HAY (TONS)	GRASS-CLOVER (AUM)
	NIRR IRR.	NIRR IRR.	NIRR IRR.	NIRR IRR.	NIRR IRR.	NIRR IRR.	NIRR IRR.	NIRR IRR.
ALL	1	28	1600	340	0.3	4.5	5.0	8.5

WOODLAND SUITABILITY (C)

MANAGEMENT PROBLEMS

CLASS-DETERMINING PHASE	ORD SYM	EROSION HAZARD	EQUIP-LIMIT	SEEDLING MORT'LY	WINDTH'W HAZARD	PLANT COMPET.	COMMON TREES	SITE INDX	TREES TO PLANT
ALL	30	SLIGHT	SLIGHT	SLIGHT	SLIGHT	SLIGHT	EASTERN WHITE PINE		EASTERN WHITE PINE
							SUGAR MAPLE	70	RED PINE
							RED PINE	63	BLACK WALNUT
								70	EUROPEAN LARCH

POTENTIAL PRODUCTIVITY

WINDBREAKS

CLASS-DETERMINING PHASE	SPECIES	HT	SPECIES	HT	SPECIES	HT	SPECIES
	NONE						

WILDLIFE HABITAT SUITABILITY (C)

CLASS-DETERMINING PHASE	POTENTIAL FOR HABITAT ELEMENTS								POTENTIAL AS HABITAT FOR:			
	GRAIN & SEED	GRASS & LEGUME	WILD HERB.	HARDWD TREES	CONIFER PLANTS	SHRUBS	WETLAND PLANTS	SHALLOW WATER	OPENLD WILDLF	WOODLD WILDLF	WETLAND WILDLF	RANGE WILDL
ALL	GOOD	GOOD	GOOD	GOOD	GOOD	–	POOR	V. POOR	GOOD	GOOD	V. POOR	–

POTENTIAL NATIVE PLANT COMMUNITY (RANGELAND OR FOREST UNDERSTORY VEGETATION)

COMMON PLANT NAME	PLANT SYMBOL (NLSPN)	PERCENTAGE COMPOSITION (DRY WEIGHT) BY CLASS DETERMINING PHASE				
POTENTIAL PRODUCTION (LBS./AC. DRY WT):						
FAVORABLE YEARS						
NORMAL YEARS						
UNFAVORABLE YEARS						

FOOTNOTES

A ESTIMATES OF ENGINEERING PROPERTIES BASED ON TEST DATA OF 6 PEDONS: 3 FROM MASSACHUSETTS AND 3 FROM MAINE.
B RATINGS BASED ON NATIONAL SOILS HANDBOOK. PART II. SECTION 403. MARCH 1978.
C RATINGS BASED ON SOILS MEMOS 26. SEPT. 1967; OR 74. JAN. 1972.

Figure 4. Sample soil interpretation sheet for Hadley soil in Vermont.

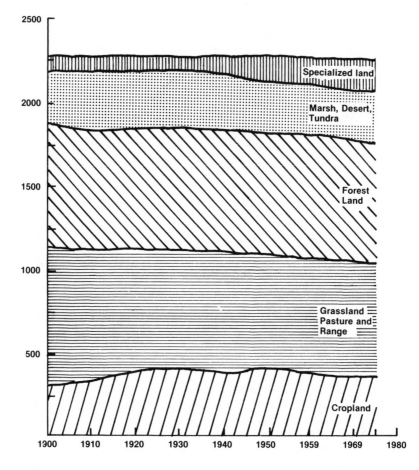

Note: *Forest Land* excludes reserved forest land in parks, wildlife refuges, and other special-use areas. *Specialized Land* is urban and built-up areas (including cities and towns, rural highway and road rights-of-way, railroads, airports, and public institutions in rural areas) and nonurban special-use areas (including Federal and State parks and other rural parks, recreational areas, Federal and State wildlife refuges, national defense sites, flood-control areas, Federal industrial areas, farmsteads, and farm roads).

Figure 5.   Major uses of land in the United States, 1900–74.[4]

that they may produce. Eventually all of the above mechanisms could deplete our cropland resource.

Specialized land (see Figure 5) includes the many different land uses that we often refer to as developed land. While this category of land

---

4. Council on Environmental Quality. *Environmental Quality* (Washington, DC: U.S. Government Printing Office, 1979).

use appears rather insignificant in terms of acres, the use of land for these purposes is expanding very rapidly as population increases and as the demands of society for these land uses increases. While this phenomenon in and of itself may give little cause for alarm, it is the type of land selected for use under this category that has caused some alarm. It is easier to develop land that is flat. Croplands are therefore prime targets. Wetlands are also flat, inexpensive and many people like to live near water. Consequently there are pressures to develop wetlands. It is not that there may not be enough land for these specialized developed uses, but rather it is the conflict between the specialized use and some other land use practice that causes concern. Wetlands are reservoirs for water, breeding grounds for various forms of wildlife and feeding areas for other kinds of wildlife. Viewing the choice of what land to develop from another perspective, even though people want to live someplace, that does not mean that such a place can support them in terms of needed resources. Witness the recent migrations to the sunbelt areas of the Southwest. While the climate is hospitable in many ways, the demands for water have all but eliminated any sustained supply and have necessitated the proposal of various large-scale engineering masterpieces to transport water to these water-impoverished areas. This type of solution, even if technically and economically feasible, masks the problem, and may be only a short-term solution.

Forest land is a major land use category in the United States (see Figure 5). About 27% of all forest land was government-owned in 1978, with 21% being owned by the federal government. Management of such lands has received various forms of attention over the years, but many people believe that a comprehensive approach to the management of forest land is yet to come. Maximum growth-sustained yield was and is one concept that forest management has championed. This concept emphasizes harvesting trees at a time that achieves maximum productivity of the forest rather than allowing trees to reach their mature growth size (see Figure 6). While this approach would keep forests actively growing, it does not allow for old age stands useful for wildlife habitat as well as aesthetics and soil rejuvenation. It could also eventually lead to the management of forests totally for commercial production, with the selection of only fast growing, highly marketable tree species for cultivation. This could eliminate tree species considered unprofitable and consequently the gene pool of such species. Once this extinction occurs, the species cannot be retrieved.

Grassland, pasture and range also constitute a major portion of the land use of the United States. Much of this land is federally owned and leased to ranchers, or is privately owned by ranchers. As with cropland, the owner/investor is interested in a maximal dollar return. This situa-

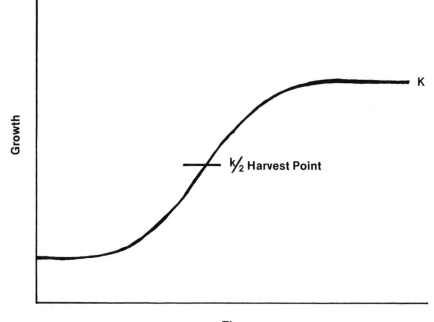

Figure 6.   Harvest point of trees in relation to growth, where K equals the maximum size a tree would reach.

tion has led to a drastic deterioration of our rangelands through overgrazing. A recent survey of our national rangelands indicates that there have been too many animals allowed to feed on much of the vegetation, with the result that the better grazing plants have been all but eliminated while the less useful plant species are proliferating. Until grazing was introduced into many desert areas, cacti were not the dominant form of vegetation. While overuse of an area may only lead to a shift in the kind of plants located there, the shift may be to a variety of plants that are less palatable to grazers and ultimately reduce the utility of the land for grazing.

Marshes, deserts and tundra also deserve consideration as natural resources. Man has and continues to use these areas without an understanding of their role in nature. These areas are not simply there to be developed; they are areas that support various gene pools of plant and animal species that may be very necessary for the continued functioning of the ecosystem even though we may not today fully understand their utility.

4.   The Need to Control

The above discussion of land and its uses has focused largely on land use problems related to topics like agriculture, forestry and wildlife. There are many additional land use problems that are of greatest significance in heavily populated areas. One example of these problems might be the question of whether retail stores should be located in numerous small clusters within residential areas or kept out of residential areas and instead grouped into one huge shopping center area. Another example is whether a 25-acre suburban housing development should have 25 one-acre building lots or 25 houses clustered on 10 acres with 15 acres of common open space. Sections B and C of this chapter will concentrate on land use control mechanisms that most often come into play when pressures are created by population growth in a specific location. Section D will then emphasize agriculture, forestry and wildlife when it addresses controls on federally owned lands. As a further introduction to our sections on control mechanisms, we note that when considering the need for land use controls in any context, one could contend that control is necessary only when things get "out of hand." When is the point at which things are "out of hand" is an issue upon which reasonable people could differ. Also, most people are of the opinion that land use issues should be resolved before they become major problems rather than later. Thus we will see that many of our "control" mechanisms will really be land use "planning" mechanisms that try to prevent problems rather than remedy them.

B.   PRIVATE AND QUASI-PRIVATE LAND USE PLANNING AND CONTROL

In Chapter 3 we discussed the doctrine of "nuisance" that prevented one landowner from using his land in a way that would interfere with the peaceful enjoyment by another landowner of that other landowner's land. The common law of nuisance thus exists as a bottom rung control mechanism that society has placed on what one can do with his land and as a bottom rung protection mechanism that a landowner has available against those who interfere with his use of his land. This level of control is imposed by society but is still a "private" mechanism since it merely gives litigants the opportunity to seek a remedy if they so choose. Beyond this private control mechanism created by society are private planning and control mechanisms which can be created by individuals themselves. These privately created control mechanisms are called easements and restrictive covenants.

If one is the owner of an easement, it can be said that he holds an interest in someone else's land. If your rural neighbor has a good water source on his property and you want to use it to supply your pond, you might purchase the right to use that water source and to go on his land to lay and repair pipe to bring the water to your land. Your neighbor would convey this right to you by deeding you an easement on his land for the stated purposes. The benefit of that easement would pass to subsequent owners of your land unless the easement were created for the personal benefit of the holder ("easement in gross") rather than to benefit the land owned by the holder of the easement ("easement appurtenant to the land"). Most easements are created by voluntary transactions between the parties, but easements can sometimes come into existence in other ways. For example, if you were to use your neighbor's water source for a long enough period of time (often fixed by statute), with his knowledge but without his consent, and adverse to his interests, you may acquire a "prescriptive easement" to use the source.

Restrictive covenants do not give one landowner the ability to make active use of another landowner's land. Rather, a restrictive covenant will give to A an interest that allows A to restrict how B will use B's land. These restrictions by covenant go beyond limits that would be imposed by the nuisance doctrine and beyond public controls such as zoning. Thus if A owned fifteen adjoining lots that were zoned to allow either single-family or multifamily residential housing, A might sell one lot to B, and others to other buyers, with restrictive covenants that the lots be used only for single-family housing. In general, if the parties intend that a restrictive covenant shall bind subsequent owners, it can be written to do so, i.e., to "run with the land."

While restrictive covenants are generally enforceable and are well accepted as private land use planning tools, we should note some circumstances where the law has precluded their use. The clearest situation in which restrictive covenants may not be used is where the covenant would lead to the exclusion from housing on the basis of race. *Shelley v. Kraemer*[5], a United States Supreme Court case decided in 1948, held that racially restrictive covenants could not be enforced by courts because to do so would violate the equal protection clause of the Fourteenth Amendment to the United States Constitution. The equal protection clause makes it unconstitutional for a *state* to "deny to any person within its jurisdiction the equal protection of the laws." In *Shelley* the court decided that for a state to use its court system to enforce covenants that provide restrictions based on race would be *state action* denying persons equal protection of the laws.

---

5. 334 U.S. 1 (1948).

The prohibition on the use of racial restrictions with respect to housing and some of its related facilities has gone far beyond *Shelley v. Kraemer. Shelley* prohibited state action to enforce a racially restrictive covenant. What about situations where there is no state action but a completely private land use restriction mechanism operates in a racially discriminatory manner? In *Sullivan v. Little Hunting Park, Inc.,*[6] a corporation had been formed to operate recreational facilities for the residents of a subdivision. A homeowner could have a share in the corporation that entitled him to use the facilities, and that share could be assigned to a tenant but only with the approval of the corporation's board of directors. The board refused to approve an assignment to a Negro tenant and the court held that the tenant had a right to the assignment. Even though no state action was involved, a statute that had been enacted by Congress, the Civil Rights Act of 1866,[7] prohibited private individuals from discriminating in housing on the basis of race. The Civil Rights Act of 1866 states: "All citizens of the United States shall have the same right...as is enjoyed by white citizens...to...purchase, lease, sell...real...property." The Court had earlier held that Congress had the constitutional power to prohibit private as well as public racial discrimination with respect to the sale and rental of property, and that Congress' words in the statute meant just what they said: all racial discrimination, both private and public, in the sale or rental of property is prohibited.[8]

A somewhat less clear situation in which restrictive covenants are limited in their effectiveness involves the law's long adhered to policy against "restraints on alienation." This policy is based on the belief that restrictions on the ability to transfer one's interest in land inhibits economic and commercial development. Thus a covenant that kept a property owner from selling his land except to members of a designated property owners association was unenforceable.[9] There are, however, policies that compete with that of free alienability of property. One such policy is freedom of contract — courts enforcing the terms of an arrangement into which the parties have voluntarily entered. Some courts have adopted the position that covenants that restrict the alienation of property are invalid only if they are unreasonable. Possible factors bearing on the reasonableness of the restriction might be how long it lasts or whether it is absolute in that it makes no provisions for hardship situations. Thus a covenant prohibiting a condominium owner from

---

6. 396 U.S. 229 (1969).

7. 42 U.S.C.A. §§ 1981, 1982.

8. *Jones v. Alfred H. Mayer Co.,* 392 U.S. 409 (1968).

9. *Mountain Springs Association v. Wilson,* 196 A.2d 270 (1963).

leasing his unit was found reasonable and therefore valid since provisions were made for hardship situations and the duration of the restriction was not necessarily forever.[10]

But for the possible need to resort to the courts to enforce them, restrictive covenants and easements are wholly private land use planning tools. Let us next look at a quasi-private mechanism. We call this quasi-private because though it is not mandatory and is utilized on the initiative of private parties, government has created the mechanism for use by the private parties. The mechanism seeks to keep land from being built upon by providing an income tax incentive to the owner to act in ways which will keep the land perpetually undeveloped.

Assume that Mr. Rich is in the 50% tax bracket for federal income tax purposes. For every dollar of taxable income he receives above the upper limit of the next lowest tax bracket, he pays fifty cents of that dollar as income tax. Mr. Rich owns a large and valuable piece of real estate in a rural area. Adjacent to that real estate is a parcel owned by someone else. That parcel is about to be subdivided into 100 lots with a house to be put on each lot. Mr. Rich does not like this subdivision from an environmental point of view and, possibly, because he also believes it will reduce the value of his real estate holding. The owner of the 100 lots is willing to sell them all together for $500,000 which is their value as land for a housing development. What action can Mr. Rich take to prevent the subdivision and what will it cost him?

First, he could just buy the adjacent parcel for $500,000 and keep it from being developed. He will have protected the environment (and his other property) from development at a cost to him of $500,000 minus whatever comparatively small income he can obtain from the property in its undeveloped state. Let us see if we can do better for his interests. Under Section 170 of the Internal Revenue Code, Congress has provided that individuals may deduct the amount of a "charitable" contribution that they make to a qualifying "charitable" organization. A "charitable" organization is much more broadly defined than merely those that give help to the poor. An organization whose purpose is to keep land from being developed may qualify under Section 170, with the result that gifts that are made to it are tax deductible. These organizations are usually called land trusts. Mr. Rich can buy the proposed development for $500,000 and donate the land to the land trust. The land trust will then sell the land for a lesser amount but with restrictions that allow it to be used only for such activities as agriculture or forestry. Mr. Rich takes the

---

10. *Seagate Condominium Association v. Duffy,* 330 So.2d 484 (1976).

value of his donation to the land trust, $500,000, as a tax deduction and he removes the adverse effects of the development at a cost to him of $250,000 rather than $500,000. This is because on $500,000 of his very high income he would have paid income tax of $250,000. By giving the $500,000 to the land trust and taking a deduction, he saves having to pay $250,000 in income tax. Of the $500,000 he gave to the land trust, only $250,000 is a net out-of-pocket cost to him — the other $250,000 is money that he has just chosen to send to the land trust instead of to the United States Treasury. Mr. Rich has now accomplished his objective at a cost to him of $250,000 rather than $500,000. Can we do still better for him?

Instead of having Mr. Rich give all 100 lots to the land trust after he buys them, let us have him keep ten of them. Since he paid $500,000 for the whole parcel and is donating 90 out of 100 lots, his tax deductible charitable contribution is 90/100ths of $500,000 or $450,000. Being in the 50% tax bracket means he saves paying taxes on $450,000 at the 50% rate. He thus saves $225,000 in taxes. He has spent $500,000, saved $225,000 in taxes and is therefore out-of-pocket $275,000 — but he still owns ten building lots for which he paid $5000 apiece. These ten lots are now surrounded by 90 lots that the land trust has perpetually restricted for development, and since these ten building lots will be *forever* surrounded by open space instead of by 90 houses, their value is greatly increased over the $5000 that was paid for each of them. Mr. Rich sells these prime building lots for $35,000 each and receives $350,000. On this sale he has made a profit of $300,000 (paid $5000 each and sold them for $35,000 each). Assuming that he kept them for more than one year after he bought them, his profit would be taxed as a capital gain, which means he would pay tax on only 40% of the gain, pursuant to Section 1202 of the Internal Revenue Code. He would be taxed on 40% of his profit of $300,000. He is thus taxed on $120,000. Being in the 50% tax bracket means he will pay a tax of $60,000 on his profit. He has taken in $350,000 on the lots he sold and pays a tax of $60,000, leaving him with $290,000 on the sale. His donation of $450,000 to the land trust left him out-of-pocket $275,000 as we saw above. The donation and the sale taken together have left him with a minus $275,000 and a plus $290,000 for a net gain of $15,000. The 100-lot subdivision that threatened the environment and Mr. Rich's other real estate has been reduced to ten prime building lots, the cost to Mr. Rich has been nothing, and in fact he has $15,000 in the bank to pay his legal fees for all the transactions.

The reader may want to question the justification for Congress allowing and even encouraging the above actions by Mr. Rich. On one hand, Congress' environmental and land use objectives of preserving agricultural and forest land are furthered, and the rich are the ones with the capital, the land and the risk taking ability that can help Congress achieve its land use objectives. On the other hand, it can be argued that the United States Treasury (all taxpayers) is subsidizing Mr. Rich's achieving his objective of protecting the value of his real estate. Furthermore, even if we look only at the environmental objective that Mr. Rich may have and not at his property value objective, should Mr. Rich's environmental projects be heavily subsidized by the treasury when someone named Mr. Poor will not be subsidized to anywhere near the same level to accomplish those things that he believes are environmentally important? That is because the lower the donor's tax bracket, the less is the percentage of the donation that actually is provided by the treasury instead of the by the donor. A $1 donation by someone in the 50% bracket is really 50¢ of his money and 50¢ of money that does not get sent by him to the treasury. A $1 donation by someone in the 20% bracket is 80¢ of his money and 20¢ of money that he does not have to send to the treasury. Is then the proper perspective from which to view the above-described tax mechanism: (1) "should more government money be spent on the environmental goals of the rich than on those of the poor?" or (2) "should government accomplish its environmental objectives by encouraging the use of privately initiated voluntary methods wherever possible?"

C. PUBLIC PLANNING AND CONTROL AND THE "TAKING CLAUSE" LIMITATION ON CONTROL

While the federal government exercises some control over how privately owned land is used, most public planning and control of privately owned land is done by local governments under authority given to them by the states. The degree to which states get directly involved in land use control varies from state to state. Some states do very little. Vermont, however, has a Land Use and Development Law[11] that requires, in addition to local requirements, a state permit for developments which might have significant environmental impact. We will focus on local land use controls and then look at the extent to which the "taking clauses" of the United States and state constitutions limit public control of land use.

1. Local Control

The dominant local land use planning and control mechanism is zoning. There are numerous different forms of zoning controls and

---

11. 10 V.S.A. § 6001 et seq.

numerous purposes for enacting them. The most well known type of zoning is "use zoning." Use zoning categorizes different activities which people may seek to undertake on land and prescribes which activities can be conducted on which parcels of land within the local government's jurisdiction. For example, a suburban city may have its land allocated for five types of "uses" and thus call its use zones R-1, R-2, R-3, C-1 and C-2. R-1 could be single-family residential, R-2 could be two-, three- or four-family residential buildings and R-3 could be apartment buildings of 5 or more units. C-1 areas might be for light commercial operations providing consumer goods and services on a retail basis while C-2 might be for heavy commercial operations conducted at the wholesale level. Some of the possible purposes for segregating these uses to different areas might include keeping heavy traffic out of places where people live, protecting property values by assuring people that a movie theater will not be built next door to their ranch house, or facilitating the efficient provision of city services like trash collection or police protection.

The uses designated for a given zone may be "permitted uses," which are activities that are allowed in that zone as a matter of right, or "conditional uses," which may be allowed in the zone if the user meets certain conditions. These conditions may either be stated in the zoning ordinance or imposed with specificity and with discretion by a local body such as a Zoning Board of Adjustment. Our C-1 zone described above could provide that all uses allowed in it are permitted uses unless the use will involve more than 30 people being on the premises at any one time. If more than 30 people will be there, the use may be conditioned on the landowner providing a specified number of off-street parking spaces.

In addition to the distinction between permitted and conditional uses, we should note the distinction between two other terms, exclusive zones and cumulative zones. If a zone is established as an exclusive zone, only the activities specified for that zone may take place there. If a zoning scheme provides for cumulative zoning, then in addition to the activities specified for a particular zone, any "higher" (i.e., less intensive) use may also take place in that zone. Thus under cumulative zoning, a light commercial zone could be used for residential use but not for "lower" (i.e., more intensive) heavy commercial activities. Exclusive zoning can be said to have the advantage of better serving the health and safety protection purpose of zoning by ensuring that people cannot choose to live in a heavy traffic commercial area or in an industrial area with high air pollution. Also, if residential uses are allowed in an area zoned for industry, industries that want to locate there may be deterred from doing so because they could be subject to liability as a nuisance to the residential landowners. Cumulative zoning, however, has the advantage of flexibility and diversity. Perhaps people should be able to choose to live in a commercial area if they can pay a lower rent there, if it is simply more convenient for them, or if they like living in an area where nonresidential activity is happening. Depending on the character and planning objectives of a city, it may choose to have some of its zones be cumulative and some exclusive.

Many other types of zoning ordinances exist besides use zones. Maximum height limitations may be provided for purposes such as added fire safety, aesthetics, or to ensure adequate availability of light. Distances may be established as a required "setback" of a building from a street for reasons such as planning for possible future widening of streets or to provide greater visibility at street corners. Communities may establish agricultural zones to preserve the character of the community by protecting it from invasion by intensive development. Regardless of the type of zoning that a local government may want to enact, it must get its authority to impose its zoning scheme from the state, since local governments are the creations of the state.

The zoning power is a part of the state's police power—the power to protect the public health, public safety and general welfare. In general the states have delegated the zoning power to local governments, with the most common mechanism for the delegation being zoning "enabling acts" which enable or permit local governments to zone but do not require them to do so. Whether the zoning power was a valid part of the state's police power was questioned in the 1926 case of *Village of Euclid, Ohio v. Ambler Realty Co.*[12] A landowner contended that a use and a height and minimum area requirements zoning scheme that restricted his use of his land and thereby reduced its market value was not a valid exercise of the state's police power. The United States Supreme Court found that a comprehensive zoning ordinance bears a rational relationship to the public health and safety and is therefore a valid exercise of the police power. *Euclid* thus clearly established the validity of comprehensive zoning, but that is not to say that all attempts at zoning are necessarily valid. One type of zoning where the trend has been in the direction of invalidity is exclusionary zoning.

Exclusionary zoning was the subject of a New Jersey case, *Southern Burlington County N.A.A.C.P. v. Township of Mount Laurel.*[13] The Township of Mount Laurel had a zoning ordinance that provided for varying minimum lot sizes and widths and dwelling unit sizes for each of its residential zones. The zones with the least restrictive requirements had

---

12. 272 U.S. 365 (1926).

13. 336 A.2d 713 (1975).

very little land still available for development. Most of the available residentially zoned land required a minimum lot size of about one-half acre. Although the New Jersey Supreme Court noted that Mount Laurel's requirements were not as restrictive as those in many similar municipalities, it said that a developing municipality may not, by a system of land use regulation, make it physically and economically impossible to provide low and moderate income housing in the municipality and thereby exclude people from living within its confines because of the limited extent of their income and resources. The result of such a system would be presumptively contrary to the general welfare and therefore outside the scope of the zoning power.

Two other factors that tend to attenuate harsh results which may otherwise flow from the exercise of the zoning power should be mentioned briefly. These are variance and nonconforming use provisions often contained in local zoning ordinances. A variance will allow someone to put his land into use in a way which is not allowable under the zoning ordinance as it applies to his land. The purpose of having a variance procedure is to account for special situations involving the property itself, rather than its owner, which in fairness or good sense should result in the property not being required to be used in compliance with the zoning laws. This might include situations where a lot is so small that to enforce compliance with minimum lot size requirements would preclude putting a building on the lot and make it useless. Another example might be where a restaurant will be located near ample public parking facilities. A variance from zoning requirements for off-street parking for restaurants would appear to be in order. As a matter of practice, zoning variances are often given where the legal criteria for a variance have not been met. In the absence of significant adverse effects on neighboring property or on the public, a variance is often issued even though the property has nothing in the way of physical characteristics that make it different from other property that is zoned the same way.

Nonconforming use provisions also attempt to mitigate possible hardships by allowing a use to continue in violation of the applicable zoning ordinance if it lawfully existed prior to the adoption of that zoning. The nonconforming use provisions do reduce hardship to the landowner, yet if the use has been made unlawful for the public benefit and would not be allowed had it not already been there, is not that public benefit being partly sacrificed by allowing the nonconforming use to be there just because it was there before the zoning enactment? Might not a better remedy for any unfairness to the owner be to compensate the owner for losses due to his having to give up his nonconforming use?

Besides zoning, local governments have other land use control mechanisms available to them. State statutes often authorize local governments to require local approval of subdivisions of land. In exchange for providing this local approval, local governments have sometimes sought "exactions" from developers who want to subdivide. For example, if a developer wants to subdivide his land for residential use, the local government may require that he dedicate land to the community for park or recreational purposes. Such exactions have been found valid for reasons such as, using the above example, an influx of new residents brought in by the subdivision will increase the need for park and recreational facilities. The subdivision will also make the developer's land more valuable. Part of his benefit can be required to be used to provide for the local needs he will be creating.[14] The subdivision approval mechanism has also been used to regulate the rate of growth of a community by restricting the number of subdivision permits that will be issued within a given period of time. A discussion of this approach is presented in Section B of Chapter 8.

The source of power for the local land use planning and control mechanisms discussed above is the police power. Another source of power to control land use is the eminent domain power, which is the power of government to take private property for public use. Rather than being an explicitly stated power, the eminent domain power is an inherent power of the sovereign—either the federal government or the state government and the state's authorized offspring, the local governments. Acknowledgment of the existence of the eminent domain power comes by way of limitations on that power that are expressed in the United States Constitution and in various forms in state constitutions. The "taking clause" of the Fifth Amendment to the United States Constitution reads: "nor shall private property be taken for public use, without just compensation." Thus the taking of private property by government is acceptable so long as just compensation is paid to the owner. If a local government wanted to establish a park, it could "take" or condemn private property and use it for a park. Similarly, if a local government wanted certain land to be used only for agriculture, it might, instead of zoning it for agricultural use only, "take" or condemn the land and resell it with restrictions that it be used only for agriculture. The key difference between accomplishing these local government objectives by using the eminent domain power, as opposed to the police powers of zoning or subdivision exactions discussed above, is that when government is acting under the eminent domain power, it must pay "just compensation." While in many instances

---

14. *Associated Home Builders v. Walnut Creek,* 484 P.2d 606 (1971).

government will voluntarily act under its eminent domain power to handle a land use situation, since regulation under the police powers does not require payment of compensation to the landowner, there is a strong inclination for government to "regulate" rather than to "take." Landowners who have found themselves subjected to uncompensated regulation often have contended that government has gone beyond the scope of its police power authority and either does not have the power to do what it seeks to do at all or, if it can act, it can do so only under the eminent domain power and with the payment of just compensation. These limits on public control of land use are the subject of our next section.

2. The "Taking Clause" Limitations on Public Control

In this section we will consider two issues involving the taking clause. First, if it is conceded that government can act as it wants to act and that its action is for the public benefit, when does that action exceed its police powers and amount to a taking requiring the payment of just compensation? In other words, what distinguishes an eminent domain "taking" from a police power "regulation?" Second, if government is admittedly seeking to act under the eminent domain power and willing to pay compensation for its taking of private property, what will qualify as a "public use" to bring its action within the confines of those words and thus within the scope of the eminent domain power?

In trying to define the line between a police power regulation and an eminent domain taking, a realistic beginning point is the United States Supreme Court's opinion in *Goldblatt v. Town of Hempstead*. [15] The Court acknowledged that the line is a fuzzy one: "There is no set formula to determine where regulation ends and taking begins." Let us then look at some of the factors that have been used by courts to determine whether a government action is a compensable taking or a noncompensable regulation.

Goldblatt concerned a town ordinance that placed restrictions on mining excavations. Those restrictions included fencing requirements, prohibited further excavation below the water table and required filling of any existing excavation below that level. The landowner had operated a gravel pit on his property for many years and contended that the ordinance was not regulatory but completely prohibitory and confiscated his property without compensation. The Court said that although a benefi-

---

15. 369 U.S. 590 (1962).

cial use of the property had been prohibited, that does not mean that the ordinance is beyond the scope of the police power and thus a taking. The owner was not disturbed with respect to his control or use of his property for other purposes, and his right to dispose of his property was not restricted. Besides factors of control, disposability and use, the *Goldblatt* opinion also referred to how onerous the government action might be in terms of its effect of decreasing the value of the property. A comparison of property values before and after the government action was said to be relevant but by no means conclusive.

Other courts and writers have used other factors in addition to or instead of the degree of diminution in value of the property or remaining uses for the property. Actual physical use by the government or the public may be a taking, whereas prohibiting uses by the owner may not be a taking. A 1982 United States Supreme Court opinion held that "a permanent physical occupation authorized by government is a taking without regard to the public interests that it may serve." A New York statute that requires landlords to allow installation of cable television facilities on rental properties is a permanent physical occupation and is thus a taking for which just compensation is required.[16] Another possibility is a sliding scale approach to the taking/regulation distinction may be used to say that the higher the type or degree of public interest, the greater the infringement on property rights that should be allowed without there being a taking. For example, action X should be a taking if government does X for historic preservation purposes, but the same action X should not be a taking if done to protect the public health.

Regardless of the factors that have been used by individual courts to draw the taking/regulation line, it is fair to say that the result has been that government can go a long way in restricting private property rights and reducing private property values by those restrictions without needing to pay compensation. At the extreme are cases like the California case in which the California Supreme Court found that the application of a local zoning ordinance did not result in a taking requiring compensation even though the trial court had determined that the ordinance precluded the landowner from making any economic use of his property.[17] To the extent that Americans believe that they are secure from their government acting in ways that reduce their property value from $200,000 to $100,000, that feeling of security is a myth. Yet there is a limit. Beyond some ill-defined point, government action that adversely affects private

---

16. *Loretto v. Teleprompter Manhattan CATV Corp.,* No. 81-244, June 30, 1982.

17. *Consolidated Rock Products v. City of Los Angeles,* 370 P.2d 342 (1962).

property will be a taking and constitutionally require the payment of just compensation.

One might want to consider the wisdom of allowing government to act in ways that substantially reduce individual property values without compensating the owners for the loss. Would it not be better to say that when government acts for the public benefit, all citizens should pay the price for that benefit rather than having the cost fall on one property owner or a small group of property owners who stand to bear the cost because of fortuitous circumstances? Thus, perhaps all government action that results in a substantial loss in property value should be compensated and the question of whether there has been a "taking" or a "regulation" should not be relevant. Furthermore, should compensation be limited to losses related to land use? For example, if a company has been operating lawfully for 20 years and even been encouraged to expand its operation by federal income tax incentives, should new pollution laws enacted for the public benefit be allowed to put this company out of business without compensating its shareholders? Are there land use and/or nonland use compensation systems that might be workable and yet fairer than the results of the taking/regulation distinction are to those whose economic interests may be injured by action taken by the government for the public benefit? If one looks for them, one will find many possibilities.[18]

Our last topic in this section concerns the reasons for which government can take private property even if it will pay just compensation for it. The taking clause says: "nor shall private property be taken for public use, without just compensation." There is thus a recognition that while the inherent eminent domain power allows a taking for public use, there cannot be a taking by government for private use even if just compensation is paid. The issue is what is meant by the words "public use." Is it a public use and thus an allowable exercise of the eminent domain power for a municipality to condemn private property, paying compensation to the owners who do not voluntarily want to sell it, and then transfer that property to another private owner like the General Motors Corporation?

Quite clearly, if a municipality were to condemn private land for a park to be used by the public, that would be a taking for public use. Our General Motors question would appear to be a taking for private use and thus not within the eminent domain power. But let us add some additional facts. If the municipality were the City of Detroit and General

---

18. Hagman, D., and D. Misczynski. *Windfalls for Wipeouts* (Chicago: American Society of Planning Officials, 1978).

Motors were going to use the property to build a new plant, thereby promoting industry and commerce and adding badly needed jobs and taxes to the economic base of the city and the state, do we now have a "public use?" A narrow interpretation of the words "public use" would still result in our answer being no. The use is still a private use — use by General Motors. The courts have not, however, given the words "public use" a narrow interpretation. Public use has been held to include serving public purposes or providing public benefits, and so long as the public interests are dominant, the fact that private interests will also benefit from the condemnation does not mean that the condemnation is outside the scope of the eminent domain power. In the General Motors example, the Michigan Supreme Court said:

> "The power of eminent domain is to be used in this instance primarily to accomplish the essential purposes of alleviating unemployment and revitalizing the economic base of the community. The benefit to a private interest is merely incidental."[19]

When we discussed the line between what is a police power regulation and what is an eminent domain taking, we concluded that government can go quite far in restricting property use and still be on the regulation side of the line. To conclude our discussion of the limits on public control of land use, we should also note that if government is acting either under its eminent domain power or its police power, it has a substantial amount of latitude with respect to what it chooses to call a public purpose or public benefit. In *Berman v. Parker,* the United States Supreme Court decided that aesthetics is a valid public purpose. The Court said: "It is within the power of the legislature to determine that the community should be beautiful as well as healthy, ..."[20] Thus there are legal limits on public control of land use, but the legal limits are not very limiting. Perhaps the more significant limits are political.

D.   USE OF FEDERALLY OWNED LANDS

Over 700 million acres of land are owned by the federal government. Additional acreage is controlled through the federal government holding various interests in land that do not amount to an ownership interest.

---

19. *Poletown Neighborhood Council v. City of Detroit,* 304 N.W.2d 455 (1981).

20. 348 U.S. 26 (1954).

Currently the use or control of use of these lands includes 75 million acres under the National Park System, 84 million acres for Wildlife Refuge and Ranges, 190 million acres in National Forests, 340 million acres managed by the Bureau of Land Management (mostly for grazing), and 80 million acres of Wilderness with an additional 180 million acres under study for inclusion as Wilderness. Two of these uses of federal land will be discussed here. Use of federal land for energy production is discussed in Chapter 7.

1. Wildlife Habitat

Prior to 1966, the wildlife refuges run by the federal government were administered as many separate administrative units and by different federal agencies. With the passage of the National Wildlife Refuge System Administration Act of 1966,[21] these units were consolidated into the National Wildlife Refuge System. Under this statute the Refuge System is to be administered by the Secretary of the Interior to

> "permit the use of any area within the System for any purpose, including but not limited to hunting, fishing, public recreation and accommodations, and access whenever he determines that such uses are compatible with the major purposes for which such areas were established. . . ."

This statutory standard for administration adopts the management concept of "dominant use" as opposed to "single use" of the land in the Refuge System. Wildlife is the dominant use but it is not the single use to which the land can be put since other uses compatible with wildlife are allowed. The dominant use management approach appears to provide for a more efficient use of land; however, it also raises the issue of when are other uses compatible and when are they not compatible. With the pressures that are often applied to use land for economic yields such as recreation or grazing, use as wildlife habitat is subject to being compromised in ways that could not happen under single use management. In enacting the dominant use approach, Congress has decided that the administrative tool of requiring compatibility of other uses with wildlife is sufficient protection, and that to go beyond the compatibility level to protect wildlife would be an unwarranted waste of land resources.

---

21. 16 U.S.C.A. § 668 dd.

The dominance of wildlife as the dominant use for Wildlife Refuge land has been called into question by the 1982 Montana Federal District Court case of *Schwenke v. Secretary of Interior.*[22] In *Schwenke,* the Department of Interior had argued that grazing was permitted on the Charles M. Russell Wildlife Refuge only to the extent it was compatible with wildlife values. Reductions in the existing grazing levels were proposed because of evidence of overgrazing and destruction of wildlife habitat. Cattle ranchers contended that management of the refuge ought to give equal priority to livestock and wildlife. The court ruled in favor of the ranchers, instructing the Interior Department to administer the refuge land under both the Refuge Administration Act and the Taylor Grazing Act.[23] An appeal of the District Court decision was filed by the Interior Department in March, 1982. Thus while wildlife is the dominant use under the Refuge Administration Act itself, the issue of whether it is dominant over uses established by other federal laws such as the Taylor Grazing Act is still being contested.

2.   Forest Land

A combination of the Forest Reserve Act of 1891,[24] authorizing national forests, and the Organic Act of 1897,[25] which limited the purposes for which national forests could be established, resulted in the establishment of national forests (1) for the protection of the forest, (2) for securing favorable waterflows or (3) to furnish a supply of timber. While these were the only purposes allowed by law as the basis to establish a national forest, once a national forest was established, the practice was to manage it for other purposes also, such as for grazing and recreation. In the Multiple Uses—Sustained Yield Act of 1960,[26] Congress addressed itself to the question of what in fact were to be the allowable uses for national forest land. The statute declared that in addition to the previously authorized purposes for establishing national forests, the national forests were to be administered as well as established "for outdoor recreation, range, timber, watershed, and wildlife and fish purposes." The Secretary

---

22. Unpublished at this writing. Decided January, 1982, Docket No. CV-79-133-BLG.

23. 43 U.S.C.A. § 315.

24. 26 Stat. 1103.

25. 30 Stat. 34.

26. 16 U.S.C.A. §§ 528–531.

of Agriculture was instructed "to develop and administer the renewable surface resources of the national forests for multiple use and sustained yield of the several products and services obtained therefrom." The multitude use approach to forest land management was thus codified by Congress with the five above-quoted purposes being the allowable multiple uses.

The Multiple Use-Sustained Yield Act gives us an example of how Congress often provides guidance to an administering agency but still leaves much in the way of how the statute will work in the control of the agency and, in part, in the hands of the courts that will interpret Congress' intent in its statute. The statute requires management for a sustained yield of products and services and defines sustained yield in terms of striving for perpetual output. In defining multiple use the statute speaks of managing the resources in the combination that best meets the needs of the American people, while recognizing that some of the land may be used for less than all of its resources. The combination of uses selected for each piece of forest is to take into account competing uses by considering the relative value of the various resources, but the use pattern is to be "not necessarily the combination of uses that will give the greatest dollar return or the greatest unit output." Perpetual output management, a combination of uses, not necessarily maximizing dollar return or unit output—these are reasonably clear boundaries set by Congress within which the agency must work, but the statute also says that in administering the national forests, "due consideration shall be given to the relative values of the various resources in particular areas." What is "due consideration?" This question is not clearly answered by Congress since the statute just says "due consideration." It has been argued that due consideration means equal consideration of the various competing uses and that a use plan that is formulated by giving anything less than equal consideration to any potential use is invalid. The courts have, however, taken the position that "due consideration" means merely "some consideration" and that "the decision as to the proper mix of uses within any particular area is left to the sound discretion" of the administrative agency.[27] The courts have thus adopted an interpretation of the statute that, even with the boundaries discussed above within which the agency must work, allows substantial agency discretion in the actual determination of what uses will be emphasized for our national forest land.

---

27. *Sierra Club v. Hardin,* 325 F. Supp. 99 (1971).

ADDITIONAL READINGS

Council on Environmental Quality. *Environmental Quality* (Washington, DC: Government Printing Office, 1981).

Department of the Interior. *A Year of Change: To Restore America's Greatness* (Washington, DC: Government Printing Office, 1982.).

Hagman, D. G. *Urban Planning and Land Development Control Law* (St. Paul, MN: West Publishing Co., 1971).

CHAPTER 5

SOLID WASTE AND RESOURCE RECOVERY

A. THE SCOPE OF THE SOLID WASTE PROBLEM

"Gee whiz mom, my bicycle finally fell apart and now I need a new one. What should I do with this junker?" "Put it out in front son and the garbageman will take it away," she said. And take it away he did, just like that garbageman you hired to take your garbage away. But, as we observed in Chapter 1, you cannot always take it away and put it someplace else. So, where do we put it? Well, "it" is really a collection of stuff we assume we do not have a use for anymore and is defined by our federal government under the general heading of solid waste. According to federal statute, we define "solid waste" as;

> "...any garbage, refuse, sludge from a waste treatment plant, water supply treatment plant, or air pollution control facility and other discarded material, including solid, liquid, semisolid, or contained gaseous material resulting from industrial, commercial, mining, and agricultural operations, and from community activities, but does not include solid or dissolved material in domestic sewage, or solid or dissolved materials in irrigation return flows or industrial discharges which are point sources subject to permits under section 402 of the Federal Water Pollution Control Act, as amended, or source, special nuclear or by-product material as defined by the Atomic Energy Act of 1954, as amended."[1]

In the United States, in 1978, we discarded 154 million tons of "it," or about 1400 pounds per person, or 3.85 pounds per person per day. That

---

1. 42 U.S.C.S. § 6903.

is a lot of solid waste. Furthermore, estimates indicate that our annual rate of solid waste production from residential and commercial sources will continue to increase (Figure 1), as will the generation of solid wastes per person per day (Figure 2).

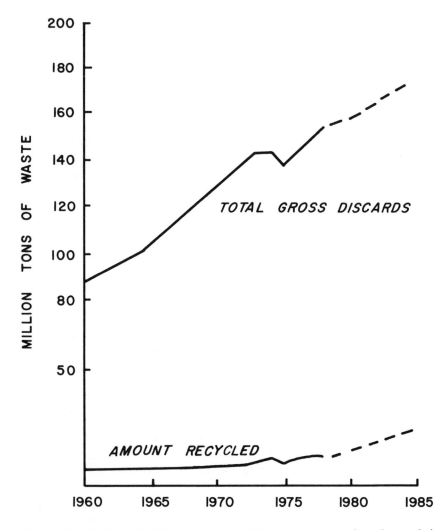

Figure 1. Estimated U.S. consumer solid waste generated and recycled, 1960–1985.[2]

2. Council on Environmental Quality. *Environmental Quality*. (Washington, DC: U.S. Government Printing Office, 1979).

To further complicate this issue we must add the fact that hazardous waste is a "species" of solid waste. A hazardous waste is generally identified by the federal government as a solid waste (remember the above definition of solid waste) that may cause or significantly contribute to increased mortality or illness or threaten human health or the environ-

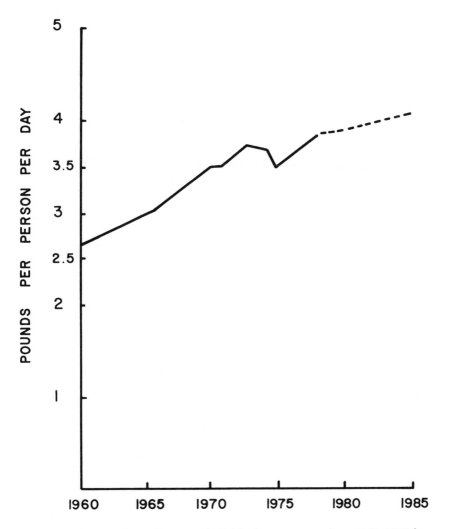

Figure 2.   Estimated average individual waste generation, 1960–1985.[3]

3. Ibid.

ment when improperly handled *and* can be measured using a standard test or easily detected by generators of hazardous waste.[4] Most hazardous waste is further characterized as a solid waste that is ignitable, corrosive or reactive. In the United States, we produce about 57 million metric tons of hazardous waste (2200 lb/metric ton) per year (1980 estimate). We usually consider three methods of coping with this waste; incineration, chemical detoxification or landfills. Currently, incineration is done on the Vulcanus, a large ocean ship that travels in the North Atlantic. One incineration ship can process 200,000 metric tons per year. If we therefore wished to incinerate all our hazardous waste (we cannot really incinerate all of it for various reasons) the United States would need 285 ships like the one currently used. Needless to say, this is not a viable approach for all our hazardous waste or even half of it. Chemical detoxification is a somewhat recent development that basically involves mixing a hazardous waste or numerous hazardous wastes together with some other chemical to make a relatively harmless solid waste. The approach of using landfills for storing hazardous waste is today's most common method and is receiving much attention. The major worry here, as with nonhazardous waste sanitary landfills, is that leakage will contaminate groundwater and thus our drinking water with "poisons." However, proper storage of these hazardous wastes in a landfill will allow their recovery at some future date when some means is developed to render them nonhazardous or to use them in some useful process. These hazardous wastes are generated by industrial sources during the manufacture of products we all use daily and expect the marketplace to provide. Such industries as cosmetics, petroleum, leather, rubber, plastics and jewelry are generators of hazardous waste. Also, hazardous wastes are generated at home when we discard such materials as drain cleaners, nail polish remover, crankcase oil and garden pesticides. It is interesting to note that these are not regulated, but the aggregate load from home generation must be high.

The major components of our solid waste are paper, glass, metals, food and a catchall category called "other" (Figure 3). "Other" is mostly hazardous waste. As one can easily see, the largest solid waste component is paper, from packaging paper to textbook paper. The discarding of almost anything contributes to the solid waste load of the United States, and this is where the real problem begins. Now that we have looked at what "it" is, the question becomes: What can we do with "it"? Conventional wisdom tells us to burn "it" or bury "it." These solutions

---

4. 40 CFR § 261.0 et seq.

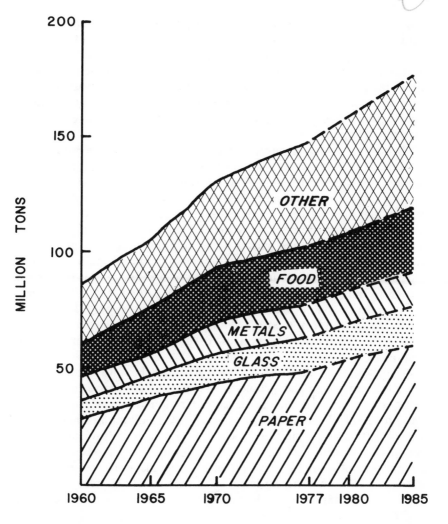

Figure 3. Estimated generation of residential and commercial solid waste by material, 1960–1985.[5]

seem perfectly reasonable until we consider that the latter answer requires land area, hopefully close to the source, that is inexpensive and of a soil quality that will allow this alternative to be implemented. Many communities are near the point of having exhausted their disposal capacity.

5. Council on Environmental Quality. *Environmental Quality*. (Washington, DC: U.S. Government Printing Office, 1979).

The former solution requires some guarantees as to air quality deterioration and cost effectiveness (a larger facility is more cost efficient). Furthermore, if we consider that every solid waste may not really be a waste but rather a resource out of place, then it becomes even more meaningful to discuss alternatives for dealing with solid waste other than those mentioned above. The importance of this loss of resources can be emphasized by keeping in mind the idea of "finite resources," as discussed in Chapter 1.

The raw materials (resources) that were used to make the product that is eventually discarded as a solid waste are theoretically limited in their supply (as is the "land resource" which is used for disposal sites). Therefore, as more people use more of a resource it is eventually depleted. If we consider alternatives to disposal such as recycling, reuse, or conservation, the period of use can be extended beyond that which is currently projected. What these alternatives do not address is the necessary replacement of a resource by another resource, since no program can give a 100% efficiency in the reuse or recycling of a resource. Also, energy is needed to implement these programs and, as can be seen in Chapter 7, current energy source patterns use a finite energy supply that is itself being depleted and, in theory, eventually totally dissipates as heat. The wisdom of the various alternatives to "disposal" will be considered in Section C.

Regardless of the resource depletion aspect of the solid waste problem, the other environmental problems associated with waste disposal are sufficient to demand that some consideration be given to regulating waste disposal. Waste disposal is related to air pollution (smell, air pollutants created by the burning process). Waste disposal is related to water pollution (runoffs from the dump site). Improper disposal results in disease transmission by rats and birds, and disposal sites are clearly aesthetic pollution. The existence of problems which stem from solid waste are difficult to deny. We next take a look at how those problems might be solved.

B. MECHANISMS FOR CONTROLLING WASTE DISPOSAL—FEDERAL INCENTIVES FOR STATE CONTROL, FEDERAL REQUIREMENTS FOR NONHAZARDOUS AND HAZARDOUS WASTE DISPOSAL

The two interrelated facets of the solid waste problem are, as noted in Section A, collection and disposal of solid waste and the fact that waste "disposal" results in the depletion of natural resources. Both the disposal and resource depletion aspects of the problem received substantial Congressional consideration in the Resource Conservation and Recovery Act of 1976.[6] This section will consider regulatory mechanisms which are addressed to disposal. Mechanisms addressed to the resource depletion problem will be discussed in Section C.

1. Nonhazardous Wastes

Collection and disposal of solid waste was a local government function until the 1960s. There was little federal involvement other than studies and advice. The mechanisms which regulated disposal were local health laws, other local ordinances such as zoning to restrict where a dump could be located, and private lawsuits. If you were bothered by a disposal activity, your recourse was to bring a nuisance action against those private parties who were interfering with your use of your property or against the local government that ran or planned a dump near your property.* Your remedy might take the form of receiving money damages to compensate you for the harm you suffered, a court-issued injunction to prevent the harmful conduct from continuing, or the imposition of a wide variety of conditions which the disposing party must adhere to in order to be allowed to continue the disposal activity. Examples of such conditions might be time periods when burning is prohibited or requirement of treatment of certain types of waste prior to disposal. While a wide array of private law remedies was available, they were generally only available with respect to harm inflicted on real estate. Also, the remedies tended to come into play after a harm had been done rather than as a preventative measure against harm, and those harmed had to go through the process of a lawsuit to attempt to obtain a remedy. Local legislative efforts to control waste disposal encountered enforcement problems and a lack of technology to provide a sound disposal system. Perhaps of greater significance with respect to local efforts was the lack of funds to effectively deal with waste disposal. The costs are high and, since there was little political glamour involved with promising a strong waste disposal program, waste disposal never got proper local funding.

In the 1960s, the federal government began to try to correct the deficiencies in the then-existing waste disposal controls. The 1965 Solid

---

6. 90 Stat. 2795.

*See Chapter 3 for a discussion of nuisance actions and remedies.

Waste Disposal Act[7] brought in the federal government with its money for technical and financial assistance to states to encourage states to take the responsibility for waste management. The Act also provided for grants to support and promote research, demonstration studies, and the development of methods to dispose of solid waste and to reduce the amount of waste being generated.

The next major piece of federal legislation was the 1970 Resource Recovery Act.[8] This statute changed the emphasis of the federal effort from disposal to recovery. The purposes of the 1970 legislation were stated more in the vein of resource recovery and the studies and demonstrations to be financed were also recovery oriented. Although Congress enacted the above-described legislation to further solid waste and resource recovery purposes, little was accomplished. The administrative and budgetary processes led to few grants actually being made, and grants and studies are not, in and of themselves, likely to lead to any massive change in a local government regulatory approach. The significance of these pieces of legislation, whether you consider it to be positive or negative, is that they were the wedge that opened the door to serious federal regulation of solid waste disposal. The existence earlier of legislation helped set the stage for public and Congressional acceptance of federal control over what had been historically a local matter.

In the Resource Conservation and Recovery Act of 1976, RCRA, Congress undertook to impose a federal scheme for regulating solid waste disposal. That statute seeks to control the disposal of solid wastes by providing financial incentives for the adoption of state or regional plans which will comply with federally established requirements. In addition to dealing with "general" solid wastes through the use of an incentive approach, the statute also established a mandatory regulatory system for the management of "hazardous" wastes.

With respect to nonhazardous solid wastes, if a state adopts a solid waste plan which is approved by the federal government (EPA), then the state qualifies for federal financial and technical assistance involving many facets of the development and implementation of the state plan. In order for a state plan to be approved, it must meet federally established requirements for approval which include a prohibition on the establishment of new open dumps and a phasing out of existing open dumps. Approved plans must also provide that disposal be in sanitary landfills, through resource conservation and recovery methods, or by other environmentally sound methods.

---

7. 7 Stat. 992.

8. 84 Stat. 1227.

A point of contrast between the Resource Conservation and Recovery Act and both the Clean Air Act and the Clean Water Act is that while the latter two statutes provide that in the absence of an approved state implementation plan, EPA will impose a federally prepared plan on the state; no such federal imposition takes place with respect to solid waste. The only sanction in the event of state noncompliance with the federal requirements for state plan approval is the state's ineligibility to receive federal financial and technical assistance. Why then, without compulsion, do the states go along with the federal objectives and requirements? The answer is twofold: money and money. First, the offer of a significant amount of federal money is hard for a state to pass up. Federal money provides jobs and other elements of economic well being. Furthermore, state administrations which pass up "free" federal dollars usually take a sound beating in the press for doing so. Being efficient in bringing federal money to the state is good politics for state officials. Perhaps a more substantive money argument for states accepting the federal solid waste disposal requirements is an awareness that, sooner or later, the waste disposal problems will have to be faced. States may feel that they may as well address the problem while the federal government is picking up a good share of the bill rather than wait to address the problem after other states have gotten federal assistance and the federal program is no longer available to help.

Although there is now substantial federal prodding and federal assistance, nonhazardous solid waste management is still largely a matter of state control. One step which some states took to attempt to reduce the magnitude of their solid waste problem even prior to the 1976 federal statute was to prohibit the disposal within the state of waste which originated or had been collected outside of the state. New Jersey enacted such a prohibition in 1973 and the validity of the New Jersey law was challenged repeatedly in the courts until a final decision was reached by the United States Supreme Court in 1978.

The first attempts to have the out-of-state prohibition declared invalid were made in the New Jersey state court system in a case called *City of Philadelphia v. New Jersey*.[9] The major grounds on which invalidity was alleged were (1) that the enactment of solid waste disposal legislation by the federal government preempted the field of solid waste disposal regulation and thus the state law was invalid under the Supremacy Clause of the United States Constitution, and (2) that the New Jersey statute was invalid because it violated the Commerce Clause of the United States Constitution by unjustifiably discriminating against articles of commerce

---

9. 68 N.J. 451 and 73 N.J. 562.

coming from outside of the state. Let's consider the preemption and Commerce Clause issues one at a time.

The Supremacy Clause, contained in Article VI of the United States Constitution says that the "Constitution, and the Laws of the United States...shall be the supreme Law of the Land;...any Thing in the Constitution or Laws of any State to the Contrary notwithstanding." It is thus clear that the state laws which are in direct conflict with the federal law are invalid. The Supremacy Clause has, however, been given broader scope by the courts. If it is found that Congress intended to *exclusively* control or "preempt" the field of regulation of certain subject matter, then state laws which seek to regulate the same subject matter are invalid even though they do not directly conflict with the federal law. Whether Congress has intended to preempt a field of regulation is often analyzed in terms of how pervasive is the scheme of federal regulation which Congress has created and whether Congress has indicated in that legislation that it is willing to accept additional, nonconflicting state legislation.

In the New Jersey Supreme Court cases decided both before and after the Resource Conservation and Recovery Act of 1976 was enacted, the New Jersey Court found that Congress' statutes, rather than evidencing a hostility to state regulation, affirmatively encouraged state action with respect to the disposal of solid waste. Thus there was no Congressional intent to preempt the field of regulation and the state law prohibiting out-of-state waste was not invalid under the Supremacy Clause. When *City of Philadelphia v. New Jersey* found its way to the United States Supreme Court in 1978, the United States Supreme Court agreed with the New Jersey Supreme Court on the issue of preemption.[10]

The New Jersey Supreme Court had also determined that the out-of-state prohibition did not violate the Commerce Clause of the United States Constitution. The Commerce Clause, contained in Article I, Section 8 of the Constitution gives Congress the power "To regulate Commerce...among the several States...." The courts have interpreted this constitutional grant of power to Congress to preclude states from enacting laws which discriminate against articles of commerce coming from outside the state unless there is some reason, apart from their origin, to treat them differently. This interpretation is consistent with the policy of preventing a state from engaging in protectionism by treating out-of-state commerce in a less favorable way than it treats its own commerce. That policy was much on the minds of the drafters of the Constitution who were well aware that many of the economic woes of the

---

10. 437 U.S. 617.

country under the Articles of Confederation were a result of states practicing protectionism.

The New Jersey Supreme Court had found that the out-of-state prohibition advanced vital health and environmental objectives with no economic discrimination against and with little burden upon interstate commerce. The United States Supreme Court reversed that judgment. It decided that solid waste is an item of commerce and is thus under the protection of the Commerce Clause. Even if an object of interstate trade is valueless, it is not outside the scope of the Commerce Clause. Furthermore, unlike diseased cattle, there are no dangers inherent in the movement of solid waste from one state to another which would justify a prohibition against its crossing a state line. The Court found that while it was true that some items of commerce may be validly subjected to state regulation, such regulation cannot take place where the purpose is basically protectionism. Although New Jersey may have an interest in conserving its remaining landfill space, it may not attempt to isolate itself from a problem common to many states by erecting a barrier against interstate movement of an item of commerce such as solid waste. The New Jersey statute prohibiting disposal of out-of-state waste in New Jersey was unconstitutional, and, while Congress has given the states a large role to play under the Resource Conservation and Recovery Act of 1976, states may not seek to limit their solid waste problems by prohibiting the entry of out-of-state waste. A question which may, however, remain open after the decision in *City of Philadelphia v. New Jersey* is whether a state may prohibit the disposal of hazardous waste which is generated outside of the state.

In addition to the 1976 statute using the lure of financial assistance to seek to encourage states to establish solid waste disposal plans, Congress also decided to encourage sound solid waste disposal action by having the federal government itself set a good example. Ordinarily the federal government is immune from having to comply with state or local laws. To set a good example, Congress waived this immunity in the 1976 statute and made all departments, agencies and instrumentalities of the federal government subject to compliance with state and local laws with respect to solid waste disposal. Since federal government facilities are among the larger generators of solid waste in the country and since these facilities had a rather poor record in the waste disposal area, using the mechanism of subjecting them to state and local controls would not only set a good example, but would also be a significant substantive contribution to alleviating solid waste problems. In Section C, we will again see how the federal government can use the mechanism of taking the lead and getting its own house in order and thereby contribute to solving another environmental problem, that of diminishing resources.

2.   Hazardous Wastes

A primary focus of the Resource Conservation and Recovery Act of 1976 (RCRA) was how to manage those wastes which, because of their hazardous nature, raised problems which might not be raised by nonhazardous wastes and which problems are so significant in character that they must be controlled by a stricter regulatory approach than that used for nonhazardous wastes. Hazardous waste, as defined in the 1976 statute, is waste which because of its quantity, concentration, or its physical, chemical or infectious characteristics may significantly contribute to an increase in mortality or serious illness or may, when improperly managed, pose a substantial hazard to human health or the environment. Thus, while a pesticide could be a hazardous waste, and a chemical substance under the Toxic Substances Control Act could be a hazardous waste, the definition of hazardous waste under the 1976 statute is much broader and can also include many other types of wastes. Among the factors which EPA and the states use to determine whether a material is hazardous are toxicity, corrosivity, flammability and potential for bioaccumulation. Examples of what are hazardous wastes are industrial wastes containing heavy metals, infectious hospital wastes, waste oils like crankcase oil and waste paint.

The two main operative mechanisms used by RCRA for controlling hazardous wastes are the "manifest system" and the requirement of permits for the treatment, storage or disposal of hazardous wastes.[11] RCRA focuses on the disposal stage in the life of a hazardous substance; however, its methodology for ensuring proper disposal is to provide a tracking of the substance through its entire life or what is commonly referred to as from "cradle to grave." This tracking approach is the manifest system. Furthermore, those who handle the hazardous waste at various stages after it has been created will have to have a permit and/or conform to federal standards in order to be allowed to handle the substance. By knowing who has the hazardous waste at every point in time and by controlling who can have the waste and making those who have it be responsible for what they do with it, Congress hopes that improper and hence environmentally unsound disposal will be avoided.

The tracking process begins with the generator of a hazardous waste. If you generate something which falls within the statutory definition of "hazardous waste," unless you are exempted, you are part of the mani-

---

11. 42 U.S.C.A. § 6921 et seq.

fest system for tracking the material's location at any time. You must initiate the manifest process by completing the "Generator Completes" section of the Hazardous Waste Manifest and Shipping Paper, a sample of which is shown in Figure 4. The manifest has seven copies, with the original staying with the waste from the point of generation until it reaches the hazardous waste facility where it will be disposed of, treated or stored. Other copies are kept by those who come into contact with the waste in its journey to the hazardous waste facility, and copies are also sent to the state where generation took place and the state of destination. The idea is to keep track of who has the hazardous waste, with the intent that it ultimately end up in a proper hazardous waste facility for treatment, storage or disposal.

One important exemption from the manifest system should be noted because to some extent it cuts back on the protection which the system was designed to provide. That exemption is for "small generators" of hazardous wastes. Under federal regulations, one is exempt from the manifest system if one generates less than 1000 kg per month of hazardous waste or less than 1 kg per month of acutely hazardous waste. While it is clear that many small, and thus exempt, generators of hazardous wastes can, in the aggregate, have very significant effects on the environment, the federal government has decided that to require small generators to be part of the manifest system would be placing an excessive administrative burden on them which would not be justified by the potential for harm which they may cause. This is the balance that the federal government has made; however, states, if they choose, can and do tighten up on the exemption for small generators and do impose regulations on them. State control which is stricter than federal control is specifically allowed by RCRA with respect to hazardous wastes. For example, in Vermont one is exempt from the manifest process only if he generates less than 100 kg per month of hazardous waste, or less than 1 kg per month of acutely hazardous waste. Also, the state requires small generators to notify the state of hazardous waste activities and to send any hazardous waste to a sanitary landfill.

The complementary mechanism to the manifest system which tracks the hazardous waste to its ultimate location is RCRA's requirement that the ultimate location of hazardous waste be one which has a permit evidencing that it meets specific standards with respect to such matters as recordkeeping, using satisfactory treatment, storage or disposal methods, contingency plans for minimizing unanticipated damage, proper personnel and financial responsibility. Unless the applicable standards are met, the facility will not receive a permit and, unless the facility has a permit, a generator of hazardous waste may not cause the hazardous waste to be transported to the facility. Various types of violations of the

HAZARDOUS WASTE MANIFEST AND SHIPPING PAPER

VT 0003089
MANIFEST NUMBER

NAME | MAILING ADDRESS | PHONE NUMBER | STATE/E.P.A. I.D. NO.

GENERATOR

PRIMARY TRANSPORTER

CONTINUING TRANSPORTER

H.W.F.

IF MORE THAN ONE MANIFEST/ SHIPPING PAPER IS USED | TOTAL NO. OF FORMS ARE | THIS FORM NO. IS | MANIFEST NO. OF FIRST FORM | DATE SHIPPED | EXPECTED ARRIVAL DATE

U.S. D.O.T. SHIPPING NAME | D.O.T. HAZARD CLASS | U.N./N.A. NO. | W.T./VOL. | UNITS | UNIT CODE | CONTAINER NO. | TYPE | E.P.A. WASTE NO. | DESCRIPTION OR WASTE ANALYSIS IF WASTE IS N.O.S

MONTH DAY YEAR | MONTH DAY YEAR

1
2
3
4
5
6

SPECIAL HANDLING INSTRUCTIONS INCLUDING ANY CONTAINER EXEMPTION, AND EMERGENCY RESPONSE INFORMATION.

IN THE EVENT OF A SPILL, CONTACT THE NATIONAL RESPONSE CENTER, U.S. COAST GUARD 1- 800-424-8802

REQUIRED LABELS
YES ☐ NO ☐

PLACARDS REQUIRED
YES ☐ NO ☐

THIS IS TO CERTIFY THAT I AM THE PRIMARY TRANSPORTER AND HAVE ACCEPTED THE DESCRIBED SHIPMENT IN PROPER CONDITION FOR TRANSPORT TO THE IDENTIFIED H.W.F.

DATE SHIPMENT ACCEPTED
MONTH DAY YEAR

VEHICLE I.D. | STATE | COMPANY NO. FOR TRAILER, MARINE OR RAIL.

SIGNATURE OF TRANSPORTER

THIS IS TO CERTIFY THAT I AM THE CONTINUING TRANSPORTER AND HAVE ACCEPTED THE DESCRIBED SHIPMENT IN PROPER CONDITION FOR TRANSPORT TO THE IDENTIFIED H.W.F.

DATE SHIPMENT ACCEPTED
MONTH DAY YEAR

VEHICLE I.D. | STATE | COMPANY NO. FOR TRAILER, MARINE OR RAIL

SIGNATURE OF TRANSPORTER

INDICATE ANY DIFFERENCES BETWEEN MANIFEST AND SHIPMENT AND LIST REJECTED MATERIALS, INDICATE DISPOSITION OF REJECTED SHIPMENT

DATE OF DELIVERY
MONTH DAY YEAR

DATE OF DELIVERY
MONTH DAY YEAR

I CERTIFY THAT THE DESCRIBED WASTE(S) WAS DELIVERED BY THE AFOREMENTIONED DELIVERING TRANSPORTER AND THAT THE INFORMATION ON THIS MANIFEST IS CORRECT TO THE BEST OF MY KNOWLEDGE.

SIGNATURE | MONTH DAY DATE YEAR

HANDLING METHOD
1. 2. 3. 4. 5. 6.

THIS IS TO CERTIFY THAT THE ABOVE NAMED MATERIALS ARE PROPERLY CLASSIFIED, DESCRIBED, PACKAGED, MARKED AND LABELED AND ARE IN PROPER CONDITION FOR TRANSPORTATION ACCORDING TO THE APPLICABLE REGULATIONS OF THE DEPARTMENT OF TRANSPORTATION AND THE U.S. ENVIRONMENTAL PROTECTION AGENCY.

GENERATOR SIGNATURE

GENERATOR'S EMERGENCY PHONE IF DIFFERENT FROM ABOVE | DATE

GENERATOR COMPLETES | TRANSPORTER COMPLETES | H.W.F. COMPLETES

Figure 4. Sample hazardous waste manifest and shipping paper.

federal control mechanisms which we have discussed can subject the violator to sanctions which range from the issuance of an EPA compliance order to criminal penalties of up to $250,000 and five years imprisonment or up to $1,000,000 if the violator is an organization such as a corporation.

As mentioned above, Congress' goal is to have hazardous waste find its way to a "proper" facility. A practical problem which bears on the fulfillment of that goal is the availability of "proper" facilities. Realistically, no one wants a hazardous waste facility in his or her backyard even if it is financially responsible and has contingency plans for unanticipated damage due to the activities of the facility. State and local governments or the federal government will have to work out an approach which will result in an adequate number of proper facilities located in places where their use by generators is not prohibitive in cost. Even with stiff penalties for violations, the effectiveness of RCRA's hazardous waste provisions may well be diluted if it is economically prohibitive for a generator to send his waste to a proper facility. This problem is currently being addressed by many state and local governments, some of which are coming to the realization that local vetos on the location of a hazardous waste facility may not be capable of being tolerated from either an economic or an environmentalist point of view.*

The hazardous waste controls imposed by RCRA address hazardous waste problems by trying to prevent them from occurring. There are, however, situations where substantial problems are caused by hazardous waste incidents. Congress provided remedial mechanisms to help solve some of the problems which result from hazardous waste incidents by enacting what is known as the Superfund Act.[12] This statute establishes a fund to finance cleanup and restoration of the environment following a hazardous waste incident. While the Superfund Act does not provide victims with compensation for personal injury and property damage, the EPA has provided for relief in some situations by requiring that hazardous waste facilities must carry liability insurance to compensate victims for personal injury and property damage caused by the release of hazardous wastes into the environment.[13]

---

*An example is the Massachusetts Hazardous Waste Facility Siting Act, Chapter 21D, Annotated Laws of Massachusetts, which does not provide a means by which a community can absolutely veto a proposed facility. The December, 1981–January, 1982 issue of the *New England Sierran,* a Sierra Club publication, took the position of not supporting any proposal which would insert an effective veto.

12. Comprehensive Environmental Response, Compensation, and Liability Act of 1980, 94 Stat. 2767.

13. 40 CFR §§ 264.147 and 265.147.

Although the safety net for the public and environmental protection from hazardous wastes has been established by the typical balancing of environmental interests with other interests, public concern about the types of harms which can result from hazardous wastes and the magnitude of those harms has led to the creation of a massive federal and state regulatory scheme in the comparatively short period of five years.

C.   RECYCLING, REUSE AND CONSERVATION

As we have seen, there are many control mechanisms that affect the disposal of waste materials. In addition, there are mechanisms that encourage the recycling, reuse and conservation of those materials. Let us begin by discussing alternatives to the "dump it or burn it" philosophy.

By far, the most popular alternative strategy for dealing with the solid waste dilemma is recycling. This method encompasses everything from glass bottles and beer cans to sludge application on forests and crops, the recycling method depending on the resource in question. We generally take two approaches to municipal solid waste recycling, the centralized approach using high technology (Figure 5) or the decentralized approach using low technology (Figure 6). Centralization accepts the idea that the more economical approach to recycling, in the long run, is to collect all the solid waste from an area such as a large city and bring this material to a central location where all processing (sorting) takes place. There are several assumed advantages to this system. The weight and volume of materials needing a landfill will be drastically reduced while, at the same time, a municipality can use revenues gathered from resource separation (iron, aluminum, glass) to pay for the operation of the program. The biodegradable remainder could be burned to heat water and get steam to make electricity or heat for municipal offices or, using a more efficient energy recycling strategy, the biodegradable portion could be properly digested under low-oxygen conditions. Using this process, methane gas is produced and burned to heat water and provide heat or electricity. In fact, if properly executed, the above plan could reduce or stabilize the tax burden on residents of the municipality participating in such a program. However, the initial cost of such a facility is high and the amount of organic waste needed on a continuous basis for the energy recovery portion of such an undertaking is very high. Recent figures indicate this type of project requires an investment of over six million dollars, and the investment is usually much higher.[14] Other data indicate that such sys-

14. Council on Environmental Quality. *Environmental Quality* (Washington, DC: U.S. Government Printing Office, 1979).

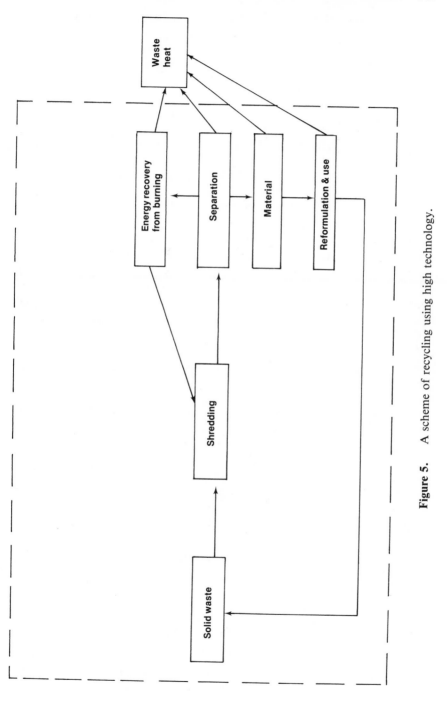

Figure 5.   A scheme of recycling using high technology.

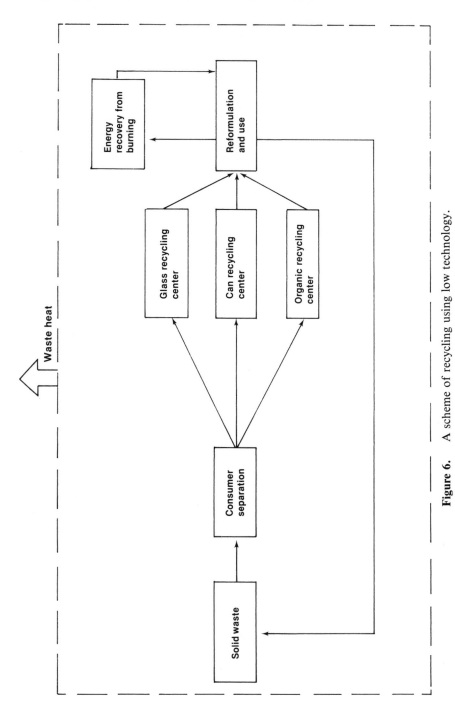

Figure 6.   A scheme of recycling using low technology.

tems do not totally recover all operating expenses but have substantially reduced the net annual cost of operation.

The other strategy for recycling municipal solid waste is source separation (Figure 6). The object of this alternative is to convince the consumers that it is to their advantage to separate paper, glass, metals and organic material before collection. This is the only practical means for paper recycling. Once this separation is complete, a municipality could either collect the resource or attempt to get the consumer to deliver the resource to a recycling center. The center then sells the resource and uses revenues to keep the center operating. This type of system usually is operated by volunteers or governmentally subsidized employees because most centers cannot support themselves. In order to sell a recovered resource to a potential reformulator, it is usually necessary to provide a continuity of supply. Since this decentralized system relies on many people to keep the outflow of recovered resources constant, there are often problems. Consider what might happen at a glass recycling facility during a "boycott" of all nonreturnable glass containers. Furthermore, remember that spring cleaning time is when everything gets sorted out. So, in addition to needing interested people as volunteers, this type of recycling requires interested consumers who are willing to take the time to sort out the stuff. On the positive side, however, this type of operation requires little initial investment. In the long run, neither of these alternatives can, by itself, provide the solution to the problem of recycling consumer solid waste. A combination of the approaches, using each where it is most appropriate, has the potential for serving as a basis to increase our recycling efforts.

Up to now our recycling discussion has considered mainly domestic solid waste, not municipal solid waste such as sewage sludge or industrial solid waste such as fly ash. While a complete discussion of each of these would be informative, we will focus on the sludge issue. Sewage sludge is usually a product of the municipal sewage treatment plant. Since sewage treatment plants may receive sewage from domestic sources, industrial sources, and storm runoff, the potential for recycling is problematical because of possible metal content. Recent advances in removing metals from industrial sewage at the industrial site may, however, eventually eliminate the problem-causing metal content of these sludges. In addition, if we assume that municipal sludge which is domestic in origin has a greatly reduced probability of having any toxic or potentially toxic content, then it becomes useful to consider a number of possibilities that are currently available or under research for sludge use. Since this material contains many nutrients crucial to the maximal productivity of crop plants, sludge has been and can be used for fertilizer on crops. Other benefits are gained in this effort since sludge is usually 80–95% water and the organic portions not only act as fertilizer but also can effectively alter soil growing potential in other positive ways. In essence, using this process means we are returning to the soil an array of nutrients that we got from the soil to begin with, and we are truly recycling so we can get new proteins, fats and carbohydrates.

Although recycling is more in vogue today, there are other strategies for dealing with solid waste, and reuse is one of them. Underlying this idea is the concept of "do not throw it away but use it again." If that glass bottle is empty, why not fill it again with the same stuff? This eventually leads to the idea of selling all possible consumer products in containers that can be used over and over again. While this notion seems to give us some advantage in material consumption, there are several drawbacks. One of these is convincing the consumer to buy the contained product, use the product, clean the container if circumstances so require and bring the container back to the retailer for a refill. Sounds easy, the cooperative food stores do it and it works—sometimes. But consider some of the other problems like what happens if you break the container or it inadvertently gets destroyed? How do we get a new one? How many do we make to start? How do we make sure the container is clean in the case of dispensing some products? Also, what about products of limited life? How much bulk storage can a retail refill station accommodate and continue to make a profit without having to increase the cost of the product to the consumer? The reuse idea is a good one, but the mechanics still need to be refined, especially when viewed in conjunction with the question of what to do about workers who used to make the containers we no longer need now that reuse is taking place.

Probably the least formally exercised approach to the solid waste dilemma is the alternative of conservation. Conservation can be viewed in many forms. Although we may consider conservation to mean only no use or limited use of a resource such as newspaper or food, there are other ways of being conservative. Buying products, such as cars, that have proven long-term use expectancy with highly efficient utilization is a way of conserving. Conservation is a disadvantage to those dependent on the principle of planned obsolescence, and, until very recently, the concept of unlimited resources allowed planned obsolescence to be a producer's managerial strategy. With increasing awareness of global resource limitations, conservation, coupled with resource recovery and reuse, appears to be forming a viable matrix for better utilization of resources, and can in fact be considered a "growth industry."

Let's next consider some examples of how the federal government has acted to encourage recycling, reuse and conservation of materials. Subchapter V of the Resource Conservation and Recovery Act[15] assigns certain duties to the Secretary of Commerce which are designed to encourage resource recovery. The Secretary is given the responsibility of stimulating the development of markets for recovered materials by identifying existing or potential markets and identifying economic and technical barriers to the use of recovered materials as well as encouraging the development of new uses for recovered materials. It would appear that the taking of such steps should lead to a reduction in the amount of waste which will have to be dealt with by disposal and also should result in a reduction in the amount of virgin materials which would be used in the absence of those steps. Consistent with these goals, the Secretary is also directed to promote resource recovery technology by evaluating its commercial feasibility, publishing the results of the evaluation and assisting those interested in making a choice of a recovery system. He is further charged with initiating the process of developing specifications for secondary materials. If reliable specifications are available for secondary materials, it is hoped that users will be more likely to avail themselves of such materials.

A summarizing phrase for the above-described federal mechanisms relating to stimulating resource recovery might be "information dissemination." A more direct approach to resource recovery is contained in that part of RCRA which addresses itself to federal procurement policy.[16] When we were discussing waste disposal we noted that one step that the federal government took in the direction of sound waste disposal was to take the lead and set a good example by voluntarily making itself subject to state and local laws concerning solid waste disposal. In the area of resource recovery the federal government has also sought to set a good example. Under RCRA, federal procuring agencies are required to procure items composed of the highest percentage of recovered materials practicable consistent with maintaining a satisfactory level of competition. Unless such items are not reasonably available, fail to meet quality standards or are unreasonably priced, their procurement is mandated if it is consistent with administrative guidelines prepared to achieve Congress' objectives. This "taking the lead" approach can spur the use of recovered materials in various ways including providing a substantial demand for a product which should attract a supplier. In turn, that supplier may very well attempt to market to others the product that he is now producing in

---

15. 42 U.S.C.A. § 6951 et seq.
16. 42 U.S.C.A. § 6962.

order to satisfy a large customer, the federal government. Also, having large amounts of items made from recovered materials in general use throughout the country may serve to reduce psychological barriers to the use of secondary materials. Thus, with respect to resource recovery, Congress has utilized relatively noncoercive mechanisms to help achieve its goals — information dissemination and the use of the federal purchasing power.

There are other examples of government involvement in resource recovery, such as beverage container deposit laws, which are intended to impact on waste disposal, resource recovery, or both of these often related concepts. Perhaps a good point on which to end this chapter is to note that government may not need to continue to expand its efforts with respect to resource recovery. Resource recovery will likely mushroom on its own through the free enterprise system as many resources become more limited in supply. Resource recovery as well as resource conservation will likely turn out to be plain good business.

ADDITIONAL READINGS

Brown, M. *Laying Waste: The Poisoning of America by Toxic Chemicals* (New York: Pantheon Books, Inc., 1979).

Council on Environmental Quality. *Environmental Quality* (Washington, DC: U.S. Government Printing Office, 1979).

Council on Environmental Quality. *Environmental Quality* (Washington, DC: U.S. Government Printing Office, 1980).

Environmental Protection Agency. *Waste Disposal in the Ground* (Washington, DC: U.S. Government Printing Office, 1977). EPA-625/1-77-008.

Meyer, S. "Compensating Hazardous Waste Victims: RCRA Insurance Regulations and a Not So "Super" Fund Act" *Environ. Law* 11:689–719 (1981).

CHAPTER 6

PESTICIDES AND TOXIC SUBSTANCES

A. WHERE DO THEY COME FROM AND WHY DO WE NEED THEM?

While pesticides are considered to be toxic substances, there are other toxic substances which are not pesticides. The regulatory scheme is different for pesticides than for other toxic substances, so let's begin by considering them separately with respect to their origins and uses.

1. Pesticides

A pesticide can be defined as a chemical agent that can be used to cause the death of, or the regulation of, nonhuman organisms that man considers detrimental to his existence. The intended target species of pesticides are then the insects, plants, fungi, rodents, mites and any other organisms that negatively affect man. These insults to man are usually in the form of reduced crop yields, disease infestation, general nuisance situations (flies, mosquitos) or real estate destruction (termites, powder post beetles, nematodes).

To illustrate the extent of pesticide development let's take a look at the history of three forms of pesticides; herbicides, fungicides, and insecticides. Herbicides (chemicals to control plant growth, usually resulting in death) were first noted in modern times around the turn of the century with the use of arsenic compounds as soil sterilants. The way arsenic compounds work is to degrade cell membranes and thereby disrupt normal cell metabolism, resulting in death of the organism. About the end of World War II the first organic herbicides (phenoxy herbicides), 2, 4-D and 2, 4, 5-T, and silvex were developed. These three herbicides act like plant auxins (growth stimulators) and virtually cause the plant to grow itself to death. The two latter compounds are commonly known to contain dioxin, sometimes known as agent orange. Later, in the 1950s and 1960s the urea base nonselective soil sterilants were developed. These act by inhibiting the photosynthetic process. Durion and linuron are examples. Still later came the dessicant herbicides diquat and paraquat which disrupt plant membranes and cause the plant to dry up. These have been followed by the carbamate and phenolic herbicides, again herbicides that disrupt membranes, as we try to produce more effective and more specific herbicides.

Fungicides (chemicals that destroy fungi) were first used in modern times in France in the 1850s, with the use of lime-sulfur on ornamental plants. Later, Bordeau mixture, mainly copper sulfate, was used to protect the French grapes. In the early 1900s, mercurial fungicides were developed to protect seeds. Some of these are still used today. Organic fungicides (PCP) were developed in the World War II time period. These fungicides alter enzyme action in cells and thus kill the fungus. The fungicide business really came of age with the appearance of captan, a foliar (leaf) spray, in 1951 and systemic fungicides in 1966. The systemic fungicides are carried in the transport vessels throughout the plants, giving a more certain effect. These fungicides inhibit chemical reactions and eventually leave cells unable to breathe.

By far, the most researched pesticides are the insecticides. In fact, it has only been recently that entomology has returned from the near total devotion to insecticide pursuits to more traditional areas of endeavor. The first insecticides (1860s) were arsenic compounds which are stomach poisons that eventually cause muscle paralysis and death to organisms that eat it. In the 1880s came the cyanide insecticides and a natural insecticide, rotenone (still used today). Around World War II (1939) the most widely recognized insecticide ever developed was placed in the market. The organic chemical is DDT, a long-term, highly effective, broad-spectrum insecticide that causes repetitive nerve discharges and eventually kills the insect. The cyclodiene insecticides (chlordane, dieldrin, aldrin) were developed about 1945 and are all neurotoxins operating on the junction between sensory and motor neurons, causing a malfunction which results in death. The organophosphorus insecticides, parathion and malathion, came along later. These cause muscles to keep tensing and never relax, eventually causing death. Recently the carbamate insecticides such as Sevin have been developed which operate much the same as the organophosphorus ones. More recently the juvenile hormone insecticides, which disrupt metamorphosis, and the chitin synthesis inhibitors, which make exoskeleton formation difficult, have been developed to combat insects. One interesting note is that most of our insecticides were developed around World War II, are organic in nature, and have spawned an industry of multinational proportions. The United States pesticide industry currently receives $7 billion per year in sales.

The fact that we have pesticides "forces" us to need pesticides. This is a Catch-22 situation. We all enjoy being free from disease or the threat of disease, keeping our meat foods the same, and eating unblemished food as well as producing as much food for mankind as possible per unit area. We also demand wood for a variety of purposes including your reading of this book, and we have found monoculture raising of timber and food crops more economical to harvest than mixed crops and timber. We have also found that the use of pesticides enhances our chances of maximizing our control in each of the above categories such that our quality of life is maintained and even increased. A little closer look at one of these instances, one-culture raising of food crops, should illustrate the Catch-22 progression.

Our farm crop raising efforts are primarily concentrated in a few families of plants, the grasses (corn, sorghum, barley, oats, rice, wheat), the nightshades (tomatoes, potatoes, peppers), and the legume family (beans, peas, peanuts). Because we plant large areas in a single crop (monoculture) so we can easily plant, cultivate, fertilize, protect and harvest the crops, we invite pests that prey on a particular crop to attack that crop by providing a concentrated food source. We make these crops even more susceptible to pest attack by selecting genetic strains that maximize food output at the expense of producing defense mechanisms. Therefore, the crops we have created through genetic selection require protection from various pests and necessitate the use of pesticides so we get abundant food and the farmer makes a reasonable profit (estimated cash loss due to pests in the U.S. exceeds $2 billion per year even with pesticides).[1] Since pests themselves have a varied genetic make-up within the pest species population, some individuals of the species population will be resistant to the pesticide and we will therefore "select" in favor of these organisms when we apply the pesticide. These resistant members of the species population will then be free to breed and eventually a pest species population will be present that resists the previously effective pesticide to such an extent that the pesticide is considered useless and a new one is needed. This vicious circle is made even more vicious because it appears that insect pests "adapt" more quickly to pesticides (become resistant) than do pest plants or fungi.

---

1. Pimentel, D. Extent of Pesticide Use, Food Supply and Pollution. *J. N.Y. Entomol. Soc.* 81:13–33(1973).

Although pesticides create many evils and also create the above described dependency on pesticides, there certainly are sound arguments favoring their use. One example of our need for pesticides is the economic need. If one assumes that pests destroy 10% of a crop and this reduces profit by an amount X, and if the use of pesticides will cost less than 100% of X, then pesticides would probably be used to increase profits and yields (see Table I). As can be seen, it is more profitable in terms of food yield and money to use a pesticide, and thus most people are satisfied that there is a real need for pesticides.

Table I.   Hypothetical Relationship Between Use and No Use of Pesticides on Profit from Raising Silage Corn

	Pesticide	No Pesticide
Yield/acre	25 tons	22 tons
Selling price/ton	$ 20	$ 20
Total price	$500	$440
Cost pesticide/acre	$ 5	0
Profit/acre	$495	$440

2.   Toxic Substances

In the broadest sense, a toxic substance can be defined as any chemical or mixture which could, under proper circumstances, do harm to health or the environment. Therefore, a toxic substance is essentially any chemical or mixture that is manufactured and consequently distributed and eventually discarded. Although Congress has not explicitly defined a toxic substance, Congress has, through its findings, implicitly defined a toxic substance as any chemical or mixture whose manufacture, processing, distribution, use or disposal may present unreasonable risk of injury to health or environment.[2] The Council on Environmental Quality further defined the situation by identifying classes of toxic substances (Table II).

As you can see by reading the table, toxic substances include almost everything we use in modern manufacturing. But, we do need these toxic substances. After the proliferation of organic chemicals following World

---

2. Toxic Substances Control Act, 15 U.S.C.A. § 2601, et seq.

Table II.   Toxic Pollutants by Classes[3]

Pollutant	Characteristics	Sources
PESTICIDES Generally chlorinated hydrocarbons	Readily assimilated by aquatic animals, fat-soluble, concentrated through the food chain (biomagnified) persistent in soil sediments	Direct application to farm- and forest-lands, runoff from lawns and gardens, urban runoff, discharge in industrial wastewater
POLYCHLORINATED BIPHENYLS (PCB) Used in electric capacitors and transformers, paints, plastics, insecticides, other industrial products	Readily assimilated by aquatic animals, fat-soluble, subject to biomagnification, persistent, chemically similar to the chlorinated hydrocarbons	Municipal and industrial waste discharges disposed of in dumps and landfills
METALS Antinomy, arsenic, beryllium, cadmium, copper, lead, mercury, nickel, selenium silver, thallium and zinc	Not biodegradeable, persistent in sediments, toxic in solution, subject to bio-magnification	Industrial discharges, mining activity, urban runoff, erosion of metal-rich soil, certain agricultural uses (e.g., mercury as a fungicide)
OTHER INORGANICS Asbestos and cyanide	Asbestos: May cause cancer when inhaled, aquatic toxicity not well understood Cyanide: Variably persistent, inhibits oxygen metabolism	Asbestos: Manufacture and use as a retardant, roofing material, brake lining, etc.; runoff from mining Cyanide: Wide variety of industrial uses
HALOGENATED ALIPHATICS Used in fire extinguishers, refrigerants, propellants, pesticides, solvents for oils and greases and in dry cleaning	Largest single class of "priority toxics," can cause damage to central nervous system and liver, not very persistent	Produced by chlorination of water, vaporization during use

Table II., continued

Pollutant	Characteristics	Sources
ETHERS Used mainly as solvents for polymer plastics	Potent carcinogen, aquatic toxicity and fate not well understood	Escape during production and use
PHTHALATE ESTERS Used chiefly in production of polyvinyl chloride and thermoplastics as plasticizers	Common aquatic pollutant, moderately toxic but teratogenic and mutagenic properties in low concentrations; aquatic invertebrates are particularly sensitive to toxic effects; persistent; can be bio-magnified	Waste disposal vaporization during use (in nonplastics)
MONOCYCLIC AROMATICS (excluding Phenols, Cresols, and Phthalates) Used in the manufacture of other chemicals, explosives, dyes and pigments, and in solvents, fungicides and herbicides	Central nervous system depressant; can damage liver and kidneys	Enter environment during production and by-product production states by direct volatilization wastewater
PHENOLS Large-volume industrial compounds used chiefly as chemical intermediates in the production of synthetic polymers, dye-stuffs, pigments, pesticides and herbicides	Toxicity increases with degree of chlorination of the phenolic molecule; very low concentrations can taint fish flesh and impart objectionable odor and taste to drinking water, difficult to remove from water by conventional treatment; carcinogenic in mice	Occur naturally in fossil fuels, waste water from cooking ovens, oil refineries, tar distillation plants, herbicide manufacturing and plastic manufacturing; can all contain phenolic compounds

POLYCYCLIC AROMATIC HYDRO-CARBONS Used as dyestuffs, chemical intermediates, pesticides, herbicides, motor fuels and oils	Carcinogenic in animals and indirectly linked to cancer in humans; most work done on air pollution; more is needed on the aquatic toxicity of these compounds; not persistent and are biodegradable though bioaccumulation can occur	Fossil fuels (use, spills, production), incomplete combustion of hydrocarbons
NITROSAMINES Used in the production of organic chemicals and rubber; patents exist on processes using these compounds	Tests on laboratory animals have shown the nitrosamines to be some of the most potent carcinogens	Production and use can occur spontaneously in food cooking operations

3. Council on Environmental Quality. *Environmental Quality*, Ninth Annual Report (Washington, DC: U.S. Government Printing Office, 1978) Stock No. 041-011-00040-8.

War II we became a society dependent upon these for our quality of life. Organic chemicals did improve our quality of life. We need motor oil, plastics, paint, pesticides, film and car batteries. Because of the way we live, the occurrence of toxic substances in our environment is inevitable. This is not to say that society is wrong, nor is this to say that such products should not be used. What the reader should have is an awareness of the scope of the toxic substances situation such that the following sections will seem more realistic. Toxic substances are with us. Our problem is to ensure that the least amount of damage to health and environment occurs during the process of using and not using these chemicals and mixtures.

B.   WHY DO WE NEED TO REGULATE THEM?

As with any undertaking, it seems appropriate to first define the scope of this issue and then examine the need for regulation. Pesticide production in the United States between 1950 and 1975 increased sevenfold from 102 million kilograms (224 million pounds) to 727 kilograms (1600 million pounds).[4] In 1975, 275 pounds of pesticides per square mile were applied in the United States. If one considers that pesticides are not applied everywhere, there is a lot of pesticide being applied to some areas. By 1976, there were over 1000 registered pesticides in the United States. In 1980, the pesticide industry in the United States sold $7 billion dollars worth of pesticides, exporting about 40% of its production in 1979. Of the 1979 pesticide exports, 25% were either banned in the United States or not registered here.[5] Economically, between 1976 and 1978, the amount of United States pesticide usage for agriculture accounted for 3.1% of average farm production expenses.[6] With the above facts about pesticide production and use, consider the following facts about new chemicals. During the period from 1965 to 1979, over four million new chemicals, potentially toxic substances, were manufactured. Currently, there are about 6000 new chemicals synthesized every week or

---

4. Council on Environmental Quality. *Environmental Quality.* (Washington, DC: U.S. Government Printing Office, 1977).

5. Wolterding, M. "The Poisoning of Central America," *The Sierra Club Bull.* 66:63–67 (1981).

6. Environmental Protection Agency. *Pesticide Industry Sales and Usage* (Washington, DC: Environmental Protection Agency, 1980).

about one million every three years. There are now over 70,000 chemicals or mixtures in active use and about 1000 new ones are added each year. The current EPA list of toxic substances exceeds 50,000.[7] While all these facts may seem alarming, the picture so far presented is really not what is of major concern. It is not the fact that we produce so many pesticides and toxic substances that is most alarming, it is what we do with them after they are "invented" and why we do it and what the results are that give cause for the alarm and the need to regulate.

We normally use pesticides to increase crop yield, to control weed growth on rights of way, and to kill disease-carrying or annoying pests. While all of this use creates an environment seemingly pleasant to live in, there are certain "other" biological effects of pesticide application besides market considerations. These effects force us to consider regulation.

Pesticide application in agriculture is viewed today as a necessity. Because we have genetically selected for strains of crop plants that maximize the yield of usable product, we have removed the plant's natural defenses against most pests. Therefore, we protect these crops by applying large quantities of pesticides to them, based on the assumption that if we did not, marketable yields would be drastically reduced, possibly causing pockets of starvation and definitely causing reduced profits. The reason we produce so many different pesticides is because target species become resistant to a pesticide after long-term exposure. What happens in this instance is that some individuals of the target species are not killed by a particular pesticide application. These individuals breed and produce many offspring that are resistant to that particular pesticide. Then, we either use more of the particular pesticide per unit area, hoping that quantity will kill, or we shift to another pesticide and use it until the same resistance is evidenced. The extent of this phenomenon and the consequent need for different pesticides is illustrated in Figure 1.[8] These are the main reasons we use pesticides and the reason we keep needing to invent new ones. The reasons we need to regulate pesticides are scattered among several concerns which we will consider now.

One case usually made for regulation of pesticides deals with the notion of United States industry only wanting to make a profit by selling products without any care as to the effects of those products on non-target species, including man. While industry might argue that all their

7. National Wildlife Federation, *The Toxic Substance Dilemma.* (Washington, DC: National Wildlife Federation, 1980).

8. Brown, A.W.A. *Ecology of Pesticides.* (New York: Wiley Interscience, 1978).

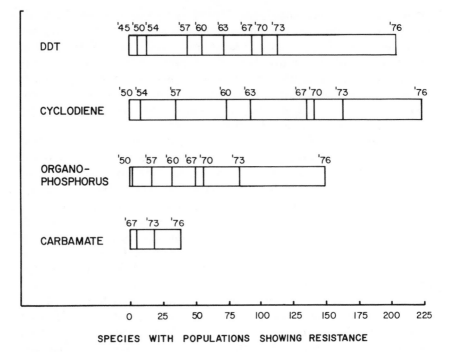

Figure 1.   Numbers of anthropod (insects, spiders, etc.) species showing resistance of insecticides discussed in text. Cumulative totals indicated by year [adapted from Brown, 1978 (See Additional Readings)].

pesticides are properly labelled, many unregistered and banned pesticides as well as regulated pesticides are currently sold outside this country. These unregistered pesticides have usually not been tested according to United States standards. Interestingly, it has been shown that many of the crops sprayed with these pesticides are crops raised by foreign agriculture efforts for export to the United States. So, in some instances we are getting imported food that contains levels of registered or unregistered pesticide residue far above those allowed by United States law.[9] It appears in this case we need to regulate to protect us from us.

Other concerns of those stressing regulation deal mainly with biological effects on nontarget species coincidental with pesticide application and long-term effects of pesticide application. We know that when pesti-

---

9. Wolterding, id.

cides are applied, species other than the target species are killed. In many instances, the other species are predators on the target species (natural controls) or economically useful species such as honeybees. Persistence of a pesticide is also a concern. Ideally, a pesticide should eliminate a target species and dissipate into a harmless end product. However, many of the first pesticides, DDT in particular, did not degrade for a long period of time and consequently were consumed along with any crop to which they were applied.

Two very significant environmental concerns with respect to pesticides are the biological effects of pesticide degradation products and the phenomenon of biological magnification. Probably the most publicized pesticide degradation product is DDE, a decay product of DDT. DDE has been implicated in the decline of many carnivorous bird species such as the brown pelican and the perigrine falcon because DDE affects the shell gland in these birds to such a degree that the egg shells of chicks are so fragile the mother crushes them during incubation. Therefore, many individuals believe we should know of these decay products ahead of time and should regulate pesticides accordingly. A major concern only recently receiving widespread attention is biological magnification. What this means is that organisms higher on the food chain get more and thus concentrate the most pesticide in their systems, sometimes to levels detrimental to their health. Let's illustrate this. Suppose that organism A contains 1 part X in one million parts of everything. If a fish ate 100 of these organisms the fish could theoretically contain 100 parts X in one million parts of everything. If you ate two of these fish you could contain 200 parts X in one million parts of everything. This is called biological magnification. If 150 parts X in one million parts of everything causes death to humans, you could theoretically eat only one and one-half fish until your body metabolized the pesticide. If your body never metabolized the pesticide then you would have to stop eating fish. Consider the problem with DDT as outlined in Figure 2. As you can see in Figure 2, if a man ate a lot of fish and no crop, he would accumulate high levels of DDT in his system rapidly. Therefore, food source will have much to do with how healthy you are in terms of pesticide accumulation.

Suffice it to say that many similar arguments could be advanced concerning toxic substances other than pesticides. With other toxic substances an additional concern is human health in terms of cancer-causing agents. While agent orange is a pesticide, benzene, naphthalene and other possible carcinogens are not. The need to regulate all toxic substances is apparent when one considers not only the volume of potential industrial production but also the preservation of human health. While

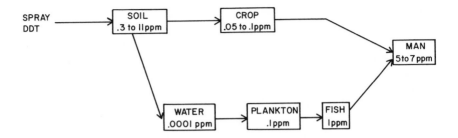

Figure 2. Simple example of biological magnification of pesticide residue through a food chain.[10]

one might consider industry to be at fault in the production of such chemicals and mixtures, industry is satisfying a demand of the human populace for food, less disease and a better quality of life. Furthermore, industry's responsibility is not only to produce a useful product but also to make money for stockholders who have invested in the production process. While industry may be said to be at fault, perhaps the fault is really that of the public as consumer and the public as investor.

C. HOW WE REGULATE THEM

Having considered the benefits which society derives from pesticides and other toxic substances as well as the harms which such products might create, we next turn to how we try to keep the benefits while reducing or eliminating the harms. How far we should go in controlling our use of pesticides and toxic substances is a question to be left for the reader's own determination. The question that will be addressed here is how far the law has gone in establishing control mechanisms. We will first focus on control through the private law control mechanism of a lawsuit where someone (a plaintiff) will be asking a court for relief without the request for relief being based on any action of a legislative body. Relief will thus be based on the "common law" or judge-made law. We will then examine public law control mechanisms in the form of legislation directed at pesticide use and at the manufacturing of toxic substances.

---

10. Edwards, C.A. 1974. *Persistent Pesticides in the Environment.* (Cleveland: CRC Press). Woodwell, G. M. et al. 1971. "DDT in the Biosphere: Where Does It Go?" *Science,* 174:1101–1107.

1. Private Controls—Negligence Actions

Our example of a private control mechanism will be where a plaintiff seeks a remedy for harm caused to the plaintiff by someone's (the defendant's) improper use of a pesticide. The plaintiff's lawsuit will likely be a negligence action since injuries caused in pesticide cases are usually one-time occurrences such as aerial spraying of pesticides in high winds or failure to stop spraying when the defendant's airplane has flown onto the plaintiff's land.* A brief description of the theory of negligence is that: (1) society has established a duty of care, e.g., do not spray in a high wind, (2) the defendant has breached or acted inconsistently with that duty (sprayed in a high wind), (3) the defendant's breach of his duty brought harm to the plaintiff of a type which was foreseeable, and (4) the defendant had no justifiable excuse for his conduct. If the plaintiff is successful in establishing these elements of negligence by the defendant, the court will award plaintiff money damages to compensate him for the harm he has suffered. The defendants in negligence suits involving pesticides are usually applicators of pesticide or the person or company for whom the applicator is working but other possible defendants might be manufacturers of pesticides. Manufacturers might be responsible for breaches of duties of care such as failing to warn the user of possible harms to the health of the user or of the harms which would occur to species other than those which were intended to be adversely affected by the pesticide.

While the theory of negligence is available to an injured party with respect to improper pesticide use situations, there are hurdles to be crossed before that theory leads to an actual remedy. The hurdle of establishing "causation" (number 3 above) is especially difficult in some pesticide cases because the plaintiff must show that the defendant's actions are connected to the resultant injury to the plaintiff. There are substantial problems in proving such a connection when the injury is delayed in manifesting itself or if the injury could have resulted from other causes in addition to or instead of the defendant's actions. If the lifespan of dairy cattle that were subjected to negligent crop-spraying activity is reduced by three years, that effect will likely not make itself known until a time in the future when demonstrating the cause of the reduced lifespan is difficult. Similarly, if a beekeeper's bees die over the

---

*Continuing infliction of harm would likely result in a "nuisance" action, with the plaintiff asking the court to stop the nuisance by issuing an injunction requiring the defendant to stop the harmful conduct. See Chapter Three.

winter it may be difficult to determine whether they died due to negligent pesticide spraying the previous spring or due to climatic conditions or due to a combination of both. While not all cases present problems of proof such as those noted here, many of them do. Situations where the cause of harm is in doubt can result in a worthy plaintiff being left without a remedy, but can also result in a defendant being found responsible and liable for a harm which the plaintiff has suffered but which the defendant did not cause.

Through use of the negligence theory, the common law seeks to provide help for those harmed by pesticide use by making compensation available. Also, the common law seeks to deter people from acting in a negligent manner. Deterrence will hopefully result from one's knowing that if he is negligent he will have to pay damages. While the common law mechanism has proven somewhat helpful in deterring negligent conduct, it has been criticized as an inadequate deterrent due to the ability of negligent parties to pass on the costs of paying damages as a cost of doing business or to insure themselves against liability for negligence. In addition, compensatory damages in a negligence action come after the harm has been inflicted. For these reasons it has been felt that additional protective mechanisms are needed to prevent harm from happening rather than to merely compensate for harm after the fact, and to prevent harm in a more certain way than through the deterrence mechanism of the possibility of a judgment for damages. To answer this need, public controls in the form of statutes were enacted.

2.   Public Controls – Pesticide Control Act, Food, Drug and Cosmetic Act, Toxic Substances Control Act

a.   Pesticide Control

The major tool for public control of pesticides is the Federal Environmental Pesticide Control Act of 1972 (FEPCA),[11] which amended the 1947 Federal Insecticide, Fungicide, and Rodenticide Act (FIFRA).[12] Prior to FEPCA, the mechanism of statutory control focused on labeling of pesticides and finding a pesticide "misbranded" in situations such as where directions for use were inadequate for the protection of the public or cautionary statements did not provide the desired degree of

---

11. 86 Stat. 973.

12. 61 Stat. 163.

injury prevention. If a product were misbranded it could not be registered, and if it were not registered, it could not be sold in interstate commerce. Under FEPCA, misbranding will result in a denial of registration and in a prohibition on sale of the pesticide, but, in addition, FEPCA creates a registration system which is more encompassing and more restrictive than that which was previously in effect.

FEPCA defines what is a pesticide very broadly. Substances intended to prevent, destroy, repel, or mitigate any "pest" (a term also very broadly defined) or to be used as a plant regulator, defoliant or desiccant are all pesticides. The prerequisite to the approval of the registration of a pesticide by EPA (and thus to its qualifying to be lawfully sold) are that the pesticide composition is such that it will do what it is claimed that it will do, that its labeling complies with the law and that "it will perform its intended function without unreasonable adverse effects on the environment" and "when used in accordance with widespread and commonly recognized practice it will not generally cause unreasonable adverse effects on the environment." If these criteria are met without any need for limiting who can use the pesticide and without any need to place restrictions on its use, then the pesticide will qualify to be registered as a "general use" pesticide. If, however, unreasonable adverse effects on the environment may generally result unless restrictions on who may use the pesticide or other restrictions on its use are imposed, the pesticide may still be registered but it will be as a "restricted use" pesticide. If the pesticide cannot satisfy the criteria even with restrictions placed on its use, its registration will be denied.

In those situations where a pesticide has been classified as a restricted use pesticide, unreasonable adverse environmental effects are sought to be avoided by restricting who may use the pesticide or placing other restrictions on its use. Pesticides which the EPA Administrator has classified as "restricted use" because they present a hazard to persons due to the pesticides' acute dermal or inhalation toxicity may only be applied by or under direct supervision of a "certified applicator." If the pesticide has been classified as "restricted use" because it may cause unreasonable adverse effects on the environment other than the toxicity to humans mentioned above, then application is allowed by or under the supervision of a certified applicator or subject to whatever other restrictions on use EPA may impose by administrative regulation.

From the above description of the registration system and the fact that most dangerous pesticides are restricted to use by certified applicators, we can see that a key mechanism of public control and protection with respect to pesticides is the process by which applicators are certified. Applicators may be certified either by federal certification or by state certification under a state plan approved by EPA. In either situation, the standard for qualifying for certification which Congress has established in FEPCA is that the applicator be "competent." The factors which affect competency are determined administratively by EPA and include topics like safety, equipment use and application techniques. For "commercial applicators," competency with respect to these topics is determined by written examinations and performance testing;[13] however, FEPCA exempts "private applicators" from being required by the federal government to take any examination to establish competency in the use of the restricted use pesticide. A "private applicator" is one who uses the restricted use pesticide on his own land or that of his employer or on property of another person if done without compensation other than trading of personal services between producers of agricultural commodities. Under an approved state plan, a "private applicator" can certify himself by merely completing a certification form. While EPA can require a private applicator to affirm that he has completed a training program, EPA may not require that a private applicator be examined to establish competency.

The above-described self-certification provision, which was added by amendment in 1975, recognizes that farmers working on their own land or that of their neighbors in an agricultural services exchange will likely be very careful in their use of pesticides and are also probably quite knowledgeable concerning pesticide use. Congress has thus been satisfied that such people need not pass examinations to determine their competency. It is true that farmers have strong motivations to use pesticides properly. In addition to the protection of their own health and land and the health and land of their neighbors (items which will likely be of importance to them even without the possibility of sanctions), they are also motivated to be careful by the possibility of lawsuits against them if they are not careful. It is also true that courses and examinations would be bothersome to many farmers. Yet the same or similar motivations for care are present for commercial applicators and have been present for many years, and still Congress found that these motivations need supplementation in the form of a system which restricted the use of our most dangerous pesticides to those we were sure were competent to use them. Farmers (and agribusiness) are large users of pesticides and if Congress was concerned enough about environmental hazards of pesticide use to create the "restricted use" classification, one may want to question the wisdom of allowing such large users of "restricted use" pesticides to use

---

13. 40 CFR, § 171.4(b).

them without a real check on their competency. The words of the statute allow a large agribusiness corporation to have its employees apply restricted use pesticides on the corporation's land without those employees being examined as to their competence. While the corporation may be motivated to make sure its employees are competent in order to protect itself against lawsuits, if the threat of lawsuits had successfully controlled the problems associated with pesticide use, FEPCA would not have been needed. Some states have closed the "private applicators" loophole by requiring, as a matter of state law, that all users of restricted use pesticides, private applicators as well as commercial applicators, be certified by passing a competency examination.[14] As an example, the following is one question which appeared on a state examination for commercial applicators:

> Q: If a 100-gallon sprayer sprays 5 acres per tankful and the spray recommendations call for 2 pounds actual per acre, how many pounds of 50WP pesticide must be added to the sprayer?
>
> A: 50WP means 50% active; to get 2 pounds actual, you need 4 pounds of product. The sprayer treats 5 acres per load and you want 2 pounds actual per acre, so you add 4 pounds of product for each acre treated or 20 pounds of product.

One further protection which is provided by the FEPCA registration scheme should be noted, and that is the set of mechanisms for ending registration and thus ending the sale of a pesticide. First, registration is automatically cancelled after a five-year period unless the registrant takes affirmative action to continue the registration in effect. This automatic cancellation provision should then result in an automatic review of the pesticide's acceptability under the established criteria for registration. Second, cancellation or a change in classification from general use to restricted use may take place if the EPA Administrator determines that the registration criteria (labeling, performance, unreasonable adverse effects on the environment) are not currently being met. In order to protect the registrant against unjustified cancellation or classification changes, procedural requirements for notice and hearings are a part of the cancellation process and thus the time for the "cancellation" process is measured in months or years. If, however, the Administrator determines that quicker action is needed to prevent an "imminent hazard" during the time required for cancellation proceedings, a third mechanism may be triggered—an order of "suspension" of the registration may be

---

14. Vermont Regulations for Control of Pesticides, IX.

issued. The suspension order process still carries with it the procedural safeguards of notice and hearing for the registrant, but the timing of the process is much shorter — days and weeks, rather than months and years. An imminent hazard can be an imminent hazard to human health or a situation which will likely result in unreasonable adverse effects on the environment during the time required for cancellation proceedings or will involve an unreasonable hazard to the survival of a species declared endangered under the Endangered Species Act. Finally, if the Administrator determines that an "emergency" situation exists, the suspension or stopping of sales and use of the pesticide may be made effective immediately and prior to any notice or hearing for the registrant.

In addition to FEPCA, Congress has sought to protect the public health from problems associated with pesticide use by enacting provisions of the Food, Drug, and Cosmetic Act to limit pesticide residues on food.[15] If an amount of residue in excess of a federally established "tolerance level" is present in or on the food, that food is considered "adulterated." Introducing adulterated food into interstate commerce is a criminal offense and the food is also subject to seizure. "Tolerance levels" are the maximum amounts of residue consistent with protecting the public health and vary for each pesticide and for each food on which that pesticide is used. For example, the tolerance level of the insecticide malathion is eight parts per million on celery and one part per million on sweet potatoes.[16] The tolerance level for the fungicide 2, 6-dichloro-4-nitroaniline is 15 parts per million on celery and 10 parts per million on sweet potatoes.[17]

The "private applicator" exception contained in FEPCA and discussed above raises one possible problem with the federal statutory approach to control of pesticide use. Another possible hole in the shield of protection was noted earlier when we considered that pesticides which are made in the United States but do not qualify for registration may still end up in our food by being sold for use in other countries and returning on food we import from those countries. Many criticisms have been levelled at the controls which exist with respect to pesticides — criticisms that the controls hamper effective use of important agricultural tools as well as criticisms that the controls are not strong enough to properly protect the environment and especially the health of people. Whether the controls now in place are appropriate will certainly be reevaluated in light of the

---

15. 21 U.S.C.A. §§ 346, 346(a), 348.

16. 40 CFR § 180.111.

17. 40 CFR § 180.200.

conduct by manufacturers and users under existing law and the nature of any evils of pesticides which have not manifested themselves today but may surface in the future.

b. Toxic Substances

Many substances which would certainly qualify as being "toxic" are regulated under laws other than the Toxic Substances Control Act (TSCA).[18] We discussed above legislation which is directed at pesticides. Examples of other legislation controlling "toxics" are the Clean Air Act which regulates hazardous air pollutants, the Atomic Energy Act which regulates nuclear materials, and the Resource Conservation and Recovery Act which establishes controls on hazardous waste disposal. In enacting TSCA, Congress took the position that chemical substances were being developed and introduced into the marketplace in such volume and with such a high degree of potential harm that they should be the focus of a particularized regulatory framework.

The basic operative mechanism of TSCA is that new chemical substances may not be manufactured unless a notice of intention to manufacture is filed with EPA at least 90 days before manufacture. The manufacturer must submit information such as the test data which it has on health and environmental effects, estimated volume of manufacture and methods of manufacture and disposal of the substance. The thrust of the legislation is to provide EPA with the opportunity to review risks to health or the environment in advance of the manufacture of the chemical substance rather than leaving such review until sometime after the substance has been manufactured when harm may already have occurred. If EPA does not take action within the 90 days to prohibit or restrict manufacture of the substance, manufacturing may commence unless EPA, for good cause, extends the review period for up to 90 additional days. If EPA concludes that the new substance presents or will present an unreasonable risk of injury to health or the environment, it may prohibit or limit the manufacture of the chemical. Action to temporarily prohibit the manufacture of the chemical may be taken where EPA finds that it needs additional information in order to evaluate the potential effects of the new chemical.

EPA also has regulatory power with respect to existing chemical substances. If there is a finding of unreasonable risk to health or the environment, EPA may invoke remedies which range from labeling require-

---

18. 15 U.S.C.A., § 2601 et seq.

ments and notifying purchasers of risks to prohibitions on manufacture and distribution of the product.

Although TSCA likely does in fact provide an increased level of protection for the public, this chapter should not end without expressly noting some potential costs of that protection. Obviously, there are the administrative costs of establishing, implementing and enforcing the regulatory scheme. Less obvious costs might be negative effects on society of not having the benefit of what would prove to be valuable and safe new chemical products due to disincentives on the chemical industry to provide those products. One rather direct potential disincentive may be that companies which have choices to make concerning whether to invest in new product development or use their capital in other ways may be deterred from developing new chemicals because the cost and the time needed to get a new product on the market may be substantially increased. A less direct disincentive may lie in the fact that going through the TSCA process of information disclosure can result in a company's competitors acquiring the company's trade secret concerning its new product. Since the trade secret may represent a substantial share of the worth of the new product, the risk of losing trade secrets may dilute the profit potential of developing new chemicals and thus shift companies away from chemical product development. While TSCA does seek to protect the confidentiality of information submitted to EPA, not all information submitted will remain confidential, either because of exceptions to confidentiality allowed by the statute or merely through inadvertence by agency employees. There is thus a price for TSCA's protection, but Congress has determined that the health and environmental protection provided by TSCA are worth the decrease, if any, in new chemical development and availability to the American public.

ADDITIONAL READINGS

Brown, A. W. A. *Ecology of Pesticides* (New York: Wiley Interscience, 1978).

Carson, R. *Silent Spring* (New York: Fawcett Publishing, 1962).

Council on Environmental Quality. *Environmental Quality* (Washington, DC: Government Printing Office, 1979).

Druley, R. M., and G. L. Ordway. "The Toxic Substances Control Act" *Environ. Rept.* 7:45:1–53 (1977).

Miller, G. T., Jr. *Living in the Environment,* 3rd ed. (Belmont, CA: Wadsworth Publishing Co., 1982).

CHAPTER 7

ENERGY

A. AN ENERGY PERSPECTIVE – KNOWN FORMS OF USABLE ENERGY

Energy may be considered the lifeblood of the ecosystem. Energy can neither be created nor destroyed, but it can change state such as by burning wood and releasing its energy for heat. These changes of state can be spontaneous or externally generated by the addition of a little "startup" energy. We use trapped energy to do work such as turning turbines for electricity, moving cars, moving trains and heating homes. The gross energy consumption of the United States over time is shown in Figure 1. This figure shows the 1979 level of energy consumption as 80 QBtus or "quads." One quad is equal to 1,000,000,000,000,000 British thermal units. A British thermal unit (Btu) is the amount of energy required to raise the temperature of one pound of water by one degree Farenheit. Therefore, each of us consumes enough energy in a year to raise the temperature of about 345 million pounds of water one degree Farenheit. Expressed in different terms, the 1979 level of energy consumption was equivalent to 14 tons of coal or 2600 gal of oil per year for each person in the United States. Two questions that are critical with respect to the energy issues that involve the environment are: from where does all this consumable energy come, and how long can it last?

Our energy needs are supplied by two very broad categories of energy resources – nonrenewable energy and renewable energy. Nonrenewable energy is viewed as a resource base that is depletable on a time scale measured in generations. Renewable energy is an energy supply that is always there and is not considered finite (exhaustible). Examples of non-renewable energy resources are fossil fuels, nuclear fuels and geothermal energy from pockets of heat, while renewable energy supplies are thought

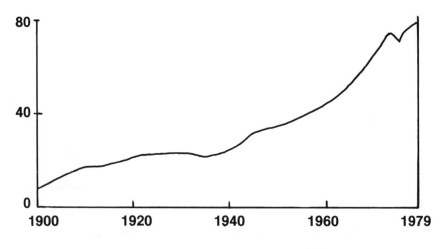

Figure 1.   U.S. gross energy comsumption (1900–1979).[1]

to be direct solar energy, water power, ocean tides, wind, plant biomass and geothermal energy from heat deep in the earth. Now, let us take a closer look at these energy sources in terms of their relationship to our needs.

As shown in Figure 2, fossil fuels provide the largest portion, over 90%, of our energy needs, followed by nuclear power and hydropower at 4% each. Fossil fuels include petroleum, natural gas, coal, oil shale and tar sands, as well as derived fuels like gasoline and kerosene. The other nonrenewable energy sources currently contribute little toward meeting our energy demands. The main problem with nonrenewable energy resources is just what the category name implies, the sources are nonrenewable. Once used up, they are gone.

In contrast to the concept of nonrenewable energy sources is that of renewable ones. Those renewable sources most mentioned and successfully utilized today include hydropower, wind energy and solar energy. The main concerns with our current nonrenewable energy sources are the cost per unit of energy (solar and wind), the dependability of the source (wind and hydro) and the amount of space devoted to the source conversion (solar, tides and biomass). While the renewable energy sources offer the clear advantage of not running out, two additional problems with their use must be considered. First, as we begin to run out of some of our nonrenewable energy sources, the implementation of any strategy to replace one energy source by another or group of others often requires a

1. United States Department of Energy. *Monthly Energy Review,* DOE/EIA0035/80 (06). (Washington, DC: U.S. Government Printing Office, 1980).

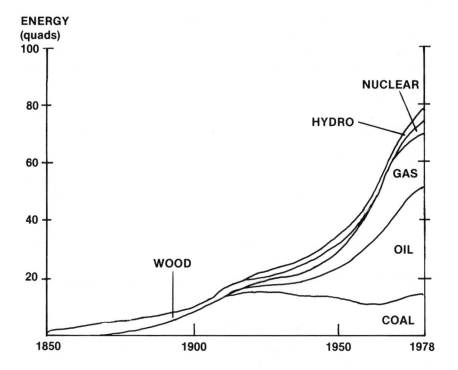

Figure 2. Energy consumption in the United States (1850–1978).[2]

long lead time and long-term planning. We may not be able to accomplish a minimally disruptive transition if we wait too long to make a serious beginning. Second, our long-term planning must allow for a balance that considers not only our energy needs but also long-term costs in terms of environmental factors. For example, commitments to hydroelectric power have had in the past, and will have in the future, the potential for interfering with fishing as both a food resource and a recreation resource. Achieving a balanced approach in energy planning may be difficult and certainly requires ample lead time for thoughtful consideration.

B. THE NEED FOR ENERGY DEVELOPMENT AND CONTROL OF DEVELOPMENT AND USE

While one might argue about the need to stimulate the development of energy resources, let us step back from this issue for a moment and

---

2. DOE. 1979. *Report to Congress.* Washington, D.C. doe/EIA-0173/2. (adaption).

examine our nonrenewable and renewable energy resource base and specific problems associated with the utilization of these resources. A summary of the energy resource situation in the United States for some of our nonrenewable energy resources is given in Table I. These figures might lead one to believe that there is really no energy supply problem at all and that most of the experts who claim that a problem exists are really quite mistaken; however, let us take a closer look at the implications of assuming full use of these nonrenewable energy resources. All oil resources listed as recoverable are not necessarily recoverable through the use of current technology or at a price that is competitive in the current market. With respect to oil, only the 160 billion bbl figure shown in Table I would be competitive in price. Shale oil and tar sands will provide

Table I.   Nonrenewable Energy Resources in the United States[3]

Resource	Recoverable[a]	Estimated Depletion Time[b]
Oil	160 billion bbl	11 years
Shale Oil	1,026 billion bbl	76 years
Tar Sands	15 billion bbl	1 year
Heavy Oil	30 billion bbl	2 years
Natural Gas	5,200 trillion ft^3	63 years
Coal	≈ 2 trillion tons	635 years

[a]We assume that technology will eventually allow almost complete recovery.
[b]This estimate is based on the use of 62 bbl of oil or 372,000 ft^3 of natural gas, or 14 tons of coal per person per year assuming the population of the United States to be 225 million people.

oil, but the technological cost is high and the cost in terms of water use is astronomical.[4] Much of the geographic area of the United States where these energy resources are available receives the least amounts of annual rainfall. The geographic area where most of our coal and all of our shale oil and tar sands are located is in the western United States, the short-grass prairie areas that receive minimal rainfall and where it takes over 10 acres of land to support one head of cattle for one year. Therefore, the

3. Based on data from a National Geographic special report, Energy. February, 1981.

4. Neuman, J. C. "Obtaining Water Supply for Energy Development in the Western United States," *Denver Law Journal* 58:80–130 (1980).

demand for water by individuals, animals, crop irrigation and recreation leaves very little water to be used as part of an energy extraction process.

There are other environmental concerns with oil extraction for energy. Oil deposits are usually associated with salt water deposits where drilling is done on land, and adequate removal of this salt water must take place so that plants in the area are not destroyed nor ground water contaminated. Another land-related concern may be slumping of land areas when the liquid support from below is removed. Ocean drilling presents another set of problems. When oil is removed from underneath the ocean, formation water is also encountered. Many environmental groups have encouraged the government to require that this water be collected and transported to land for disposal. Their concern centers around the belief that dumping such water around the drilling site will cause the death of many young fish and fish eggs and eventually destroy fisheries. Unfortunately, most of our coastal ocean areas that are ripe for oil drilling are also areas where many different oceanic organisms, including but not limited to fish, live and reproduce. In summary, without significant technological advancements, domestic oil resource utilization offers us little in the quest for energy "independence" because of the small amounts readily recoverable using conventional technology, the technology costs and water resource costs associated with recovery of oil in shales and tar sands, and environmental detriments presented by the oil recovery processes.

Natural gas seems to offer some hope for a long-term, U.S.-based supply of energy; however, only 1200 trillion ft³ of the recoverable natural gas mentioned in Table I is recoverable by conventional means. That means that the estimated depletion time is really 14 years for conventionally recovered natural gas. Again, additional recovery will require the development of new technology that is cost-effective to enable people to buy the gas after recovery. Environmental concerns with respect to natural gas center mainly on the extent of pipelines necessary to transport the natural gas in a liquified form and the probabilities and consequences of pipeline breakage.

Coal is by far the most abundant nonrenewable energy resource the United States has at its disposal. It is also much cheaper to make electricity with coal than with oil (about 1.5¢/kWh for coal and 5¢/kWh for oil), and coal can also be used to heat homes and factories. The technological and economic aspects of coal production as well as its fitness for a diversity of uses might make coal the answer to all our energy needs; however, numerous health and environmental factors must be evaluated with respect to the use of coal. Coal—be it anthracite, bituminous, subbituminous or lignite—is either deep mined or strip mined. Deep mining creates more human health problems than strip mining (gases in mine shafts, collapse of shafts, black lung disease). Strip mining, on the other hand, removes land surfaces that are either not reclaimed, reclaimed slowly or are unable to be reclaimed within a reasonable time. The process of reclaiming strip mine spoil requires water, a resource in very short supply in the western areas where much coal is available for strip mining. This western land area is also used for ranching to raise the meat we demand for our tables, and it takes a lot of land to raise one head of cattle. We thus have a conflict between the energy resource of coal and the food resource of cattle. To accommodate the need for both of these resources requires that we return the land from which coal was removed to its former uses as quickly as possible so that our food supply will not suffer. While this task would be considered relatively easy in Pennsylvania or Ohio, the strip mining sites in places like Wyoming are not so easily reclaimed. Even if the topsoil is put back in place, and even if the whole topography is restored, it takes a long time to establish the integrated ecosystem that is destroyed by strip mining. Again, the lack of large quantities of water makes the process of land reclamation after strip mining of coal a long-term project in the West.

Other environmental concerns relating to coal are the sulfur content of coal and its association with acid rain as well as the metal content of coal (mercury) which could eventually contribute to human health problems. Coal mined in the eastern United States is mostly bituminous coal that has a high enough sulfur content so that its use is a major contributing factor to acid rain. This problem can be resolved using current technology, but the cost is significant and there is disagreement about the extent of the benefits that will result from incurring these costs. Western coal is subbituminous coal and contains virtually no sulfur. Therefore, this coal would not contribute to the acid rain situation in terms of sulfuric acid. However, western coal contains larger quantities of heavy metals than does eastern coal. Some of these metals, mercury in particular, are considered harmful to humans and can accumulate in biological systems. For example, bacteria can use mercury and thus allow it to enter the food chain. For a price, technology can resolve this problem by removal of the metals. This then leads to the question of what to do with the waste substances that we now have removed. Lastly, and by no means of least significance in deciding on which type of coal to use under which circumstances, is the fact that eastern coal has a cost per ton of about half that of western coal and a heat content per unit weight of about twice that of western coal. Our domestic coal supply clearly offers us great potential, but it just as clearly leaves us with major environmental questions that cannot be ignored.

Our other nonrenewable energy resources are subject to criticisms similar to those for oil, coal and natural gas. Geothermal is localized, advanced technology is needed to utilize it, and it is not transportable unless it is converted to electricity. Nuclear fission power, while atmospherically considered safer than other more conventional forms of energy, has other problems. Construction cost and time for construction, reliability of the plant, possibilities of meltdown and consequent water contamination by radioactive substances, the ultimate cost of a generated energy unit, and the problem of radioactive waste all detract from the appeal of a nuclear energy society. Nuclear fusion and breeder reactors are not yet at the stage of development where they could contribute to the energy resource pool; however, if these types of energy sources are eventually utilized, the potential environmental harms are of such a magnitude that serious consideration about the use of these types of energy is mandated. Not only could there be large-scale contamination of water and air by radioactivity, but also the storage of the radioactive wastes as well as the contaminated materials used to build the buildings must be undertaken. In essence, there is a necessity to eventually store the whole facility, as even the nuts and bolts will be contaminated.

With all of the problems involving supply and use of nonrenewable sources of energy, it is unfortunate that one cannot immediately say that renewable energy resources are the answer. These too have technological as well as environmental problems. Renewable energy resources such as solar and wind are used to make electricity which must be stored. Large capital costs plus slowly developing technology of utilization of these resources makes these energy pathways currently very costly compared to the nonrenewable sources. Besides costs, these alternatives have their own environmental constraints. Solar energy requires space as well as long daylight periods free of cloud cover. These problems appear to be easy enough to resolve — i.e., build in the southwestern desert and transport the electricity around the country. Leaving aside the substantial questions of technological and economic feasibility of such a scheme, there are still potential environmental problems. If sunlight is intercepted on a very large scale by collectors, what will warm the earth beneath these collectors? Will the very large-scale placement of such facilities change weather patterns, induce warmer or cooler global climate or generate some other environmental problem the nature of which is currently unknown? Wind energy generators require space and substantial amounts of wind. Again, geographic location and transport of electricity as well as lack of cost-effective technology currently present problems. Even if these are resolved, the idea of a windmill everywhere raises aesthetic questions. Biomass for energy also requires space as well as energy inputs to plant and harvest the biomass and time to grow the biomass. Once the biomass is generated it must be transported to a facility and prepared for energy production. This energy pathway also removes land from some other use and will eventually conflict with other land use practices. Hydroelectric power, while inexpensive once it is in place, is dependent on weather and must also deal with environmental problems such as the dams as impediments to fish migration.

Our current energy situation is one of high dependence on other countries to meet our energy needs. As these countries have more energy demands of their own, and as more competition develops for energy in the world markets, the flow of foreign energy to us may become cost-prohibitive or may simply be curtailed for home country use or for use by a political ally. It would therefore appear to be in our best interest to stimulate the development and utilization of our own renewable and nonrenewable energy resources. From the above discussion it is clear that there are ample opportunities for us to achieve domestic independence with respect to energy, but it is also clear that none of our choices is free of environmental problems. A balance must be struck which will provide our needed supply of energy while leaving us with the quality of life that we find desirable. Inherent in such a balance is the giving up or compromising on some environmental concerns in order to obtain our needed energy. Also inherent in the balance is the fact that energy should not be provided at the minimum possible cost regardless of the effects on the environment. If the adverse effects on the environment are to be kept within reason, we must accept some controls on how we obtain our energy supply. We must also seek to conserve energy to the maximum degree consistent with our desired standard of living so that we do not need to supply ourselves with more energy than we really need and thus do more harm to our environment than is really necessary. In the next section we will investigate some of the mechanisms that government uses to stimulate our supply of energy and some of the controls that have been imposed on obtaining that supply in order to protect the environment. The last section of this chapter will consider approaches to encouraging conservation of our energy supply.

C. ENVIRONMENTAL CONTROLS AND THE STIMULATION OF ENERGY SUPPLY

The question of what to do about our appetite for energy is often cast in terms of two opposing camps—those who argue for the production of more energy and those who argue for conservation of energy. While the arguments for conservation vs. the arguments for more production may, if simply stated, indicate a total polarization of points of view, that is not an accurate picture. Very few people who believe in greater production as the way to resolve our energy problems also believe that conservation is unnecessary. They are in favor of conservation, but their frame of reference is one of accepting that our country's well-being requires continued economic and thus industrial growth. Such growth is largely dependent on more energy being available, and, although some of that energy may be made available by conservation, the magnitude of the need is such that production increases will have to supply the bulk of it. The production orientation also favors satisfying some of our needs by developing alternative energy sources, but it also contends that our supply from our basic current sources of energy (oil, coal, gas) can and should be increased.

The frame of reference of those who lean heavily toward the conservation philosophy often incorporates a challenge to the need for or desirability of continued growth. Ever-increasing growth creates many of the other environmental problems discussed elsewhere in this book as well as depleting our current sources of energy. Most proponents of energy conservation would not, however, take the position that all economic and industrial growth should stop immediately or that alternative sources of energy should not be developed and utilized. For most Americans the proper course is somewhere between the extremes and the question is one of emphasis — emphasis on production coupled with attempts at and hopes of conservation, or emphasis on conservation, with implementation of production increases from our current sources of energy only as a last resort for our economic well-being. Numerous efforts have been made by government to encourage both production and conservation, but we cannot answer the question of what to do about our energy appetite by merely saying that we should maximize both production and conservation at the highest levels we can technologically achieve. We must also consider the factors that compete with the policies of encouraging production and conservation.

If government is to encourage production, it must be willing to accept the accompanying financial costs, such as the decrease in tax revenues that might result from tax incentives created to encourage energy production. Encouraging production can also bring with it costs, such as interference with other land uses such as food production. Other environmental costs of encouraging energy production include water pollution from offshore drilling and aesthetic pollution from strip mining or windmills. A policy of encouraging conservation also has costs associated with it. Tax credits for those who install energy-saving equipment or materials decrease tax revenues. Furthermore, conservation of energy can create environmental costs. Small fuel-efficient automobiles (or motorcycles) may be more hazardous than larger, less fuel-efficient models, and highway safety must certainly be considered an environmental cost. The question thus comes back to one of emphasis, and government has attempted to pursue the parallel paths of encouraging both production and conservation.

One approach to encouraging production has been to focus on the price of energy. The amount of an energy resource that will be produced is greatly influenced by the price that it will sell for in the marketplace. In the Energy Policy and Conservation Act of 1975,[5] Congress sought to encourage increased production of petroleum by allowing "new" oil to be sold at a price that was not kept artifically low by government price controls. "Old" crude oil remained subject to price controls. "Old" oil was defined as that amount which was produced from a property at a level equal to or less than the amount of oil produced from that property during an earlier time period. There was thus incentive for producers to raise their volume of production from a property since this increased volume (the "new" oil) could be sold at a price substantially higher than the government controlled price for "old" crude oil. Another price-related production enhancement step was taken in the Federal Energy Administration Act Amendments of 1976[6] which exempted oil produced by "stripper wells" from price controls. "Stripper wells" are those whose production does not exceed 10 barrels per day and are often seen as the backyard oil wells in areas like Los Angeles. The above price decontrol steps were taken specifically to spur production of crude oil. All crude oil and refined petroleum products are now decontrolled with respect to price pursuant to President Reagan's Executive Order No. 12287[7] and in response to the belief of many people that oil prices should be allowed to seek their market levels in order to achieve the best mix of conservation along with optimizing levels of supply.

A major part of implementing the federal policy of increasing our energy supplies must be to take into account the vast amount of federally owned land and areas over which the federal government has authority, such as the Outer Continental Shelf (OCS). Energy is obtained from those locations primarily through leasing programs. The conditions of the leases are used to ensure that the federal energy resource actually

---

5. 89 Stat. 871 at 941.

6. 90 Stat. 1125 at 1132.

7. 46 Fed. Reg. 9909, Jan. 28, 1981.

provides a supply to the consumer. For example, leases of federal land for the mining of coal contain provisions requiring diligent development and continued operation of the mine.[8] The Code of Federal Regulations defines "diligent development" as developing the coal source such that coal is actually produced in commercial quantities (1% of the reserves of the source) by the end of the tenth year of the lease. "Continued operation" requires that an average of 1% of the reserves be produced in succeeding years.[9] Thus, those who might seek to enter into a long-term lease of the federally owned coal source for the purpose of speculating on increasing prices rather than to bring the coal to market are discouraged from doing so.

With respect to the Outer Continental Shelf, the leasing mechanisms have also been adjusted by Congress for the purpose of encouraging greater production of energy. In the Outer Continental Shelf Lands Act Amendments of 1978, Congress declared that it is national policy that the OCS should be made available, subject to environmental safeguards, for expeditious and orderly development.[10] The legislative history of the statute, as contained in the report of the House of Representatives, said that our dependence on foreign oil must be reduced, and that the basic purpose of the legislation was to "promote the swift, orderly and efficient exploitation of our almost untapped domestic oil and gas resources in the Outer Continental Shelf."[11]* One mechanism that the statute uses to expedite the development of the OCS is to provide new bidding procedures for leases. Prior to the Amendments, all leasing used a "front-end bonus system" that required a potential lessee to secure a large amount of capital to be available for payment to the government immediately upon acceptance of the winning bid for the lease. Alternative bidding and leasing procedures which do not require the making of a large front-end payment are allowed under the Amendments.[12] The intent is to make leasing more attractive to producers and thus encourage greater production. Whether in part because of the above legislation or for other reasons, the Secretary of the Interior reported that new leasing records were

---

8. 30 U.S.C.S. § 207(b).

9. 43 CFR § 3400.0–5.

10. 92 Stat. 629 at 635.

11. The material referred to here is from Vol. 3, 95th Congress, Second Session, 1978, p. 1460 of *United States Code Congressional and Administrative News.*

*A substantial amount of the history behind a piece of legislation may be found in the *United States Code Congressional and Administrative News,* West Publishing, St. Paul.

12. 43 U.S.C.S. § 1337 (a) and (b).

set for the OCS in 1981, with over two million offshore acres leased to energy companies and over \$9.8 billion obtained as federal revenue.[13]

There are numerous other approaches that government has used to try to increase our supply of energy besides the mechanisms of removing the disincentives of price controls, imposing production requirements with respect to federally owned resources, and the liberalization of leasing procedures. As our final example of production enhancement mechanisms we will note some statutory measures that provide direct financial assistance for activities that, if encouraged, are likely to make significant contributions toward an increased energy supply. Coal is currently our most abundant domestic source of fuel. To "enhance competition or encourage new market entry" and thereby increase coal production, Congress has established a loan guarantee program to enable small coal producers who could not otherwise obtain adequate financing to get financing for the purpose of developing new underground coal mines.[14] Federal financial incentives and support have also been enacted for the development of alternative sources of energy. For example, the Biomass Energy and Alcohol Fuels Act of 1980[15] provides for federal loans for the construction of municipal waste energy projects. In addition, the owner or operator of such a project may be able to get a minimum price guarantee from the federal government with respect to the energy that the project produces and sells. Loans, loan guarantees and price guarantees are also provided for other biomass energy projects which would utilize materials such as wood, agricultural crops or animal wastes. Legislation has also been enacted to encourage development of many other alternative energy sources, including solar, wind and fusion energy.

Though Congress has provided legislation that was designed to encourage energy production from alternative sources, its long-term commitment to its stated alternative energy goals and the appropriateness of the methods it has chosen to meet those goals are still being tested. One example of this testing process is the administrative implementation of the Wind Energy Systems Act of 1980.[16] That statute establishes federal assistance in the form of grants and cooperative agreements with public and private entities for the purchase and installation of wind energy systems to obtain information through broad operational experience with those systems. In April, 1982, the Department of Energy issued

---

13. *Energy Users Report,* Vol. 10, Number 3, p. 66, Jan. 21, 1982.

14. 42 U.S.C.S. § 6211.

15. 42 U.S.C.S. § 8801 et seq.

16. 42 U.S.C.S. §9201 et seq.

rules for processing applications for this assistance, but as a preface to the rules it said that they were being issued only because they were required by law and that the department intended to oppose funding under the rules. It stated that direct financial assistance would be wasteful and unnecessary because of the availability of tax credits and because market conditions were providing sufficient incentives for the private sector to install large wind energy systems.[17] The appropriateness and necessity of particular approaches and/or Congress' degree of commitment to encouraging alternative energy production have been and certainly will continue to be tested many times during the developmental stages of those alternative sources.

Having considered examples of how Congress has encouraged production of more energy, let us next look at how it and state governments have attempted to handle some of the competing factors involved with encouraging energy production—the environmental problems that energy production creates and the controls that have been enacted to deal with those problems. Congress' awareness of and concern about environmental problems associated with energy production can be seen by looking at qualifying language that exists in many of the statutes that seek to stimulate energy production. While the purpose of the Outer Continental Shelf Lands Act Amendments is to exploit the oil and gas reserves of the OCS, the statute calls for "expeditious and orderly development, subject to environmental safeguards." And although the Biomass Energy and Alcohol Fuels Act encourages the use of biomass for energy production, the Congressional findings in the statute ask for a biomass energy program "that does not impair the Nation's ability to produce food and fiber on a sustainable basis for domestic and export use."

In addition to the somewhat nonspecific language seen in our last two examples, specific provisions for environmental protection may be found both in statutes whose primary goal is to encourage production and in those that are addressed primarily to environmental issues. An example of the former is Congress' loan guarantee program for the purpose of developing new underground coal mines. That "production enhancement" statute, referred to on the previous page, appears to recognize that burning low-sulfur coal creates less air pollution than burning high-sulfur coal. The statute thus leans in the direction of low-sulfur coal by prohibiting more than 20% of the loan guarantee funds issued in any fiscal year from being used to open new mines which produce coal which is not low-sulfur coal.

---

17. 47 Fed. Reg. 16166 (April 15, 1982).

Looking at our "production enhancement/environmental control" balance from the direction of statutes whose specifics are addressed primarily to environmental controls, we come to the Surface Mining Control and Reclamation Act of 1977[18] which, while recognizing that coal supply is essential to the nation's energy requirements, looks at the obtainment of coal primarily from the viewpoint of environmental protection. The federal surface mining statute concerns itself with past harm to the environment from coal mining as well as prevention of future harm. An abandoned mine reclamation fund is established to be used largely for the reclamation and restoration of land and water resources adversely affected by past coal mining.[19] The money for this fund comes from reclamation fees imposed on current production of coal. A fee of 35¢/ton of surface mined coal and 15¢/ton of underground mined coal or 10% of the value of the coal at the mine, whichever is less, is deposited in the fund. The geographic allocation of money in the fund takes into account the geographic area (state or Indian reservation) from which the revenue was derived.

The basic statutory mechanism for addressing present and future threats to the environment from surface coal mining is the permit system.[20] Surface coal mining is prohibited unless a permit is obtained. In a manner similar to its approach in the Clean Air Act, Congress has given primary responsibility for administering its surface mining program to the states if the states want to accept that responsibility. Thus permits to surface mine coal may be issued by the state if the state has a program that is approved by the Secretary of the Interior. In the absence of an approved state program, a federal program with federally issued permits is implemented. For a state program to be approved, the state must show that it is capable, through use of a permit system and by other means, of carrying out the environmental protection purposes and provisions of the federal statute. Among these are having and enforcing a reclamation plan that will restore the affected land to a condition capable of supporting its prior use or a better use and restoring the land to its approximate original contours.

Various provisions of the Surface Mining Control and Reclamation Act have been challenged on many grounds in the courts, but the validity of the statute has been upheld. In *Hodel v. Virginia Surface Mining &*

---

18. 30 U.S.C.S. § 1201 et seq.

19. 30 U.S.C.S. § 1231 et seq.

20. 30 U.S.C.S. § 1251 et seq.

Reclamation Association,[21] it was contended that the performance standards of the statute which required that on "steep slopes" an operator must return the site to its "approximate original contour" were unconstitutional as a violation of the Tenth Amendment to the United States Constitution. The Tenth Amendment says: "The powers not delegated to the United States by the Constitution, nor prohibited by it to the States, are reserved to the States respectively or to the people." It was claimed that the regulation of land use was a traditional function of the states under the states'"police powers" and that the Tenth Amendment limited the power that Congress would otherwise have had under the Commerce Clause of the Constitution to regulate private land use activities that affect interstate commerce.[22] The United States Supreme Court decided, citing many cases involving other statutes, that the scope of the Tenth Amendment did not limit Congress' interstate commerce authority with respect to the activities of private individuals and businesses. The steep-slope provisions of the statute apply only to private activity and do not regulate "States as States." An attempt to regulate the latter would violate the Tenth Amendment. The Court thus reaffirmed that the exercise by Congress of its authority under the Commerce Clause in a manner that displaces the states' exercise of their police powers over private activity does not invade areas reserved to the states by the Tenth Amendment.

Another court challenge to the surface mining statute concerned the "prime farmland" provisions of the act. With respect to obtaining a permit to mine most surface mining sites, the statute requires that there be a reclamation plan to put the land back into a reasonable use, but not necessarily its prior use, after mining occurs. Congress' concern that we do not lose our prime agricultural land led it to impose stricter reclamation requirements for that type of land. An applicant for a permit for mining on prime farmland must show that he has the capacity to restore the land, within a reasonable time after the completion of mining, to the productivity level of nonmined prime farmland in the surrounding area. The posting of a bond to ensure that the plan will be completed is also required. In *Hodel v. Indiana*[23] it was claimed that the prime farmland provisions were a taking of private property by government without the payment of just compensation as required by the Fifth Amendment to the United States Constitution. The District Court had concluded that

---

21. 425 U.S. 264 (1981).

22. Article II, Section 8 gives Congress the power to "regulate Commerce...among the several states...."

23. 425 U.S. 314 (1981).

there was an unconstitutional taking of private property because "it is technologically impossible to reclaim prime farmland in a postmining period so that equal or higher levels of yield under high levels of management practice can be achieved."[24] The Supreme Court found that the prime farmland provisions are not a taking of private property since they do not prohibit surface mining but merely regulate the conditions under which the activity may be conducted. And even if the District Court is factually correct in its determination, there would still not be a taking that requires the payment of just compensation unless the landowner could show that there were no economically beneficial uses for his property besides mining.*

Although the validity of many of the provisions of the Surface Mining Control and Reclamation Act have been upheld by the Supreme Court, some of the goals of the legislation are subject to undermining by the practical application of one of the exemptions from coverage contained in the statute itself. The statute says that its provisions do not apply to "the extraction of coal for commercial purposes where the surface mining operation affects two acres or less."[25] This exemption was originally intended to allow small operators to mine on small areas without having to meet the requirements of the statute. The small operators were relieved of the financial and administrative burdens and the size of the sites would itself keep environmental damage at a low level.

The practical application of the exemption has been that a big company hires a small contractor to mine its coal; the contractor invokes the small operator's exemption to avoid the reclamation process and costs; then the small operator sells the coal back to the large company. Statements attributed to Virginia's chief mining inspector said that possibly the majority of Virginia's coal production comes from mines with about 2 acres of surface area.[26] The original Department of the Interior regulations denied the exemption to any operation conducted by a person that affected more than 2 acres either at physically related sites or at unrelated sites but within 1 year. The loophole in this language is that "operation conducted by" would apply only to the small operator actually doing the mining but not to the large company working through many small operators as independent contractors. As long as each of the large company's

---

24. 501 F. Supp. at 470.

*A more detailed discussion of the "taking" clause of the Fifth Amendment is given in Chapter Four.

25. 30 U.S.C.S. § 1278(2).

26. *Washington Post,* October 25, 1981, p. F1.

small independent contractors could qualify for the 2-acre exemption, no reclamation work was required.

The Department of the Interior has attempted to close this loophole by adopting a new rule with respect to the 2-acre exemption. Under the new rule, where sites whose aggregate area is more than two acres are mined within 12 months and are within the geographic proximity stated in the rule, the individual sites of 2 acres or less are not entitled to the 2-acre exemption if they are "under common ownership or control."[27] The large company owning or controlling many small sites actually mined by small independent operators is thus made subject to the provisions of the statute, including the reclamation requirements.

It should not, however, be presumed that the conflict involving the 2-acre exemption is necessarily over. The original Department of the Interior rule used language that was arguably more restrictive than the language used in the statute itself because the statute made no specific mention of denying an exemption where there are more than 2 acres as an aggregate of related sites or unrelated sites mined within 12 months. Whether the agency had the authority to use that language to deny exemptions was challenged in *Hodel v. Virginia Surface Mining & Reclamation Association,*[28] but that issue was removed from the case before the case reached the Supreme Court. It remains to be seen whether there will be a court challenge claiming that the new agency rule, which also contains language that is arguably more restrictive than the statute uses to establish the 2-acre exemption, is inconsistent with the intent of Congress and thus beyond the agency's authority and invalid.

The Surface Mining Control and Reclamation Act is federal legislation, but it allows states to regulate surface mining so long as the state programs provide for implementation of the federal requirements. If a state chooses to have more stringent land use or environmental controls on surface mining, the statute specifically allows it to do so.[29] Let us consider a situation where states appear to want to be more environmentally cautious and where they have been precluded from imposing their own controls by the existence of federal controls.

The method of energy production that has spurred the most impassioned opposition is atomic energy. Perhaps that is because the harm that might be caused by an atomic energy mishap is so direct in its impact on humans, because the type of harm is so distasteful or/and because of

---

27. 47 Fed. Reg. 33424, Aug. 2, 1982, revising 30 CFR § 700.11.

28. 425 U.S. 264 (1981).

29. 30 U.S.C.A. § 1255.

the large numbers of people who could be affected. In addition, it might be because of a belief that adequate environmental protection with respect to nuclear power is substantially less of a certainty than protection against oil spills or protection of the land against the harms that might result from coal mining. While other issues are relevant to the dispute concerning the desirability of nuclear power, protection from radiation hazards appears to be the major item of public concern.

The bulk of the responsibility for regulating nuclear power in general and providing protection against radiation hazards in particular is vested in the federal Nuclear Regulatory Commission (NRC), the successor of the Atomic Energy Commission, by the Atomic Energy Act of 1954, as amended.[30] This authority includes the licensing of nuclear power facilities. In response to some of the above-mentioned concerns, various states have indicated dissatisfaction with the sufficiency of the umbrella of protection provided by federal control of nuclear power and have enacted various types of state legislation to provide additional control over or protection from nuclear power. The leading case in the area is the 1971 case of *Northern States Power Company v. State of Minnesota.*[31]

In *Northern States,* the federal Atomic Energy Commission (AEC) had issued an operating license to the power company. Minnesota sought to impose more stringent conditions on the level of radioactive discharge allowed than the AEC had imposed. Minnesota argued that while the Atomic Energy Act of 1954 did not expressly allow more stringent state controls with respect to radioactive waste releases, it neither expressly nor implicitly disallowed more stringent state control, i.e., preempted the state's authority to more strictly regulate such waste releases. The United States Court of Appeals for the Eighth Circuit found that though there was no express declaration in the Atomic Energy Act that federal control of radiation emissions are to be sole and exclusive, Congress had manifested an intent to displace all state regulation in that field and thus preemption of state authority was implied. The implication of the preemption was based on the legislative history and pervasiveness of the federal regulatory scheme. This determination was further supported by the nature of the subject matter involved and by a finding that there is a need for uniform nationwide controls in order to effectuate the objectives of Congress under the Atomic Energy Act. Among those objectives are encouraging development and use of atomic energy to foster industrial progress, benefit the general welfare and increase the standard of

---

30. 42 U.S.C.S. § 2011 et seq.
31. 447 F.2d 1143.

living. State controls that would affect the purchase and sale of power in commerce might interfere with attaining these objectives. State efforts to regulate nuclear power plants with respect to radiation hazards were therefore held to be invalid. The Eighth Circuit's decision was affirmed without an opinion by the United States Supreme Court.[32]

The reader may want to question the justification, if any, for the federal government expressly allowing states to regulate the mining of coal in ways that are more stringent than the federal controls and yet refusing to allow the states to enact stricter provisions to protect their citizens from nuclear power-related radiation hazards. Congress has not in any way explicitly rejected the implied intentions that were attributed to it in the *Northern States* case; however, the issue of what control states may exercise over nuclear power facilities is still being hotly contested in the courts. *Northern States* says there can be no state regulation with respect to radiation hazards. Is a California statute that conditions nuclear power plant construction on findings by a state commission that adequate storage facilities and means of disposal are available for high-level nuclear waste invalid due to having been preempted by the federal Atomic Energy Act? The Ninth Circuit Court of Appeals in *Pacific Gas and Electric Co. v. State Energy Resources, Etc.,*[33] decided that this California statute was not preempted since it was based on the economic aspects of nuclear waste disposal rather than on radiation safety concerns. Yet an Illinois statute that prohibits spent nuclear fuel from coming into the state for purposes of disposal or storage would be invalid under the preemption theory according to the Seventh Circuit Court of Appeals in *Illinois v. General Electric Company.*[34] If a state wants to regulate such areas as nuclear fuel disposal or other areas involving radiation hazards, could it not frame its statutory purposes and legislative history to show economic or other legitimate concerns rather than radiation hazard concerns and thus circumvent the federal preemption that Congress was found to have intended in the *Northern States* case? Clarification and perhaps wholly new approaches to what states can and cannot do in the way of regulating nuclear power plants may emerge when the Supreme Court considers the *Pacific Gas* case, which it has decided to review, but has not yet heard at the time of this writing.

---

32. 405 U.S. 1035 (1972).

33. 659 F.2d 903 (1981).

34. 683 F.2d 206 (1982). This case was decided on other grounds but the court included its views on the preemption issue to assist the Supreme Court if it should decide to review the case and if it reached the preemption issue.

D.   ENCOURAGING CONSERVATION OF ENERGY

There are numerous legal mechanisms in use today at both the federal and state levels of government that seek to encourage conservation of energy. Some of the approaches are directed solely at reducing the amount of energy being used, while others, although they may have the effect of reducing overall use, are directed more at changing the form of energy used from a less available supply to one that is more abundant. In addition, the mechanism of removing government imposed price controls (deregulation) has the dual objectives of stimulating supply, as we have already discussed, and of diminishing consumer demand for energy or at least for the type of energy whose price is deregulated.

Our examination of governmentally created conservation measures will focus on those of the federal government, although we note in passing that states can have significant regulatory input into the conservation process. One example of state influence is that states control the price structure of electric power. Historically, electric power rate structures used the "declining-block" rate design, which said higher-quantity users paid a lower price per unit of power used than did lower-quantity users. The basis for this approach is that it is said that it costs the utility company less per unit to get power to a large-volume user than to a small-volume user. The "declining-block" structure is, however, claimed by some to provide a disincentive for user conservation of electricity. States can choose alternative structures such as "flat rates" with a constant price per unit consumed, or "inverted rates" with a higher price per unit as consumption increases. These rate structures are claimed to be more conservation oriented than the declining-block approach and also to more fairly account for actual costs of power production, since additional output capacity needed to meet high demands results in the cost per unit of electricity produced increasing as output increases. Thus, questions are presented of which rate structure is economically more reflective of the true costs of supplying power to the high- and low-volume users; whether it is fair to a high-volume user to make him pay more per unit consumed if the costs to provide power to him are lower than for a low-volume user; and do flat rates or inverted rates really result in significantly greater conservation of energy than declining-block rates, or are large-volume users' consumption patterns independent of the rate structure?

With respect to federal government action aimed at conservation of energy, we will begin with some examples of tax advantages that are available to those who take steps toward conservation. The residential energy tax credit provisions found in Section 44C of the Internal Revenue Code allow as an annual credit against one's income tax liability

15% of the energy conservation expenditures made for residential insulation or other energy-conserving components such as storm windows and automatic setback thermostats. The upper limit of annual expenditures which will qualify to have 15% of them treated as a credit is $2000. The above-described part of Section 44C addresses the matter of reducing energy consumption. Section 44C also provides a credit with respect to expenditures made for installing residential renewable energy sources such as solar or wind. Forty percent of the expenditures, with up to a limit of $10,000 of annual expenditures qualifying, is allowed as a credit against tax liability. This part of Section 44C addresses changing the form of energy that would be used.

It should be noted that both parts of the residential energy credit are "credits" taken off one's tax bill and not "deductions" that are taken off one's income prior to computing the tax bill. Thus a $1000 expenditure on insulation results in a tax saving of $150 regardless of whether one is in the 12% tax bracket or the 40% bracket. If the system were to use a full deduction of expenditures instead of a 15% credit, a $1000 expenditure would be a tax saving of $120 to someone in the 12% tax bracket and a saving of $400 to someone in the 40% bracket. Under the credit system of Section 44C, the presumably less financially well off person in the 12% bracket does not get less of a tax break than the better off person in the 40% bracket — but the less well off person also does not get any more of a break than the one who is better off. The reader may want to consider whether, if the purpose of Section 44C is conservation of energy, the uniform dollar tax saving for both rich and poor is the best tax incentive structure for accomplishing that purpose.

We should also note that the residential energy credits discussed above reduce the amount of one's tax liability. If one is poor enough not to have any tax liability, the Section 44C credits do not provide any tax relief or incentive for installing conservation items. The Department of Energy is, however, authorized to provide dwelling weatherization assistance in the form of grants to low-income persons (those near the federally established poverty level), especially the elderly or handicapped.[35] These grants are to help achieve Congress' purposes, as stated in the legislation authorizing the program, of aiding those with low income as well as saving the country needed fuel.

In addition to the residential provisions discussed above, the Internal Revenue Code also contains tax provisions to encourage desired energy-related activities of business. When business invests in various types of

---

35. 42 U.S.C.S. § 6861 et seq.

real or personal property, it qualifies for an investment tax credit under Section 46. The investment tax credit is designed to stimulate business investment in capital property. Besides the regular investment tax credit of 10% of the cost of the property, an additional 10 to 15% credit is allowable for investments in desirable forms of energy property which will reduce the amount or alter the type of energy consumed. Examples of energy property that may qualify are hydroelectric generating property, equipment for extracting oil from shale rock and intercity buses. Given the high dollar amounts that such items may cost, a tax credit of 10 to 15% of the cost may well serve to tip the balance in favor of business making some of the energy conservation investments that Congress seeks to encourage.

Congress has made extensive use of tax incentives to foster its conservation objectives; however, it must be kept in mind that the tax incentives approach to conservation is not free. Administrative costs aside, there is the direct reduction in the flow of revenue to the federal treasury. Let us next examine some examples of federal conservation mechanisms that work in ways that do not directly reduce the treasury's income. We will consider four examples in increasing order of the degree of federal government interference with the actions of private parties.

Our first example is energy conservation initiatives for federal buildings.[36] Among the steps to be taken are the implementation of a 10-year plan for energy conservation with respect to buildings owned or leased by the federal government, the establishment and achievement of energy performance targets for federal buildings, and installation of solar energy equipment in federal buildings. These steps are taken not only for the purpose of reducing energy use by the country's largest energy consumer, but also for purposes of acting as an example to other consumers of energy and to stimulate energy conservation technology and solar energy supply technology by stating that there is a large consumer for such technology. The above steps involve government action with respect to energy conservation, but they create no direct interference by government with the actions of those outside of government.

The federal labeling requirements imposed on manufacturers of automobiles and certain other consumer products such as refrigerators and television sets interfere with manufacturers to the extent of requiring the labeling, but they do not prohibit the manufacture or the purchase by consumers of inefficient or high energy consumption products.[37] Rather

---

36. 42 U.S.C.S. § 6361(a)(2) and § 8241 et seq.

37. 15 U.S.C.S. § 2006 (automobiles); 42 U.S.C.S. § 6296 (other consumer products).

the labeling requirements operate on a theory of exposing the public to information about energy consumption with the belief that such information will lead to demand for and hence the production of more energy-efficient products.

The level of interference created by the national maximum speed limit of 55 mph is somewhat greater.[38] The 55 mph limit was first put into effect to conserve fuel. It also had the effect of significantly increasing highway safety. States must impose and enforce the 55 mph limit or suffer the loss of eligibility for federal highway funds. Federal highway funds given to states are very large dollar items and few states could afford the loss. Also, the use of these highway funds provides many jobs for citizens of the recipient state. There is thus substantial arm twisting on the states from this federal conservation mechanism and, if the states use the 55 mph limit, there is the direct effect of a mandatory control on the behavior of those people using the highways. Still, although the arm twisting is great, the phrasing of the federal statute does not make it impossible for a state to refuse to accept the federal policy.

When we come to the federal imposition of average fuel economy standards on automobile manufacturers, we are beyond the level of interference that says a party will not be eligible for a privilege from the government if it fails to conform to the federal policy and we have reached the point where failure to conform is unlawful and carries penalties with it. The average fuel economy standards require that the average of the fuel economy of all the passenger automobiles manufactured by a manufacturer shall not be less than a stated number of miles per gallon in a given model year.[39] Thus the average fuel economy for all passenger automobiles manufactured by an individual manufacturer in 1980 was required to be 20.0 miles per gallon. The standard for 1985 and thereafter is 27.5 miles per gallon. Violation of these fuel conservation requirements subject the manufacturer to the possibility of large civil penalties. Congress has not, however, gone to the absolutely mandatory level of interference with automobile manufacturers by either saying that production of all inefficient automobiles is prohibited entirely or that failure to meet the average standards will result in a prohibition on the sale of any of a manufacturer's automobiles. Depending on factors such as the level of industrial cooperation, new technology, and the available supply of fuel, it is possible that conservation controls of a more mandatory nature than those described above may be imposed. Perhaps, how-

---

38. 23 U.S.C.S. § 154.
39. 15 U.S.C.S. § 2002.

ever, even the conservation controls and incentives that exist now may become unnecessary because the cost of energy itself may provide the best measure of the appropriate level of conservation.

ADDITIONAL READINGS

Goodwin, G. D., Ed. *Energy Policy in Perspective* (The Brookings Institution, Washington, DC, 1981).

Kendall, H. W., and S. J. Nadis, Eds. *Energy Strategies: Toward a Solar Future* (Cambridge, MA: Ballinger Publishing Company, 1980).

Landsberg, H. H., Ed. *Selected Studies on Energy* (Cambridge, MA: Ballinger Publishing Company, 1980).

Lovins, A. B. *Soft Energy Paths* (Cambridge, MA: Ballinger Publishing Company, 1977).

CHAPTER 8

POPULATION

A. STIMULATION OF POPULATION GROWTH AND THE NEED FOR POPULATION REGULATION

1. Upper Limits on Population Growth and Lower Limits for Species Existence

Did you ever wonder how there got to be so many fleas, mosquitoes, Mediterranean fruit flies, cattle and people everywhere and so few Atlantic salmon, Indiana bats and elephants anywhere? Well, there are numerous hypotheses to account for these observations, but before we examine some of them let us take a look at how a species population grows. The four processes — birth, death, immigration and emigration — and their relation to the size of a localized population are depicted in Figure 1. Taking the planet earth as a whole eliminates immigration and emigration as processes that influence population size. On the other hand, a localized population, such as the people of the United States, caddis flies in a temporary pool, or the Furbish louseworts of Maine, may all be influenced not only by births and deaths but also by immigration and emigration of individuals.

People who keep track of population size, growth, diversity and distribution as well as other vital statistics of populations are called demographers (demographers are usually assumed to keep track of only human populations but there are other people who keep track of plants and animals using demographic techniques and are therefore also demographers). Demographers who keep track of population growth use mathematical techniques to help them understand how a population grew and what the population *could* grow to be. In word form, the size, N, to which a population *could* grow between time, t, and some future

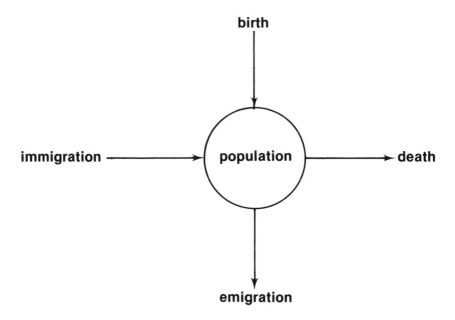

Figure 1.   Processes that may add or subtract from the size of a local population.

time, t + 1, is determined by the size of the population at time t and the intrinsic rate of increase (r) over the time period in question.* In a mathematical manner, this could read as follows:

$$N_{t+1} = N_t + rN_t$$

The intrinsic rate of increase r is the difference between the birth rate b and death rate d of the population in question ($r = b - d$). Therefore, two populations that start at the same size could have two totally different sizes after the same time period if each has a different intrinsic rate of increase r for each time interval and each reproduces in a similar time domain (Table I).

Conversely, two species populations with the same intrinsic rate of increase, but reproducing over different time intervals (one population reproduces every year while the other reproduces every two years), will also never reach the same population size over the same period of time. If

---

*The term intrinsic rate of increase has, unfortunately, several indistinct meanings that have created some confusion among population scientists. We use the term here to mean only the rate of increase of a population based on historical perspective.

Table I.   An Example of How Two Populations with
Very Different Intrinsic Rates of Increase Grow over Time

Time Period	Population 1 (r = 0.2)	Population 2 (r = 0.6)
1	100	100
2	120	160
3	144	256
4	173	410
5	208	656

one were to graph either situation through numerous time periods the result would be a curve that rises exponentially and shows *no* upper limit to growth, a concept that was rejected in principle by some researchers referred to in Chapter 1. Instead, it was recognized that the growth in a population reaches a limit of support after an elapsed time. Therefore, over any period of time, there is a limit imposed on the size that a population can reach and this is a function of the space used by the population. Space contains the resources used by the population (food, shelter). In population studies this upper limit is conceptualized as the "carrying capacity" of that environment, at that time, for the population in question. There is also another limit—the lower limit for a population to continue to exist. These limits are depicted in Figure 2.

What this all means is that if a population exceeds the carrying capacity of the environment there will be a decline of some proportion that "causes" the population numbers (number of living individuals) to decrease to some point below the carrying capacity for the population in question. If the population numbers fall even further and go below the lower limit, then the probability of that population becoming extinct is equal to 1.0, i.e., the population has a 100% chance of becoming extinct. This lower limit could be a rather large actual number like 10,000 or a relatively small number like 100. The numerical level of the lower limit is determined by the occurrence of intraspecific reproductive encounters that give at least enough viable offspring such that the number of individuals in the species population can remain stable or increase under *any* circumstances (the worst case analysis). Therefore, a population that will survive under basically "any" circumstances is one whose numbers remain between the upper and lower limit (see Figure 2). The upper limit (carrying capacity) is not really a definite number, but rather a group of numbers representing various limiting environmental parameters. The carrying capacity itself may vary because of many environmental factors external to the population in question, and could converge with the lower

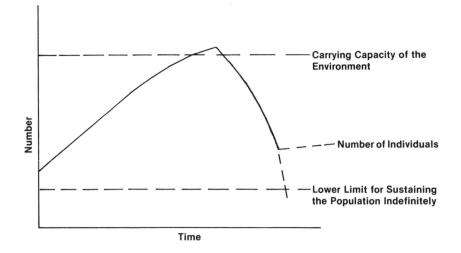

Figure 2.   Hypothetical growth curve for a population passing its carrying capacity.

limit. This would be a very precarious position for any species population. For example, suppose that one "family" of pileated woodpeckers needed 10 acres of woodlot to survive. Suppose further, that 5000 contiguous families of pileated woodpeckers were needed in order to have an indefinitely sustained population of woodpeckers. If there were not any woodlot of 50,000 contiguous acres for pileated woodpecker habitat, then there could be no pileated woodpecker population sustained indefinitely. In other words, even if there were 10,000 noncontiguous woodlots of 2500 acres each, although the overall population of woodpeckers could currently be very high, the number of families close to each other would be too small to continue the species indefinitely.

2.   Stimulation of Population Growth

What stimulates a population to grow? More importantly, what could stimulate a population to grow to a number larger than the carrying capacity for that population? Contrary to what might be one's first thought, at least with respect to humans, it is not *increased* birth rates that stimulate a population to grow as much as it is *decreased* death rates. Remember, populations increase faster when the intrinsic rate of increase (r) increases, and this increase is usually caused by a reduction in death rates. Modern medicine has contributed substantially to the stimulation of population growth by reducing infant mortality as well as preserving the lives of individuals who would have died from some disease such as heritable diabetes or hemophilia. Now all of these people may well live and reproduce. Some believe that this artificial selection (keeping people alive through medical practices until reproductive success) will not only result in a larger population but will also eventually lead to a physical weakening of the human population by perpetuating "disease" traits. Under normal circumstances it is believed that most of these people would die before experiencing reproductive success. In addition to medicine, religion has also been implicated as a stimulus to population growth. By specifically forbidding the use of contraception and encouraging reproductive output, religion does indeed stimulate population growth. This religious attitude, coupled with the medical advances noted, creates an overwhelming stimulus to population growth. Other factors that have been implicated in stimulating population growth include increased food supplies, greater mobility of the populace, industrialization and moral deterioration. Some have voiced the idea that when people get more to eat and thus are healthier they tend toward more reproduction. Also, the idea has been espoused that if individuals can get more food with the same effort or even less effort than previously made, then individuals will have more time for reproduction. Industrialization has also been implicated in stimulating population growth in much the same manner. The argument is that industrialization (any advancement that is similar could substitute) gives people more leisure time and therefore they spend more time engaged in reproductive activity, which eventually creates a population increase. While medicine and food can be viewed as manipulating death rates, religion and industrialization probably manipulate birth rates. Whichever of these one would choose to emphasize as the "cause" or "causes" of any perceived population growth problems, the fact is that the human population in the United States, as well as elsewhere, is increasing and therefore approaching the carrying capacity. To many people this condition calls for some form of regulation. The questions are: Should population be regulated and, if so, what form should such regulation take?

3. Population Regulation — Do We Need It?

There are basically two attitudes concerning population regulation — regulate and do not regulate. Since our human population is unsure about whether we really need to regulate ourselves, we have turned to an examination of nonhuman populations with the hope that by understanding the population behavior of other animal species we can shed light on our questions relating to the human population. Though this seems, at first, to be a fruitful endeavor, the controversy over what regulates populations of other animals is itself unresolved.

Current notions about animal population regulation take two fundamental approaches. One school of thought believes that populations regulate themselves by the density of the population itself. In other words, the number of individuals within the population dictates the size to which a population grows (internal control). This idea suggests that each individual, or perhaps each dominant individual, has a territory. When the total territory, summed over all individuals possessing a territory, approximates the total amount of territory available, then the species population has regulated itself. Another way of viewing this idea is that every population has some space that it can inhabit. When the number of individuals in the population has comfortably inhabited all the available space that members of the population can use, the population has reached the carrying capacity and regulation (internal) keeps increased reproductive effort at a minimum. The other school of thought argues that a species population size is independent of the population density and is a function of the environment (external control). What this means is that some external force such as temperature, wind speed, food availability, daylight period or some other factor regulates population size rather than it being regulated by density. These ideas are really the opposite poles of a continuum that allows population regulation to be a combination of the two notions (Figure 3).

The major objection to either of these possibilities or a combination of them is that the operation of each of these regulating mechanisms is supposed to occur when the carrying capacity is about to be reached. Therefore, although we know that no natural population has ever annihilated itself, we do not know whether that statement will be applicable to man and whether the mechanisms will operate to preclude man's self-annihilation due to his having reached or exceeded the carrying capacity.

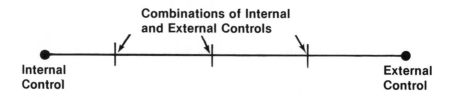

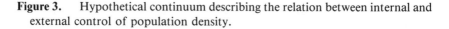

Figure 3.   Hypothetical continuum describing the relation between internal and external control of population density.

Furthermore, even if upon reaching the carrying capacity there is no annihilation of man, drastic consequences short of annihilation may occur, such as widespread famine. Yet another constraint on our thinking is that we do not know what form the real regulation among other species takes; rather, we know the result and speculate about the causes. While some scientists have attempted to study this question in experimental situations, these are generally artificial situations that examine segments of a species population. Some insight into whether we need to regulate our human population will likely be gained by studying non-human populations, but it is safe to say that no definitive answer has yet been provided.

Let's consider the need to regulate from another perspective. Every species population is assumed to start out small and grow larger over time. People keep track of localized human populations in terms of not only the number of individuals but also the distribution of individuals among age classes. Diagramatically, this effort produces a population picture like that in Figure 4. As one can see by examining the age distributions in Figure 4, the population on the left (Mexico) is and will be expanding rapidly and the population on the right (Sweden) is almost stable in population growth. The population in the middle diagram of Figure 4 (United States) is growing slowly and apparently approaching the structure of the population on the right (Sweden). The country on the left has a short time of doubling its population (≈ 30 yr) while the country on the right has a longer doubling time (≈ 125 yr). Two things are

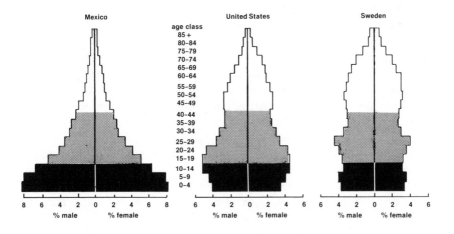

Figure 4. Age structure diagrams for Mexico, United States and Sweden as of 1974. [Adapted from Miller, 1982 (see Additional Readings)].

important to consider when examining diagrams such as these. One is the doubling time and thus the number of people. A second consideration is the age structure of the population. With respect to its numbers, any localized human population as well as a global human population places demands on our resource of space. People use space to domicile themselves, for recreation, and to provide food and other products for living. Since there is a finite amount of space that can be used for the above activities, as the number of people increases the amount of available space per individual in each category decreases. Therefore, the population may eventually stabilize itself once all the available space is used up. This may take place peacefully through mechanisms such as people reproducing less so as not to have to share space with their offspring, or it may happen through wars fought for space. If one wants to avoid the possible harsh consequences of nearing or exceeding our carrying capacity for human beings, one may opt for regulation of the growth of our population size. With respect to the age structure of population, society may need to concern itself with the burden placed on the younger members of the population in having to support the older members. As a population growth pattern becomes more stable (Figure 4), the percentage of older members within that population increases. Therefore, in stable populations where older individuals are supported by younger individuals (such as by a social security system) the financial burden on younger individuals increases. Soon it necessitates that the fewer younger individuals be supporting more older people.

Working against the idea of stable population or zero population growth (ZPG) is the expanding industrial society. As more jobs are created more people are needed to fill these jobs. Since younger workers are more acceptable to industry, there is a consequent shift in reproductive patterns to provide more younger available workers. Thus a stable population structure such as that shown for Sweden in Figure 4 may tend to change to look more like that shown for Mexico. When the industrial demands are met or the industrial demand for population declines, the structure may respond by gravitating away from the Mexican model toward the Swedish model. However, the response of industry to economic forces and the response of population to industrial forces are not necessarily equally as rapid. Population responses are usually less rapid compared to industrial responses. Therefore, some regulation to keep these responses in line with society's needs at the time may be preferable to a boom or bust scenario.

Issues pertaining to immigration and emigration also raise the question of the need for control mechanisms. A sonnet, written by Emma Lazarus, is preserved on a tablet inside the pedestal of the Statue of Liberty on Liberty Island in New York Harbor. The sonnet says, in part:

...Give me your tired, your poor, your huddled masses yearning to breathe free, the wretched refuse of your teeming shore. Send these, the homeless, tempest-tost to me, I lift my lamp beside the golden door!

A noble motto for a young and struggling country such as the United States was in 1886 when the Statue of Liberty was dedicated in remembrance of our revolutionary alliance with France. In fact, since the United States began keeping records (1820) over 50 million individuals have immigrated through the "golden door" of the United States. When there was much land to be settled and much work to be found, the idea of large-scale immigration to any country was not considered burdensome. But, since land resources have become scarcer, food resources in some countries even more scarce, and the demands for workers in an organized labor market have become stressed, the need for and the tolerance of immigrants in many countries has begun to cause at least localized if not national negative reaction. The recent episodes in the United States following the Vietnam War and the more recent mass immigrations from Cuba and Haiti have demonstrated that, within the United States at least, the attitude embodied in Ms. Lazarus' sonnet is under reconsideration. The United States, as well as other countries, is becoming more selective regarding the quality of immigrants. In a sense, nations are discriminating more closely among immigrants. What this could eventually lead to is an even greater distinction between the nations that "have" and those that "have not." In terms of the overall regulation of the human population, what this suggests is a form of density-dependent population regulation among nations based on the quality of contribution a potential immigrant might make to the overall goals of a receiving nation. Conversely, nations might counter the loss of high-quality individuals to higher-quality nations by restricting emigration, much as Britain did with scientists in recent years. While the actions described above may seem not only inconsistent with Ms. Lazarus' thoughts but also inconsistent with the historical underpinnings of our society, the institution and maintenance of immigration quotas and the calls to tighten up on enforcement of immigration laws attest to the realistic nature of the situation.

To summarize, population size relative to the carrying capacity of its surroundings, matters such as age distribution of population, population size relative to society's contemporary need for people, and immigration and emigration are all issues which could be the subject of affirmative regulation. Again the questions are: Should there be regulation and, if so, in what form? Though regulation of human population issues by legislation may seem repugnant, the alternative regulatory mechanisms may be no less acceptable. For example, internal control of the human population by birth regulation and even death regulation may prove a more acceptable alternative than waiting until the use of space through time becomes limiting. This latter alternative may foster famine, wars, infanticide and other more barbaric methods of population regulation. The question then becomes: Do we regulate before a critical density is reached or do we wait and see what happens when and if a critical density is reached? The decision is further complicated by our inability to know how long one can play "wait and see" and when we will pass a "point of no return." Therefore, one must ask not only what are the real options for population regulation but also when should such options be implemented and how will they be enforced. We will now examine some methods which might be used to regulate population and some legal issues the resolution of which may substantially affect population issues.

B.   LEGAL ISSUES INVOLVING POPULATION

1.   Matters Where Population Regulation Is the Primary Issue

When the topic of population law is raised, issues that often come to mind first are contraception, abortion and sterilization. In many countries, these issues have been addressed largely from the viewpoint of the utility of these tools as means of controlling population. For example, in India the national government uses media advertising to promote small families and has established medical camps where women and men receive cash payments for submitting to sterilization procedures. India has gone to the brink of imposing compulsory sterilization to try to control its mushrooming population, but the government which had been seriously considering compulsory sterilization was removed from power before the program was ever put into effect. Government policy of slowing population growth can also be seen by noting that in the countries containing 80% of the population of the developing world, there is some form of government-supported family planning. In some countries abortion policy has been established based largely on the effects that abortion would have on population. For example, in 1955 the Soviet Union enacted a decree that legalized abortion on request. The purposes were to reduce harm to women from abortions performed outside of hospitals and to give women the opportunity to decide questions of motherhood for themselves. Most of the socialist countries of eastern Europe soon followed suit; however, in more recent years some of these countries have become more restrictive about allowing abortions. This restrictiveness is said to be a response to those countries' concerns about low birth rates. Thus while most decisions concerning population issues that have been made on the basis of policies about population have resulted in governments acting to slow population growth, some decisions on population issues have been made with an eye toward increasing population.

In the United States, while issues such as population size, geographic distribution, and age distribution have been the subjects of some government action intended to impact on these issues, the issues of contraception, abortion and sterilization have not really been "population" issues but have been disputed and decided primarily on grounds other than their effects on population. The political and judicial decisions on these topics have been made in the context of Constitutional rights of privacy, due process and equal protection. They have also been made in the context of religion and varying thoughts on what is appropriate morality and what is the appropriate relationship between government and morality. We will begin by first discussing a few examples of our own government acting for primarily population-related purposes. We will then discuss abortion and contraception in a separate section, thereby emphasizing that in the United States these issues have not really been "population" issues.

Our first example will be a governmental entity acting to control the number of people that will be allowed to live within the geographical area of that entity. Many communities have experienced huge increases in population during very short periods of time. This has resulted in stress being placed on a community's ability to provide municipal facilities and services. Towns such as Ramapo, New York have sought to alleviate these population pressures by enacting ordinances to control the growth of the community.[1] Ramapo's ordinance tied development by residential subdivision to the availability of municipal facilities. Before a permit to subdivide would be issued, certain municipal facilities would have to be available. The facilities were to be provided in accordance with an 18-year plan or capital program. Growth would thus be allowed, but it would be slowed down to the pace at which facilities were provided. Ramapo's ordinance raised the general question of whether a town should have the right to control its growth, but in the *Ramapo* case the question was whether the town did in fact have that right. The town's ordinance was attacked on the grounds that it was a "taking" or confisca-

---

1. *Golden v. Planning Board of Town of Ramapo,* 285 N.E. 2d 291 (1972).

tion of private property by the government without the just compensation required by the Constitution,* and also that Ramapo's action was an unjustifiable exclusion of people from the community.

The court's answer to the taking without compensation argument was that the restriction on any individual piece of property was only temporary rather than permanent because the property would be able to be subdivided sometime during the 18 years. Also, the property could be used prior to its qualifying for a subdivision permit — it just could not be subdivided. A detailed discussion of what is an unconstitutional "taking" without just compensation may be found in Chapter 4. It is there shown that what will be called a "taking" by the courts is very narrow and that governments such as the Town of Ramapo have a great deal of latitude in regulating and controlling the use of land and ultimately controlling population through land use controls. On the issue of whether the ordinance amounted to an unjustifiable exclusion of people from Ramapo, the court said that the ordinance was not exclusionary but was merely the implementation of sequential development and timed growth. The court said it would not countenance exclusion, but that timed growth was acceptable. Since timed growth is, however, temporary exclusion, and results in fewer people in an area for a period of time, governmental control over the size of the population within its boundaries was found to be allowable at least to some extent.

Our second example of government acting for a population-related purpose involves not only numerical control but also control that concerns itself with the type or classification of people involved. That example is our immigration laws. In our early history there were very few restrictions on immigration. We had frontiers to settle and a demand for labor by our expanding industries. These needs dovetailed nicely with our concern for economically, politically and religiously oppressed people in other parts of the world. Later on came a desire to retain the racial and ethnic composition of our population and the Immigration Act of 1924 established quotas and formulas restricting immigrants from certain countries as the method of implementing that policy. Today's complex immigration laws are based in part on humanitarian factors such as the needs of refugees, but they also take into account the availability and competition for our country's resources such as jobs and the government's ability to provide for the needs of those who cannot provide for themselves. The Immigration and Nationality chapter of the

---

*5th Amendment: "...nor shall private property be taken for public use, without just compensation."

United States Code[2] has overall numerical limitations on the number of immigrants and thus addresses itself to numerical population control. It also provides a hierarchy for selection which accords preferential treatment for factors such as being a member of a profession or having ability in the arts or sciences and being sought by an employer in the United States, or being capable of performing skilled or unskilled labor, not of a temporary or seasonal nature, for which a shortage exists in the United States. Therefore, in addition to numerical control, the statutory framework also addresses itself to controlling the type of people that we are willing to add to our country's population.

As our last example of population parameters being directly related to actions taken by government, let's consider age. In contrast to our immigration example where the law sought to control the population parameters of "how many" and "who," the population parameter of age is not what is being controlled, but rather it may be used to control something else. To illustrate, if we want to reduce the size of the federal workforce and/or reduce unemployment by removing people from the working population, we can lower the age at which one will qualify for retirement benefits. If, however, our concern is the financial viability of the Social Security system in light of the fact that people are living longer and the percentage of older people eligible for social security is increasing, this age distribution pattern could result in pressure to raise the age at which one could qualify for retirement benefits. From these illustrations we can see that the age distribution of our population could strongly influence what we might establish as the age for retirement with government benefits.

Having considered a few examples of laws specifically intended to control population matters or being subject to possible influence by population factors, let's next turn to issues where, although their resolution will have substantial effects on population, the population aspects of the issues have not had much effect on how these issues are resolved in the United States.

2. Matters Where Population Regulation is Not the Primary Issue—Contraception and Abortion

On one level the issues of contraception and abortion involve answering the substantive question of whether the state can legally interfere with

---

2. 8 U.S.C.S. Chapter 12, § 1101 et seq.

the choice of the individual. On a second level are the problems that result from it being unclear, as a matter of law, whether the state can so interfere. If, for example, performing an abortion violates a state criminal statute, and if it is not clear whether that statute is constitutionally valid or invalid, physicians will be deterred from performing abortions and thus the existence of the doubt will itself provide an answer to the substantive question which may or may not be the correct answer. The doubt may also place physicians and patients in a precarious position. Thus, if performing or obtaining an abortion is a crime after the fetus has reached the stage of "viability," what is the time of viability given the medical profession's ability to sustain life outside the womb at ever-earlier stages of fetal development? In this section we will consider some of the substantive answers that the courts have provided to the question of what a legislature can do in the way of interfering with an individual's desire to obtain contraceptives or an abortion. Where contraception or abortion is sought to be prohibited or regulated by state government, the interests that the state may have in controlling a type of conduct are brought into conflict with the interest of the individual in her or his own privacy. That the individual has a constitutional right to privacy was first recognized in a case involving contraceptives and, that is where we will begin.

a. Contraception

A Connecticut statute which was in existence in 1961 made it a crime to use drugs, articles or instruments for the purpose of preventing conception or to counsel others in the use of contraceptives. The defendants, a physician and an official of Planned Parenthood, gave information, instruction and medical advice to married persons as to the means of preventing conception. In the case of *Griswold v. Connecticut*,[3] the defendants were found guilty in the Connecticut courts as accessories to the violation of the state statute and they asked the United States Supreme Court to reverse that conviction.

The Supreme Court did reverse the conviction on the grounds that the Connecticut statute interfered with the fundamental right of privacy contained in the United States Constitution. The Court recognized that nowhere in the Constitution could one find a "right of privacy" explicitly stated; however, it found that various parts of the Bill of Rights created a "zone of privacy" which could be invaded by government in only extremely limited ways and only under extremely limited circumstances. An

---

3. 381 U.S. 479 (1965).

example of how the Court saw parts of the Bill of Rights as creating a "zone of privacy" is the First Amendment's protection of the freedom to associate and privacy of one's associations. Although the First Amendment does not mention freedom of association, the Court said freedom of association was a peripheral First Amendment right and that the First Amendment has a "penumbra" where privacy is protected from governmental intrusion.

Other facets of the privacy penumbra can be found in places such as the Third Amendment's prohibition on quartering soldiers in people's houses in time of peace and the Fourth Amendment's prohibitions against unreasonable searches and seizures. The Court further noted that the Ninth Amendment provides: "The enumeration in the Constitution, of certain rights, shall not be construed to deny or disparage others retained by the people. . . ." A concurring opinion focused more heavily on the Ninth Amendment and said: "To hold that a right so basic and fundamental and so deep-rooted in our society as the right of privacy in marriage may be infringed because that right is not guaranteed in so many words by the first eight amendments in the Constitution is to ignore the Ninth Amendment and to give it no effect whatsoever. . . ." Thus, without it being stated in express terms in the Constitution, the "right of privacy" was recognized as a fundamental constitutional right.

The *Griswold* case involved contraceptive advice to married couples and the opinions in the case repeatedly spoke of marriage and the marriage relationship. In *Eisenstadt v. Baird,*[4] the Supreme Court was called upon to determine whether the "zone of privacy" with respect to contraceptives extended beyond the marital relationship. *Eisenstadt* concerned Massachusetts statutes that prohibited the distribution of materials for the prevention of conception unless such distribution was to married persons and by a physician or a pharmacist. With respect to the right of privacy, the Court found that this right is a right of the individual, not a right of the marital relationship or the marital couple. It said that the marital couple is not an independent entity but rather an association of two individuals, each with a separate intellectual and emotional makeup, and that the right of privacy is the right of the individual to be free from unwarranted governmental intrusion. The Court found that the Massachusetts statutes violated the Equal Protection Clause* of the Fourteenth Amendment of the United States Constitution because they provided dis-

---

4. 405 U.S. 438 (1972).

*". . . nor [shall any state] deny to any person within its jurisdiction the equal protection of the laws."

similar treatment for married and unmarried persons who are similarly situated and that there is no ground or difference that rationally explains the different treatment accorded married and unmarried persons. The Court's position was based on its findings that the statutes' unequal treatment could not be justified as either a deterrent to fornication or as a health measure when viewed in terms of what the statutes and their exceptions prohibited and what they did not prohibit.

While the right of privacy led to the invalidation of the Connecticut and Massachusetts regulatory efforts discussed above, it should be emphasized that individual rights may be subjected to governmental interference in some situations. Even "fundamental" rights such as the right of privacy or freedom of speech may be interfered with, but for governmental interference with a "fundamental" right to be found to be constitutional, there must be a very strong reason to support the interference. The required strength of the reason has been referred to as a "compelling state interest" or a "significant state interest" rather than merely a "valid state interest." In *Carey v. Population Services International,*[5] the Supreme Court examined various aspects of a New York statute to see if the strength of the state interest was sufficient to justify the interferences with the right of privacy that the statute created. The New York statute in *Carey* made it a crime: (1) to distribute contraceptives to minors under the age of 16, (2) for anyone other than a pharmacist to distribute contraceptives to persons over 16, and (3) for anyone to advertise or display contraceptives. All three provisions were found to be unconstitutional since a sufficient degree of state interest was not present to justify interference with a fundamental right. With respect to distribution to those under 16, the Court found that minors as well as adults have constitutional rights such as the right of privacy. It did, however, reaffirm that the power of the state to control the conduct of children is greater than the scope of its authority over adults. The minor's right to privacy in connection with procreation decisions could be restricted, but only if the restrictions served a significant state interest that is not present in the case of an adult. The state contended that it had a significant interest, in that by restricting access of minors to contraceptives it could decrease sexual activity of minors. Without deciding whether a state could act to discourage sexual activity of minors, the Court found that the state had presented no evidence supporting a link between the availability of contraceptives and increased sexual activity of minors. The Court noted that the state had conceded that there was no

---

5. 431 U.S. 678 (1977).

such evidence, and further, that evidence had been presented to indicate that unavailability of contraceptives did not have a deterrent effect on sexual activity of minors. There was thus no significant state interest to justify the state's interference with the minor's right to privacy.

The Court handled the distribution by a pharmacist requirement in a similar fashion. It found that the alleged state interest of allowing purchasers to inquire into the relative quality of products was perhaps not even a factually valid state interest and certainly did not reach the compelling level of state interest that would be necessary to justify restricting the distribution channel of contraceptives to licensed pharmacists. Such a restriction on access could place a burden on the freedom to make the decision of whether to bear or beget a child, and the freedom to make that decision is what the right of privacy in this area is all about. Lastly, with respect to the New York statute's prohibition on advertising or displaying contraceptives, the Court acknowledged that such activity might be offensive or embarrassing to some people; however, that is not sufficient justification for interference with another fundamental right, the First Amendment right of freedom of expression. The dissemination of information about the contraceptives, even in a commercial context, is protected from suppression under the First Amendment unless there is strong justification for such suppression. Embarrassment and offensiveness do not provide the required justification.

Given the above court decision, contraceptive distribution has overcome the major legal hurdles that have been placed in its way, and the heat of the battle has significantly subsided. In our next area of inquiry, abortion, we will see that the court cases have also upheld the right of privacy; however, because of higher degrees of moral, religious and political concern, the abortion issues are as hotly contested as ever.

b. Abortion

As with the contraception issues, the right of privacy played the pivotal role with respect to abortion. In 1973, while a few states had removed most restrictions on abortion, 30 states had statutes either prohibiting all abortions or any abortion not for the purpose of saving the life of the woman. The United States Supreme Court decided the case of *Roe v. Wade*[6] in 1973 on the basis of the constitutional right of privacy and invalidated a Texas statute making it a crime to procure or attempt an abortion unless it was to save the life of the mother. The court ap-

---

6. 410 U.S. 113 (1973).

proached the question of the constitutionality of the Texas statute by balancing the interests of the mother on the one hand with the interests of the state on the other.

The state interests alleged to be served by prohibiting abortions were to discourage illicit sexual conduct (this was dismissed by the Court as not a serious argument), to protect the mother from a hazardous surgical procedure and to protect prenatal or potential life. Against these interests are the woman's interests — her constitutional right of privacy which, because of factors like possible mental and physical health problems of child care and distress associated with an unwanted child, the Court said was broad enough to encompass a woman's decision of whether or not to terminate her pregnancy. While the right of privacy is not an absolute right, it is a fundamental right and thus could be infringed upon by the state only to serve "compelling" state interests. In *Roe,* the Court found that the state's interests in protecting the mother's health and in protecting prenatal life are compelling state interests and thus not all statutes restricting or prohibiting abortions are invalid. Why, if the state interests were found to be "compelling," was the Texas statute invalidated?

The Texas statute was held invalid because it was "overbroad" — it prohibited some conduct that it could validly prohibit but it also prohibited conduct that it could not constitutionally prohibit. Although the state has an interest in protecting the mother's health, that interest does not allow prohibiting an abortion in the first trimester of pregnancy because it was factually shown that during the first trimester abortion is a less hazardous medical procedure than childbirth. Thus to prohibit abortion beyond the first trimester (or beyond whatever point in time abortion might become a greater health hazard to the mother than childbearing) might protect the mother and be allowed. Prior to that time the statute does not protect the mother and does not serve the state interest. It therefore outlaws too much — it is overbroad — and is unconstitutional.

A similar analysis resulted in the statute being overbroad with respect to the state's interest in protecting potential life. The Court acknowledged that there are different religious, philosophical and scientific views about when life begins. It went on to say that the time at which the state's interest in potential life becomes "compelling" is the time when the fetus has reached the point of viability (24–28 weeks), i.e., it presumably has the capability of meaningful life outside of the mother's womb. After the time of viability was reached, the Court said that there was both logical and biological justification for a state to prohibit abortion. Since the Texas statute prohibited abortions not only subsequent to the time of viability of the fetus but also prior to viability, it was overbroad and invalid.

Roe v. Wade did not tell states that they could not prohibit abortions under any circumstances, but it was the turning point in abortion law because it told states that some abortions could not be prohibited and that attempts to limit or regulate abortion would be closely scrutinized by the courts. A state would have to provide substantial justification for its restraints. When the court in *Roe* told the states that there were some abortions that could not be prohibited, it answered some questions but it left open many, many others. Let us consider three illustrative examples: (1) May a state require the consent of the spouse prior to an abortion? (2) May a state require parental consent for a minor's abortion? (3) May public funds be used for abortions?

In *Roe* the court specifically stated that it was not discussing any rights that a father may have in the abortion decision. In the 1976 case of *Planned Parenthood v. Danforth,*[7] the Court faced the father's rights issue: Should a father have the right to veto an abortion? In *Danforth,* a Missouri statute required prior written consent of the spouse unless the abortion was to save the life of the mother. The Supreme Court found that that part of the statute was unconstitutional. The Court's opinion was grounded on logic and precedent relating to *Roe v. Wade* and also on practical reality. The Court reasoned that since *Roe* had decided that a state did not have the power to prohibit at least a first trimester abortion if the mother wanted it, a state could not delegate to the spouse a power that the state itself did not have. On the pragmatic level the court recognized that where mother and father disagreed, only one of them can physically prevail. On balance, the Court decided that the mother's view should prevail since it is her body and she is more physically affected by the pregnancy.

A dissenting opinion was filed in *Danforth* on the issue of consent of the spouse. The dissenters believed that where the mother and father disagree, that is the point at which the interest of the unborn child comes in and tips the balance. In such a disagreement situation, the dissent said that the cutting off of potential life should not outweigh letting it mature into a live child. One can support the position that the father should be able to veto an abortion by raising the interest of the unborn or merely by arguing that the unborn child is his child as much as it is the mother's. On the other hand, one can contend that even though the father has a substantial interest in the unborn child, the choice should be solely that of the mother because it is her body and thus her interests outweigh his. If one were to believe that the father should not be able to veto an

---

7. 428 U.S. 52 (1976).

abortion, as the Court decided in *Danforth,* should a father be able to require that the mother have an abortion? While this possibility may sound totally unsupportable to some, consider the source of the woman's right to have an abortion — her right to privacy. When that right was recognized in *Roe v. Wade,* the Court wrote:

> . . . additional offspring, may force upon the woman a distressful life and future. Psychological harm may be imminent. Mental and physical health may be taxed by child care. There is also the distress for all concerned, associated with the unwanted child, and there is the problem of bringing a child into a family already unable psychologically or otherwise, to care for it.

Might not many of these concerns, and perhaps others such as that of financial responsibility, apply to a man as well as a woman and give him a right of privacy encompassing the right to not become a father? Might additional factors such as severe mental impairment of the mother subsequent to conception ever be relevant to a possible "father's right to an abortion?" A father's right of privacy would seem to be plausible, yet it would strain the imagination to envision facts where his right of privacy would outweight the mother's and result in the law requiring a pregnant woman to submit to an abortion against her will.

Another "consent" issue with respect to abortion arises in the context of a state seeking to require parental consent prior to a minor obtaining an abortion. In *Planned Parenthood v. Danforth,* the Supreme Court held that a state may not impose a blanket provision requiring such parental consent as a condition on an abortion. Subsequent to *Danforth,* Massachusetts attempted to reconcile its interests in encouraging parental advice in abortion situations with the right of a woman to choose to terminate her pregnancy. Massachusetts required the seeking of parental consent but if that consent were refused, authorization for the abortion could be obtained through a court order with the judge basing his decision exclusively on what would serve the minor's best interests. The Supreme Court, in *Bellotti v. Baird,*[8] found that although the Massachusetts statute was not a "blanket prohibition," the requirement that the minor first consult with her parents imposed "an undue burden upon the exercise by minors of the right to seek an abortion" because of the vulnerability of a minor to having her parents obstruct her going to the

---

8. 443 U.S. 622 (1979).

court or having an abortion. Having a legal right brings with it the need to be able to assert that right.

In *Bellotti,* the Court's opinion stated:

> every minor must have the opportunity—if she so desires—to go directly to a court without first consulting or notifying her parents. If she satisfies the court that she is mature and well-enough informed to make intelligently the abortion decision on her own, the court must authorize her to act without parental consultation or consent.

Even without this independent competency showing, the court must permit an abortion if the minor shows it would be in her "best interests." Following the *Bellotti* decision, Massachusetts enacted legislation to conform to the *Bellotti* requirements of access to the courts without parental involvement. The approach of *Bellotti* and hence the Massachusetts statute appears to be fatally flawed in practical terms from the perspective of both those who favor some control over a minor's abortion decision and those who favor no control.

Those who favor control would cite a review of the post-*Bellotti* statute that appeared in the *Boston Globe* newspaper on March 31, 1982. That review found that 647 pregnant minors had received court permission for abortions while none had been refused permission. If the minor showed maturity, the abortion must be allowed. In situations where maturity is not shown, even those judges who oppose abortion could see no way to substantiate a judicial determination that the forcing of a clearly immature minor to have her baby against her wishes would be in her "best interests." Those who oppose any approval requirements prior to a minor undergoing an abortion also criticize the statute because of the traumatic and inhibiting effects that it produces. Should a 16-year-old girl have to go to a courthouse and appear in front of a male judge and answer questions pertaining to her sex life and abortion? Besides the inhibition on the exercise of her constitutional right which the prospect of such a proceeding may create for the girl, seemingly insignificant concerns such as having to go to court during school hours and possibly having her parents find out may inhibit the exercise of her rights. The practical results of the statute may include discouraging minors from asserting their constitutional right to an abortion or encouraging them to go to another state to have an abortion. Lawsuits are currently pending challenging the constitutionality of the current Massachusetts statute.

As an example of the continuing narrowing of the issues in the Supreme Court's abortion cases, let's compare the *Bellotti* case and the concerns that the Court seemed to express in that case with its position in the 1981 case of *H.L. v. Matheson.*[9] In *Bellotti* the Court appeared concerned about the inhibiting or "chilling" effect on a minor's assertion of her rights, and thus requiring her to consult with her parents or to seek their consent prior to asking for court approval for her abortion was impermissable. An additional logical result of this concern would be that a minor who could satisfy a court that she had a legal right to an abortion should be able to have it without her parents being notified. A state's requiring notification could easily be seen to be inhibiting on the minor's assertion of her rights. In *Matheson,* the Court upheld the validity of a Utah statute requiring parental notification prior to the abortion at least in cases of immature minors who had not shown that their best interests would be served by not notifying their parents. If a minor who is immature can establish in a court proceeding her right to have an abortion since the abortion would be in her best interests, is it not likely that her exercise of that right will be inhibited if her parents are to be notified since she may not be able to show that notification is not in her best interests? Thus even a very limited notification statute may provide the inhibiting effect that the Court seemed interested in preventing when it decided the *Bellotti* case.

Let's further consider the practical effect and the scope of the "constitutional right" to have an abortion by looking at the issue of public funding of abortions. Connecticut participated in the federal Medicaid program and paid for childbirth but refused to pay for nontherapeutic abortions as part of the program. In *Maher v. Roe,*[10] an indigent woman who wanted a nontherapeutic abortion contended that by paying the medical bills of women choosing childbirth, but refusing to pay the bills of those choosing abortion, Connecticut was establishing discriminatory classifications in violation of the Equal Protection Clause of the Fourteenth Amendment* to the United States Constitution. The Court in *Roe v. Wade* had found that the right to have an abortion was a fundamental right. In *Maher,* the Court found that there is no fundamental right to a free abortion. Without there being any interference with a fundamental right, and without there being any discrimination against an "inherently suspect classification" of people (race is an inherently suspect classification, but poverty is not), the state did not need to have a "compelling state interest" for treating "childbirth women" and "abortion women" unequally. Different treatment would be acceptable under the Equal

---

9. 101 S. Ct. 1164 (1981).

10. 432 U.S. 464 (1977).

*See footnote on p. 205.

Protection Clause so long as a "reasonable basis" for the classification is shown. Making references to the state's interests in encouraging normal childbirth and in choosing among competing demands for limited public funds, the Court found that there was a "reasonable basis" for the classification.

Maher said that a state was not required to fund nontherapeutic abortions through Medicaid, but it specifically said that a state was free to provide such benefits if it so decided. Federal law, in the form of various versions of the Hyde Amendment to Appropriations bills, has precluded the use of Medicaid funds even for medically necessary abortions in all but limited situations, such as those threatening the life of the woman. The question of abortion funding thus moved from the state legislative forum to Congress, and Congress' 1979 Hyde Amendment[11] was challenged with respect to its constitutionality in *Harris v. McRae.*[12]

In *McRae,* a Medicaid recipient in the first trimester of a pregnancy that she wished to terminate contended that the Hyde Amendment's prohibition on the use of Medicaid funds to pay for an abortion for her, even if the state wanted to so use the funds, was unconstitutional. She claimed that the prohibition was unconstitutional as a denial of Equal Protection, as a violation of the Due Process Clause of the Fifth Amendment,* and as an establishment of religion in violation of the First Amendment.** The Supreme Court found that the Hyde Amendment was constitutional. It rejected the Equal Protection argument along lines similar to those discussed above with respect to *Maher.* Responding to the Due Process argument, the Court said that although the "liberty" protected by the Due Process Clause affords protection against governmental interference with freedom of choice in certain personal situations, it does not confer an entitlement to the funds that may be needed to realize the advantage of that freedom. Just because government may not prevent parents from sending a child to private school does not mean that government has an affirmative constitutional obligation to provide the funding to allow all persons to implement such a decision. Concerning the Establishment of Religion argument, the Court said that even though the Hyde Amendment may incorporate into the law a doctrine of the Catholic Church, the fact that a law may coincide with the tenets of a

---

11. P.L. No. 96-123, § 109.

12. 100 S. Ct. 2671 (1980).

*"No person shall be...deprived of life, liberty, or property, without due process of law..."

**"Congress shall make no law respecting an establishment of religion...."

religion does not, without something more being present, constitute an "establishment of religion" — the aiding of religion in general or the prefering of one religion over another.

The above results in *McRae* have been simply stated and appear to be quite simply stated in the opinion of the Court. What the United States Constitution does or does not allow or require with respect to highly sensitive issues is, however, far from clear and simple. The best evidence of this is the fact that *Harris v. McRae* was decided by a 5 to 4 vote of the Court with three dissenting Justices stating:

> The fundamental flaw in the Court's due process analysis, then, is its failure to acknowledge that the discriminatory distribution of the benefits of governmental largesse can discourage the exercise of fundamental liberties just as effectively as can an outright denial of those rights through criminal or regulatory sanctions....[13]

The closeness of the Court's vote emphasizes the question of whether courts should be involved with sensitive political and moral questions such as abortion. One can say that if there is to be any governmental involvement in such an area, it should be by the elected legislature. On the other hand, one can say that a major purpose of the Constitution is to protect individuals from the imposition of the political majority's judgment of what is morally acceptable and socially desirable. Freedom of speech, freedom of religion, as well as the right of privacy are protections against the majority's elected legislature and those protections are entrusted by the Constitution to the care of the courts. Even if one advocates the position that the courts, by use of the Constitution, are supposed to protect the individual from the majority, one must be aware that the protection only exists so long as the Constitution contains the source of protection. If a constitutional amendment were enacted to prohibit abortion, the rules would all change, since a validly enacted constitutional amendment cannot be declared unconstitutional. While no such amendment currently exists, many efforts have been and are being made to incorporate some form of prohibition on abortions into the United States Constitution.

ADDITIONAL READINGS

Commission on Population Growth and the American Future. *Population and the American Future* (Washington, DC: U.S. Government Printing Office, 1972).

---

13. Dissenting opinion of Justices Brennan, Marshall and Blackmun.

Council on Environmental Quality. *Global Future: Time to Act* (Washington, DC: U.S. Government Printing Office, 1981).

Hutchinson, G. E. *An Introduction to Population Ecology* (New Haven, CT: Yale Univ. Press, 1978).

Isaacs, S. L. *Population Law and Policy* (New York: Human Sciences Press, 1981).

Miller, G. T., Jr. *Living in the Environment* (Belmont, CA: Wadsworth Publishing Co., 1982).

CHAPTER 9

INTERNATIONAL ENVIRONMENTAL LAW

A. THE NEED

1. The International Concept

"Golly dad, how come there are no fish in the lake anymore?" "Well son, our Canadian government believes it has something to do with air pollutants sent to us by the United States." "Is somebody going to do something about it, dad?" "I don't know son, I don't know." So goes the frustration of trying to cope with environmental issues that cross sociopolitical boundaries and will eventually affect practically everyone in the world. Let us examine for a moment what can lead to the above-described situation. In other words, how do things move around anyway?

There are three broad categories of items that flow around, on, or near the surface of the earth in some organized pattern. The categories may be viewed as air, water and active or passive species of migratory plants and animals which use air, water or land routes to migrate. These three categories of flow move between and upon stationary masses of land that have been apportioned and will continue to be apportioned into various sociopolitical units. The distribution of these stationary land masses is shown in Figure 1. An examination of this figure reveals that stationary land masses are not evenly distributed among all latitudes and longitudes. Further examination of this figure and some knowledge of geographical industrial distribution indicates that most of the industrial sectors of the world are distributed somewhere between the latitudes 30°N and 60°N of the equator. Between these latitudes is an area roughly described as the North Temperate Zone, and that zone includes the United States, Canada, Europe, China and the U.S.S.R.

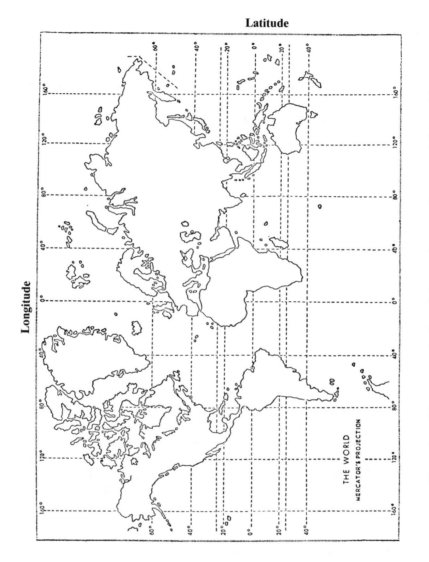

Figure 1. Mercator projection of the continents and oceans of the world.

The current understanding of large-scale air circulation patterns near the surface of the rotating earth is given in Figure 2. This understanding reasons that air above the surface of the earth tends to circulate within one of three areas north or south of the equator. As the figure indicates, air circulates almost entirely within defined regions (belts) and the air within a region is more apt to stay in that region than to migrate to another region. Consequently, any foreign material (pollutant) introduced into the atmosphere has the likelihood of being carried by that atmosphere in the direction of the prevailing air currents within the region (belt). Thus any air pollutant introduced into any belt of atmosphere has a greater probability of falling downward within that belt (as opposed to any other belt) when rains or other forms of precipitation scavenge pollutants out of the air. Since the prevailing westerlies are the dominant air circulation pattern in the North Temperate Zone, one

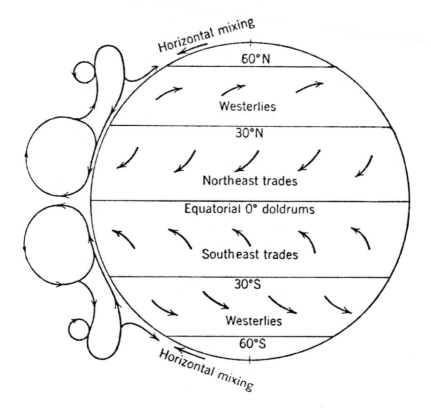

Figure 2.   The circulation of the earth's atmosphere, incorporating the effects of the earth's rotation.

would expect that air pollutants introduced into that atmosphere would be dispersed in a somewhat northeasterly direction and remain within the belt until removed in some form of precipitation. This is presumably how the United States could send air to Canada that could contribute to or cause the scenario mentioned at the beginning of the chapter. While these air pollutants must come out of the air and into the lake if they are to kill fish or keep fish from reproducing effectively, rain can act to carry these pollutants out of the air and down to earth and into the lake. This is also the basis of the argument advanced by the Scandinavian countries regarding the contribution of other European countries (England and Germany) to their lake acidification problems. The idea is that coal burning in Germany and England produces sulfur dioxide, some of which is converted to sulfuric acid and eventually falls onto the territory of other countries. There is currently a large research program investigating this phenomenon on the European and North American continents. Today acid rain is viewed by many as a world problem as well as a regional problem. It should also be noted that while pollutants tend to remain in the belt into which they were introduced, pollutants introduced into the atmosphere can be transported in the atmosphere from one defined belt (prevailing westerlies of the northern hemisphere) to another defined belt (polar area of the southern hemisphere). However, the density of an air pollutant continuously introduced into a defined belt will remain higher in that belt than in some other belt that either directly touches the belt of introduction or is farther removed from the belt of introduction.

The second category of flow—water—is partially depicted in Figure 3, which shows the circulation of major ocean currents around the continents. It is also important to remember that water *circulates* to the ocean by evaporating into the air and then falling back to earth as some form of precipitation and then running "down the hill" until reaching the ocean. And, because continents have relief (mountains and plains) and are also separated by oceans that are large sources of water for the atmosphere, precipitation patterns on the earth vary significantly before the water starts flowing back toward the oceans. Again, it is important to recognize that since, for example, fresh water from rivers flows into the oceans, any material introduced into water has the potential of being carried all over the world and could thus contaminate remote portions of the globe and eventually generate, at any point on the globe, a water situation that would be locally detrimental. There is currently evidence that DDT and other waterborne pesticides are common contaminants of ocean water around Antarctica. Ocean water around Antarctica is where many ocean animals get their food during part of the year. Therefore, a

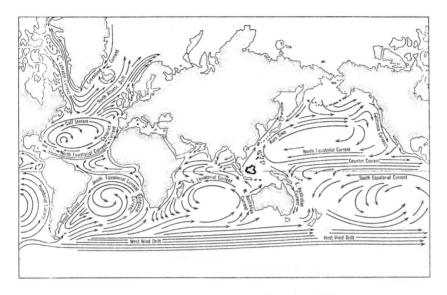

Figure 3. World pattern of ocean currents.

pollutant such as DDT, which can accumulate in organisms near the top of food chains, could actually function as a contaminant at a point far removed from the introduction point of the DDT. Thus whales or fish could become contaminated in Antarctica, a place where DDT was not used. This could also mean that pollutants introduced into the ocean by a country such as the United States could eventually contaminate the fish caught and sold in Japan.

The idea that dumping some potentially hazardous waste material into the ocean is solving a problem shows that there is little understanding of or caring about global water circulation patterns in the minds of those who make such decisions. To get some idea of this type of problem consider that New York City currently dumps sewage sludge into the New York Bight, a section of the Atlantic Ocean. This practice has reached a critical state since some of this sludge has been found on local beaches, but more importantly this sludge has been found to contain disease-causing viruses. In other words, New York City introduces additional breeding grounds for disease organisms into the ocean on a daily basis. Eventually, a disease from this area could travel around the world. A more alarming situation might be the practice of dumping radioactive wastes into the ocean. The quantities of radioactive wastes dumped over a period of years by European countries and the United States are given in Tables I and II, respectively (The United States ceased ocean disposal

Table I.   Sea Disposal of Low-Level Radioactive Wastes
from European Countries[1]

Year	Dumped weight (metric tons)	Radioactivity (Ci)	
		Alpha (actinides)	Beta, Gamma
1971	3970	630	11,200
1972	4130	680	21,600
1973	4350	740	12,600
1974	2270	420	100,000[a]
1975	4460	780	60,500[b]
1976	6770	880	53,500[c]
1977	5605	958	76,450[d]
1978	8000	1100	79,000[e]
1979	5400	1400	83,000[f]

[a] Almost exclusively tritium.
[b] Includes about 30,000 Ci of tritium.
[c] Includes about 21,000 Ci of tritium.
[d] Includes about 32,000 Ci of tritium.
[e] Includes about 36,000 Ci of tritium.
[f] Includes about 42,000 Ci of tritium.

of radioactive waste in 1970). What is not given in these tables is the amount dumped, if any, by other countries possessing capabilities of generating radioactive waste. One might ask where the material will eventually go if the containers in which the radioactive waste is dumped fail over a long period of time.

To bring the above situation to a somewhat narrower scope, let us consider the Great Lakes, four of which are jointly "owned" by the United States and Canada (Superior, Huron, Erie and Ontario). These lakes have water circulation patterns that put water that is near Canada at one time near to the United States at another time, and vice versa. Therefore, a pesticide liberally applied by a farmer in Cuyahoga County, Ohio, could enter the Cuyahoga River (parts of this *river* used to be listed as a major fire hazard) and flow into Lake Erie. This pesticide could potentially circulate throughout Lake Erie or into another Great Lake and eventually contaminate fish in the Canadian portions of the Great Lakes to a level such that the marketing of fish for human consumption

1. Dyer, R. S. *Sea Disposal of Nuclear Waste: A Brief History,* Washington, DC: George Washington University Law Center, 1980).

Table II.   Primary U.S. Radioactive Waste Dumpsites[2]

Site	Coordinates	Depth (m)	Distance from Land (km)	Years Dumpsite Used	Estimated Number of 55-gal Drums Dumped	Estimated Activity in Drums at Time of Packaging (Ci)
Atlantic	38°30'N 72°06'W	2800	190	1951–1956 1959–1962	14,300	41,400[a]
Atlantic	37°50'N 70°35'W	3800	320	1957–1959	14,500	2,100
Pacific Farallon Island (Subsite A)	37°38'N 123°08'W	900	60	1951–1953	3,500	1,100
Farallon Island (Subsite B)	37°37'N 123°17'W	1700	77	1946–1950 1954–1965	44,000	13,400

[a]This does not include the pressure vessel of the N/S Seawolf reactor, with an estimated induced activity of 33,000 Ci.

2. R. S. Dyer. "Environmental Surveys of Two Deep Sea Radioactive Disposal Sites Using Submersibles," *Symposium on Management of Radio-active Waste from the Nuclear Fuel Cycle,* IAEA-SM-207/65 (Vienna, Austria: International Atomic Energy Agency, 1976).

would have to be suspended. These types of suspensions have occurred from time to time at various locations bordering the Great Lakes in both Canada and the United States. Indeed, we know that some potentially harmful substances (such as mercury) can be carried long distances by water and can accumulate in local food chains to the extent that local food resources are contaminated.

Probably the most difficult of our flow categories to examine is the flow of plants and animals across international boundaries. Here one must consider actively migratory species such as Canadian geese, whooping cranes, bison, whales, salmon and seals, the somewhat passively migratory species such as the plants poison ivy, ragweed, kudzu vine and bearberry, as well as other passively transported species such as cereal leaf beetles, Mediterranean fruit flies, Colorado potato beetles and even disease-causing species such as swine flu and Hong Kong flu. Let us examine some of these in specific instances.

Whales migrate throughout the oceans. Each species of whale follows different migratory routes (patterns) that, at various times, cross into different political jurisdictions. At other times, these whales are in international waters rather than within the claimed territorial limits of a country. Though we all might recognize that if too many individual whales of one species are eliminated, the probability of that whale species population going extinct becomes a certainty, there is a real and important human population need among the peoples of various countries to use whales as a stable food resource and for other goods of commercial value such as whale oil and scrimshaw. One can then imagine what might happen when numerous countries and individuals collectively agree that the number of individuals in the population of some whale species (humpback whales) is near the point of being extinct. The attempted resolution of such a dilemma might result in some compact among various members (countries) of the international community to limit the taking of certain whale species to a level such that the species population will continue. In fact, the International Whaling Commission has accomplished such a compact, and set limits on whale catches (Table III). The members also agreed to cease using factory ships (slaughterhouses that float) except for minke whale taking. The unfortunate aspect of this type of international endeavor is the nonparticipation of some countries that will continue to hunt and harvest whales, and also the fact that even member countries will supplement their own catch by purchasing whale meat from nonparticipants in the compact (Table IV). In addition, many countries feel that there has not been enough research on whale population dynamics to make any reasonable estimate of the limits that should be placed on catches. This dilemma, the uncertainty of science, may

Table III.   International Whaling Commission Commercial
Whaling Quotas, 1974–81 (number of animals)

			Species			
Season	Fin	Minke	Sei	Bryde's	Sperm	Total
1974–75	1,300	7,000	4,000	2,000[a]	23,000	37,300
1975–76	585	9,360	2,230	1,363	19,040	32,578
1976–77	455	11,924	1,995	1,000	12,676	28,050
1977–78	459	8,645	855	524	13,037	23,520
1978–79	455	9,173	84	454	9,360	19,526
1979–80	604	12,006	100	743	2,203	15,656
1980–81	651[b]	10,987	100	793[c]	1,320	13,851

[a]Represents a combined quota of 2,000 Sei and Bryde's whales in the North Pacific.
[b]The official quota is 701, but Iceland has declared that it will take only 254 of its quota of 304.
[c]The official quota is 1,415, but 622 cannot be taken legally because of the moratorium on factory ship whaling and the Indian Ocean sanctuary.

Table IV.   Japanese Imports of Whale Meat From Non-IWC
Members[4] (metric tons)

	1971	1972	1973	1974	1975	1976	1977	1978
Imports	4,170	4,201	4,995	6,798	4,831	5,665	7,642	10,432
Percentage increase over 1971		1	20	63	16	36	83	150

never be resolved. The real issue has yet to be addressed, namely, what will happen when the world's increasing population demands more whale meat and whale products and virtually everyone agrees that the various whale species populations cannot tolerate the hunting pressure and will become extinct under almost any circumstances?

Another species migration example might be the situation of the restocking program for Atlantic salmon being carried on by the United

3. U.S. Department of Commerce, National Oceanic and Atmospheric Administration. *The United States and Whale Conservation* (Washington, DC: U.S. Government Printing Office, 1978).

4. U.S. Department of Commerce, National Oceanic and Atmospheric Administration. *The Moratorium Issue* (Washington, DC: U.S. Government Printing Office, 1979).

States and neighboring Canada. The United States has already invested over $150 million dollars in this program. Hatchery-raised Atlantic salmon are released into various rivers of the northeastern United States (White and Black Rivers in Vermont, Penobscott and others in Maine) where they spend about two years eating and growing as they slowly move downstream to the ocean. Upon reaching the ocean, these fish move toward Greenland where they feed and grow. It is hoped that they will later return to the United States and the stream where they were released as young salmon and breed to produce even more young salmon. In this situation there are a number of potential and actual problems that may eventually leave this and similar programs in a less than successful state. For example, who owns the salmon—the country that stocked them or the country whose waters they might be feeding in at some period during their life cycle? While these fish are in international waters does anyone have the right to catch them? The significance of these issues may become even more important as food supplies dwindle and more people are hungry, but even today many of these salmon are caught by European fishermen off the coast of Greenland. Consider further, not only the problem of dams on tributaries the salmon are trying to swim up, the expense of fish ladders and the increased mortality associated with fish ladders, but the potential contamination of breeding waters by internationally transported air pollutants. It is currently accepted by many individuals that acid precipitation resulting from oxide emissions in both Canada and the United States will eventually limit the successfulness of the Atlantic salmon restoration program because breeding areas will become too acidic for the survival of eggs and young fish. Therefore, it would seem expedient to try to resolve these problems before there is a loss of critical salmon habitat and the accompanying loss of a food resource and a recreational resource. Up to this point we have considered only species that are migratory through national and international waters, so it would seem appropriate to also discuss a species that migrates between countries using the air.

Probably everyone is familiar with the fact that numerous bird species are migratory, including Canadian geese, warblers, swallows and ducks; many of these migratory species are hunted for food and sport in areas that transcend the political boundaries of individual countries. A species such as the Canada goose migrates from places in Canada to places south of the United States during the fall period of the year. During this period hunting is usually allowed in all political jurisdictions through which the geese travel. Pursuant to treaties between the United States and Canada and the United States and Mexico, the limits for taking of migratory birds is regulated such that the species population is not eliminated. A current controversy involving migratory birds centers around the use of lead shot (bullets) to take such species. It seems that if a bird is "merely" wounded it may live for a period until the lead dissolves enough to internally poison the bird. That bird can then be eaten by predatory (scavenger) species. This results in lead accumulating in food chains and eventually creates another problem concerning human consumption of these predators.

Besides large animals, there are other species that are considered more passively migratory and are regulated by various means usually involving inspections or quarantines. For instance, the Mediterranean fruit fly might infect the fruit crops of parts or all of California. Because agricultural experts might fear the spread of this fruit fly if California fruit is shipped outside California, a quarantine may be imposed on California fruit to keep the fruit from being shipped to other parts of the United States and also into the world market. Sometimes such a mechanism is not implemented if the fruit is treated with a pesticide to levels that ensure against the spread of the pest.

Charles Darwin once reported on digging a trench about two feet wide and six feet long which contained 326 species of plants, 298 of which were not considered native to England. This suggests that plants can also be migratory by some mechanisms. Indeed, the United States used to ship uncleaned bales of cotton to England that probably contained much seed of our native weeds. Today if one attempts to cross the border between Canada and the United States or to cross the border from Mexico into the United States, the traditional border interrogation seeks to determine if one is carrying any plants with roots or in soil or soil itself. The reason for this questioning revolves around the idea that soil, transported from one country to another, usually in association with plants, may carry diseases into the country of destination. If one admits having soil and/or plant roots, these are confiscated by the examining country and presumably rendered harmless. Yet most vehicles entering a country have dust both on the vehicle surface and in the tires, as well as on the boots of the persons in the vehicles. This soil could contain larvae, spores or bacteria but is admitted freely across borders without the care taken to scrutinize soil associated with carried plants. Airplanes might act in a similar manner to transport passively migratory species.

Finally, let us consider the effect of introduced passively migratory species on the area of introduction. Kudzu vine was intentionally imported into the United States to help revegetate the barren landscape of Tennessee, which had resulted from smelting operations. While the "experiment" appeared to be a success, subsequent years of observation have indicated that kudzu is a pest, growing unchecked all over the southeastern section of the United States. The cereal leaf beetle is another example of a species spreading virtually unchecked. This pest, accidently introduced into the United States around the 1940s, is a serious pest on cereal grains. Without natural controls to check the population size (predators) this pest succeeded in drastically reducing cereal grain yields and helped foster a whole new area of pest management. Along with pesticides, numerous introductions of various predators were undertaken at a significant cost. For numerous reasons these introductions failed, although the beetle was eventually controlled by pesticides and newly recognized local predators (bluejays) which took advantage of the food resource.

From the above discussion we can see that air, water and mechanical means can act to transport almost anything to various parts of the globe. These transported entities (pesticides, acids, gases, spores, seeds, animals) may then inflict harm on the environment where they land to such a degree that it begs for some regulation to alleviate the problem. Let us next examine the movement of various resources that cannot move internationally by themselves but do move internationally when man so desires.

2.   The Not-So-International Concept

While the first section of Part A concerned natural resources that move around somewhat independently, this section concerns natural resources that are captive and move when and as man chooses to make them move. They exist within one or more sociopolitical units and move and are used within and/or between sociopolitical units in the stream of commerce. These natural resources are either nonrenewable or renewable in some sense but are all essentially finite, in that demand for these resources will eventually outstrip supply. These natural resources currently include some foods and the lands on which they grow, fossil fuels (coal, oil, natural gas), lumber for building, rare and endangered species, iron ore, bauxite for aluminum, gold, copper, uranium, manganese and vanadium.

Since all food is derived from the use of sun energy to grow green plants, we can assume green plants and their products are the actual food supply. In addition to sunlight, green plants require adequate moisture, nutrients and a benign environment in which to grow. Also, plant food crops need to be high yielding per unit area, easily harvested, somewhat nonperishable, highly nutritious and resistant to various pests and climatological uncertainties. Without consideration of the energy inputs necessary to maintain such a system, the most likely botanical candidates for such a crop are annual plants. Therefore, our crop research efforts have proceeded to develop just such "species" for use by sedentary societies. Our research developed "super" species of wheat, oats, barley, corn, lettuce, sunflowers, sorghum and many others. Through the slow process of genetic selection our scientists have "created" high-yield varieties of each species of crop plant. To help ensure that these crops are high yielding, fertilizers are used to make certain that the plants get enough food, while irrigation systems are constructed to maintain a favorable moisture condition. A benign environment for growth is provided by breeding resistance for various maladies into crops as well as inundating the growth area with various biocides to protect the crop from "enemies." The crops were made easy to harvest by planting monocultures and genetically engineering varieties of crops to place the desired harvestable portion of the crop in a uniform place above ground so machines could easily retrieve it. Other geneticists developed more nutritious varieties at the same time that science developed means of transporting these crops to distant points by using various methods to keep the product from perishing (refrigeration, canning, drying). Much of this was accomplished in the north temperate zone. That zone has seasons that are amenable to annual crop production, soils that can withstand (at least currently) the continuous use pattern established and the technology to produce large quantities of food. This procedure is currently being transferred to parts of the southern hemisphere temperate zone. This system has succeeded because of the soil and the technology available, but cannot succeed in the tropical areas of the world mostly because of the poor nutritive quality of the soil in those areas and also because of the lack of seasonality and the problems of inadequate technology or its cost. This does not mean that small-scale agriculture cannot work in the tropics much as the slash and burn nomadic agriculture of the past has functioned, but the large-scale monoculture agriculture of the temperate areas will not function in the tropics. While the more polar regions in each hemisphere have soils capable of sustained production, the lack of a long enough growing season bars their consideration for annual crop production. Therefore, large amounts of food resources and reserves on a continuous basis are captives of temperate zone countries that have the soils and space to support them. When and if the human population reaches a stage at which these captive resources cannot meet the growing demand, the questions of who owns the resource and how it should be internationally apportioned will definitely arise.

Another application of the captive resource concept is the nonrenewable energy supply of the earth. Consider the following hypothetical situation. A group of countries, OPEC, controls much of the world supply of oil. These countries are mostly warmer, more tropical, less able to produce all their required food needs—needs that will become more critical as the population increases and irrigation becomes less "cost" effective. They are also currently striving to become "first" world countries in terms of quality of life for the average citizen. Since these countries hold a captive resource that they do not really need, and since some other countries, the U.S.S.R. or the U.S.A., have food resources that these OPEC countries need or will eventually need, how are the food and the oil supplies allocated? Who owns the oil and what rights does the owner have in reference to who uses the oil? How are these rights protected? In essence, the question is really that if a sociopolitical unit possesses a captive natural resource at a time when the resource is approaching the limits of availability, what peaceful recourse does this sociopolitical unit have to guarantee any rights it has to the resource. Frameworks for addressing such questions will be examined in Section B.

Captive natural resources could also include rare and endangered species of plants and animals or even rare and endangered ecosystems. Let us examine three such instances, one pertaining to an ecosystem, namely the tropical rainforest, another a rare and endangered animal species, and, finally, the idea of endangered species of plants. The tropical rainforests come in many varieties, lowland wet and seasonal to name two. These captive natural resources, taken as a unit, have been recorded as having the greatest diversity of plants and animals of any ecosystem. Looking at this type of system as a whole unit, one discovers that all the nutrients are tied up in plant and animal matter, not in the soil that is nowhere near as rich as the soil in temperate areas. Therefore, if the plants of a tropical rainforest are harvested, there is a very high probability that nothing will grow back for a long time and what does grow back will be a system that does not resemble the system that was harvested. Most of the tropical rainforest of the world exists in countries that are somewhat overpopulated, economically somewhat "deprived" (these are mostly third world countries or recent second world countries), and currently striving to develop a quality of life similar to more affluent countries. As part of this push to become "equal" to more affluent countries, these tropical sociopolitical units are utilizing their natural resources, including the tropical rainforest, to gain a positive or "balanced" balance of trade that increases the quality of life for the country and its inhabitants. Although this captive natural resource, the tropical rainforest ecosystem, may become an extinct system because of the way it is being used by the sociopolitical units controlling its use, it seems somewhat hypocritical for a country that does not possess such a resource but does possess a higher quality of life to seek to have that resource conserved and consequently keep the standard of living of the people of the rainforest country at a lower level.

Before briefly discussing the concept of endangered species of plants and animals, it seems pertinent to examine a few other concepts germane to the situation at hand. It is estimated that 99.9% of all species that have existed are now extinct. It is also surmised that just because a species is rare is no reason to believe that extinction is imminent. Presumably, some species have always been rare, are currently rare, and will continue to be rare. Extinction is a phenomenon associated with a lack of reproductive success, and a plant species or animal species is forever faced with the possibility of extinction. Since most species are captive natural resources, the manipulation of extinction may not rest with the interest group or the country seeking to keep extinction from occurring. And, even if the interest group is able to carry out every aspect of a program to preserve a species, there is no assurance that the effort will be successful. For a species to remain viable it must have certain conditions. The basic problem is that there is never an assurance that these conditions are known or could be met. The grizzly bear and the African elephant are thought to be endangered species. Most efforts to preserve these species pursue the action of establishing a large park area for the species to use for survival. Unfortunately, little attention is paid to some very relevant questions, such as how many individuals of the species are necessary to maintain a viable population and how much space do all of these individuals require. The potential clash with human needs and wants tends toward the avoidance of this question when larger mammals or birds that have very specific habitat requirements are considered.

Plants present an even more difficult realm. It is harder to identify with plants than with animals and therefore harder to justify preservation efforts. One does not know what the exact role of plants is in any environment and a plant may not even be necessary. The problem here, as with all extinctions, is that once the species is gone it cannot be retrieved. Again, does one country have the right or duty to seek the preservation of the plant resources of another country until everyone knows what role each threatened species plays in the grand scheme of things? Is it only then that one can make a "rational" decision about preservation?

The overall problem of the need to regulate captive natural resources, both animate and inanimate, is only beginning to surface as a collective world problem. Before examining some attempts at multilateral solutions to world problems, let us look at a need to regulate even "closer" than the world need—the Canada and United States situation.

3. Canada and the United States

The longest militarily "unprotected" bilateral border in the world lies between Canada and the United States. These two nations have been on quite friendly terms for about two hundred years, sharing numerous categories of natural resources, including, air, water, migratory waterfowl and fish populations. Indeed, early in this century both Canada and the United States recognized the need for some form of bilateral environmental agreement covering the use of critical natural resources that are common to each country and tend to flow between them. We will examine some environmental resource issues that have demonstrated a continued need for some cooperation on their use between Canada and the United States.

Lakes Superior, Huron, Erie, Ontario and Champlain, as well as numerous rivers and streams, are a shared resource between Canada and the United States. We have previously discussed the concept of flow of shared lake water between these countries and the problem of pollutants being carried from the country of origin to the recipient country, where human health problems could result. Now, let us note some other possible water issues between the United States and Canada. The Pelly River flows from Canada to the United States (Yukon Territory to Alaska) while another freshwater river, the Milk, crosses into Canada from the United States and then returns to the United States (Alberta and Montana). Freshwater is a resource that can be used for irrigation and harnessed to produce electricity. While both these uses are increasing in both countries, what will be the outcome when one nation uses so much of the resource that the other country virtually loses the use of the resource? Consider what might happen if Canada decided to dam a river such as the Milk or Pelly for hydroelectric power and irrigation water for cropland to grow more grains. Suppose further that this process reduced the flow of each river to the point that not only were United States fish resources damaged in each river but also the subsequent use of either river by the United States for hydroelectric power or for irrigation water was no longer viable. The United States might have no claim to the water while it is in Canada and Canada may have no duty to let the United States have the water flowing out of Canada. Who owns the water and how could it be apportioned fairly? Consider further the situation if

Canada decides to declare ownership of the waters flowing from Canada and demands a fee from the United States for either the water itself or the electricity produced from the water flow and without such a fee Canada will hold the water captive. Although this situation has not occurred, it could. One should consider whether in the area of internationally shared resources there is a need to anticipate problems and attempt their resolution before a problem becomes so large that a peaceful resolve cannot be reached. This is but one possible scenario in the interaction between two friendly neighbors as their populations and their demands increase.

Geese, ducks and other waterfowl migrate between and among Canada, the United States and countries south of the United States. Not only do these species produce revenue from licenses, ammunition and firearms, but also economic rewards for those who provide other goods and services for individuals who pursue these fowl for sport and as a food resource. Early in this century Canada and the United States recognized the need to control bird takings in their respective countries so that each country could get some of the resource.[5] If the human population continues to expand and use the land for food, houses and recreation, then how will the countries separately and collectively manage their internal resources so that viable populations of each of these migratory waterfowl is available for sport and food resources? Certainly the experience of passenger pigeon extinction and the current threat to migratory landing areas and reproductive areas for the whooping crane should give some indication that a long-term plan is needed to conserve our collective waterfowl resource.

The most heated current environmental issue between Canada and the United States involves the long-range transport of air pollutants from the United States to Canada and vice versa and the subsequent deposition of these air pollutants as metal-containing acidic precipitation. While the uncertainty of the extent of damage to ecosystems in Canada and the United States from acid rain is arguable, there is a certainty that acid rain is falling on parts of Canada and the United States and results from the burning of fossil fuels by stationary and mobile sources in both countries. While each country has amassed tomes of literature documenting the various effects of acid rain containing metals on processes such as seed germination, animal reproduction, and plant uptake of water, there is no clear direct evidence linking acid rain exclusively to the effects noted. As with most large-scale environmental issues, the evidence is circumstantial and

---

5. Migratory Bird Treaty between the United States and Great Britain on behalf of Canada, August 16, 1916. 39 Stat. § 1702 T.S. No. 628.

some evidence indicates "positive" effects under certain circumstances. The real issue in this instance, as with other environmental issues, is not which evidence is right or wrong, legally acceptable or unacceptable, but rather the goal that is being pursued. Approaching large-scale environmental issues such as this within the adversarial process loses the goal amidst a multitude of procedural issues totally removed from the goal. While this approach will produce a "winner," there is really no "winner" when an environment is changed to a state that lowers its capability of use by man as a natural resource. That Canada and the United States recognize this problem is apparent from recent discussions commenced to help resolve the acid rain issue. However, one might pose the question of how these countries will resolve this issue in a binding manner such that little, if any, irreversible or irreparable damage to the environment will occur. Previous attempts to resolve large-scale environmental issues through multilateral or bilateral agreements have met with some success. What we will examine next are some of the means of seeking resolution of international environmental problems and some reasons why these current means of resolution may not be suited for reaching useful environmental outcomes.

B. MECHANISMS FOR REGULATION

In this part of the chapter we will first discuss two broad mechanisms through which sociopolitical units address the need for international law concerning environmental issues. In the third section of this part we will discuss some specific mechanisms by which the United States and Canada have reached agreement regarding environmental issues.

1. Treaties

While one often thinks of treaties as instruments implemented to end a war, there are many other types of treaties enacted between two or more nations, such as those that seek to regulate the use of some natural resource. A treaty has been defined as "A compact made between two or more independent nations with a view to the public welfare. An agreement, league, or contract between two or more nations or sovereigns, formally signed by commissioners properly authorized, and solemnly ratified by the several sovereigns or the supreme power of each state."[6] A

---

6. Black, H. C. *Black's Law Dictionary* (5th ed) (St. Paul, MN: West Publishing, 1979).

treaty between two sovereigns is called a bilateral treaty, while one involving more than two sovereigns is termed a multilateral treaty. Several environmental treaties (conventions, agreements, compacts) to which the United States is a party are mentioned in Table V. The process by which treaties are accepted by the various signatories to them is a function of the government of the country that signs. For example, in the United States, after a treaty is signed by representatives of the President, the treaty must be approved by two-thirds of the United States Senate. In addition, legislation will generally need to be enacted to implement the provisions of the treaty.

As mentioned in part A of this chapter, the Atlantic salmon is a species of fish that migrates among various national waters as well as international waters, and is currently undergoing a major restocking program in the United States and Canada. Because of the importance of this species for food and sport, the United States, Canada, Iceland, Norway, the European Economic Community and Denmark (acting for the Faroe Islands as well as being a member of the EEC) held a full Diplomatic Conference in Reykjavik, Iceland in January of 1982, for the purpose of adopting a Convention on the Conservation of Salmon in the North Atlantic Ocean. This treaty, a multilateral one, is available for signature in Reykjavik and goes into force when four sovereigns have ratified the treaty, provided that two members of each of the three commissions discussed below have also ratified the treaty. Since the method of operation of this treaty is quite similar to that of other fishery treaties, we will examine how this treaty is constructed, as well as what it does and what it does not accomplish, assuming that the treaty comes into force.

Table V.   Examples of Multilateral Treaties to Which
the United States is a Party

1. Agreement on the Conservation of Polar Bears, 13 International Legal Materials 13–18. 1974.

2. Convention for the Conservation of Antarctic Seals, (reprinted 133 *Cong. Rec.* S15606-08. 1976). 1972.

3. Convention for the Establishment of an Inter-American Tropical Tuna Commission. 1 U.S.T. 230. 1949.

4. Convention on International Trade in Endangered Species of Wild Fauna and Flora, 12 International Legal Materials 1085. 1973.

5. Convention on Psychotropic Substances. TIAS 9725. 1980.

6. Implementing Agreement for the Establishment of the Economic Assessment for Coal. TIAS 9775. 1975.

The agreement applies only to Atlantic salmon which migrate outside fishery jurisdictions of coastal sovereigns who are farther north than 36°N latitude. Fishing for Atlantic salmon is prohibited beyond twelve nautical miles of the coast of all ratifying sociopolitical units except off West Greenland and the Faroe Islands, where the limits are set at 40 and 200 nautical miles, respectively. These latter limits are based on tradition. This treaty establishes the North Atlantic Salmon Convention Organization (NASCO), located in Edinburgh, Scotland. A Council of NASCO will act for the exchange of information, in recommending the commencement of scientific research, and in the administration of NASCO. The treaty establishes three commissions within NASCO—the North American Commission, the West Greenland Commission and the North East Atlantic Commission—and decisions of a commission must come from a unanimous vote within the commission.

The North American Commission is composed of Canada and the United States; however, although the European Economic Community is not a member, the EEC may participate and vote, provided that they present proof satisfactory to the commission that they have Atlantic salmon in significant numbers within the jurisdiction of the United States and Canada. The West Greenland Commission is composed of Canada, the United States and the European Economic Community. The North East Atlantic Commission is made up of the European Economic Community, Iceland, Norway and the Faroe Islands (Denmark as the representative). The United States is not a member but may participate under circumstances similar to those imposed upon the EEC by the North American Commission. As one can see, the process is somewhat complicated, but does indulge the idea that "fair" representation on a commission must be given to any party that has Atlantic salmon in the area that is the responsibility of that commission.

Within its jurisdiction, each commission is supposed to provide a forum for members to exchange information and propose regulatory measures for the taking, in commission members' waters, of Atlantic salmon that originated in the rivers of parties to the treaty who are not members of the Commission. Also, commissions are charged with making recommendations to the Council regarding the undertaking of scientific research. There are other provisions within the treaty pertaining only to certain commissions, such as ones for the North American Commission, which specifically applies to the United States. This commission's members will seek to regulate patterns of fishing for Atlantic salmon such that there is no initiation of or increase in the catches of Atlantic salmon originating in the rivers of another party, such as Norway, except with the consent of that party. Members will also seek to minimize by-catches of Atlantic salmon originating in rivers of other members. By-catches are the taking of Atlantic salmon during fishing for cod, herring or some other commercial fish.

As is often the case with treaties, the Salmon Treaty has an "escape" provision that allows a country that is a party to the treaty to not be bound by it. The Salmon Treaty has an objection procedure that allows any member of a commission to lodge an objection within 60 days to any measure proposed within the commission. The measure does not become binding on that member although it is binding on other members who do not lodge an objection. This objection type procedure is the one that often receives criticism from advocates of a strong treaty. In essence, this objection procedure allows any member to not participate in any regulatory scheme for Atlantic salmon fishing if the member does not wish to participate. Besides this criticism, there are other problems presented by multilateral treaties. A participant may wish to withdraw from a treaty, refuse to comply with certain provisions of a treaty or refuse to comply totally. When governments change, the new government might cancel all treaty obligations of any previous government. In short, the effectiveness of a treaty is limited by the bounds of good faith, continuing voluntary cooperation, public opinion, or retaliatory sanctions that one government might impose upon another for noncompliance with a treaty. As more people demand more uses of international natural resources, the lack of enforcement power in any treaty is likely to become a matter of increasing concern.

2. The United Nations

Among international organizations that seek to resolve disputes on major issues including environmental ones, the United Nations is seen by many as having significant potential due to its worldwide recognition and the fact that the General Assembly probably has the most representative membership of world community organizations. There have been treaties under United Nations auspices involving minerals and exploration on the moon[7] as well as the prevention of oil spills on the oceans;[8] however, United Nations representation on the basis of equality of representation by each country of the world is not without its problems. For example, a United Nations conference on the Human Environment in 1972 proclaimed that:

---

7. 227 U.N.T.S. § 3.

8. 610 U.N.T.S. § 205.

> ...the developing countries must direct their efforts to development, bearing in mind their priorities and the need to safeguard and improve the environment. For the same purpose, the industrialized countries should make efforts to reduce the gap between themselves and the developing countries. In the industrialized countries, environmental problems are generally related to industrialization and technological development.[9]

Asking industrialized countries to restrain their technological development while at the same time aiding developing countries to become more like the industrialized countries may be more of a commitment to international environmentalism than is realistic to expect. A legitimate question is thus raised about whether the United Nations can go beyond the realm of being a forum of self-serving discussions and possible information gathering to being a body with real impact on resolving environmental problems.

Another arm of the United Nations that has the potential for acting to resolve environmental problems is the International Court of Justice. There are two paramount questions that must be considered when addressing the concept of the International Court of Justice. The first is the jurisdiction of the Court, and the second deals with the enforcement capabilities of the Court once a decision is rendered. In response to the first question it is useful to examine the position of the United States regarding the jurisdiction of the Court. Pursuant to Article 36(2) of the Statute of the Court,[10] the United States has taken the position of submitting to jurisdiction only with regard to matters that are essentially not within the domestic jurisdiction of the United States as determined by the United States. In essence then, the United States will only participate in proceedings of the International Court of Justice when the United States so wishes. This is not a position necessarily unsupported by rational thought, since it is highly unlikely that any country would willingly allow some body beyond its control to unilaterally determine the fate of said country on any issue of any real significance without that country knowing what the specific issue is in advance of its adjudication, and having an opportunity to decide whether or not it is willing to submit that issue for outside resolution.

---

9. Rüster, B., and B. Simma. *International Protection of the Environment,* Vol. I, (Dobbs Ferry, NY: Oceana Publications, 1975) p. 118.

10. Statute of the International Court of Justice. Documents of the United Nations Conference on International Organization, Vol. 15, p. 355 (1945).

The second question involves enforcement of decisions, a predicament that has led some to question the very existence of something called international "law." Recently, the Scandinavian countries were given some possible recourse to the International Court of Justice regarding the deposition of acid precipitation on them from other European sources such as England and the Rhur Valley.[11] This matter is still under consideration by the Court and no final opinion has been rendered. Even when a decision is rendered there is no assurance that any enforcement will take place. While this outcome apparently begs a solution in enforcement, the real problem may be that a dispute resolution structure that produces a winner and a loser when environmental issues are considered may really produce only losers. A court may not be a suitable forum in which to resolve such issues. What may be preferable might be a forum that offers accommodation of the various interests of the parties by seeking an understanding that we are all in this together.

3.   Canada and the United States

In this section we will discuss bilateral treaties between the United States and Canada. Let us begin by examining the bilateral treaty between Canada and the United States concerning migratory birds — the Convention with Great Britain for the Protection of Migratory Birds.[12] Since this treaty was negotiated in 1918, Great Britain acted on behalf of Canada. The treaty generally establishes three groups of migratory birds: (1) game birds, (2) insectivorous birds, and (3) other nongame birds. For each group a closed season is provided during which no hunting is to occur. Additionally, the length of any hunting season is restricted to less than three and one-half months for game birds. Special exceptions are noted for native populations (Eskimos and Indians) as well as for persons demonstrating a need to take the birds because of injury to agricultural or other interests of a community. After the treaty was approved, the United States had to enact legislation implementing the treaty, hence the Migratory Bird Treaty Act.[13] This statute was challenged in *Missouri v. Holland*.[14] Missouri had contended that migratory birds were owned by the state in which they were found and that the federal government had

---

11. 15 International Legal Materials 1218.

12. 39 Stat. 1702, T.S. No. 628.

13. 16 U.S.C. § 703.

14. 22 U.S. 416 (1920).

no authority to interfere with what was argued to be an exclusively state concern. Had the *Holland* case not involved a treaty, the decision might have rested on whether Congress had the authority to regulate migratory birds pursuant to its power to regulate interstate commerce under the United States Constitution. The Court did not, however, have to deal with Congress' power under the Commerce Clause because there was a treaty involved. Since the treaty was valid, and since a treaty dominates over state laws by virtue of the Supremacy Clause contained in Article VI of the United States Constitution, statutes that implement a treaty are constitutional as a necessary and proper means of executing federal power. The Supreme Court of the United States upheld the statute as being constitutional and denied the claim of Missouri to migratory birds within the jurisdiction. Today it is quite clear that, even without a treaty, protection of wildlife by the federal government is constitutional and the state-ownership theory would not prevail.

A more recent convention between the United States and Canada, and one that has some bearing on current negotiations between these two nations, is known as "The Trail Smelter Case," a product of arbitration resulting from the Convention of April 15, 1935.[15] The basic understanding in this convention was that three jurists of repute were to be selected to "answer" four questions concerning the Trail Smelter, located in Trail, British Columbia, and any interaction of said smelter with property located in the State of Washington. The government of Canada was to select one jurist, the United States another, and both governments would jointly choose a third jurist from a neutral country who would be Chairman. The duly constituted tribunal was to "answer" the following questions:[16]

1. Whether damage caused by the Trail Smelter in the State of Washington has occurred since the first day of January, 1932, and, if so, what indemnity should be paid therefore?
2. In the event of the answer to the first part of the preceding question being in the affirmative, whether the Trail Smelter should be required to refrain from causing damage in the State of Washington in the future and, if so, to what extent?
3. In the light of the answer to the preceding question, what measures or regime, if any, should be adopted or maintained by the Trail Smelter?
4. What indemnity or compensation, if any, should be paid on account of any decision or decisions rendered by the Tribunal pursuant to the next two preceding questions?

---

15. 3 U.N., Reports of International Arbitral Awards 1905 (1949).
16. Ibid.

The tribunal reported its final decisions with respect to these questions on March 11, 1941. During the period between the constitution of the tribunal and the final decision, scientific advisors were appointed by the tribunal and experiments conducted for the tribunal to assist them in reaching a proper decision. In the final analysis, the tribunal "answered" the questions by allowing the claim that the Trail Smelter did cause damage and awarded money to landowners in the State of Washington. They also allowed for the flexible regulation of emissions from the smelter and left open the ability of landowners to collect damages at some future date under suits filed in United States courts. The use of procedures similar in many ways to those used in *Trail Smelter* are currently being discussed by Canada and the United States with respect to a much larger problem. Under a memorandum of intent (8/5/80),[17] Canada and the United States have agreed to negotiate some resolution to the question of acid precipitation by sometime in 1983. That this is a mammoth undertaking is quite evident if one examines the extent of the issue (see Chapter 3). As opposed to *Trail Smelter,* there is not just one industrial operation to question, but rather a whole section of industrial society (stationary sources) as well as transportation (mobile sources). A major issue is also the treatment of each country by the other. In the United States, allowance may be made for adverse effects on Canada under § 115 of the Clean Air Act. However, for a foreign nation to have the right to assert its position under § 115, a foreign nation must give the United States essentially the same rights under its laws. Such does not seem to be the case in Canada regarding air pollution claims by the United States, and this currently appears to be a major obstacle to the resolution of this issue between the parties. While this hurdle will probably be overcome, the final resolution of this issue will most likely be found in some form of mediation/arbitration as was recently discussed by participants at a symposium on this subject.[18]

Probably the longest-standing cooperative agreement between Canada and the United States involving environmental issues is the agreement to form the International Joint Commission in 1909. Originally charged with governing navigation and related activities on the St. Lawrence River and the Great Lakes, the Commission has more recently become involved in evaluating water quality in the lakes and streams of the Great Lakes Basin. While the Commission has made great strides in dealing with major environmental issues confronting the Basin, the lack of

---

17. TIAS 9856 1981.

18. 4 Canada-U.S. Law J. (1981).

enforcement provisions in its charter leaves the Commission somewhat powerless and capable only of making recommendations. While each of the foregoing examples of Canadian-United States attempts at resolving transboundary environmental issues indicates some willingness to co-operate, each has also indicated an unwillingness to vest any large-scale or long-term enforcement power in some international organization. Eventually, this may well become necessary as populations place more constraints on Canadian-United States resources and on the resources of other countries as well.

ADDITIONAL READINGS

Council on Environmental Quality. *The Global 2000 Report to the President* (New York: Penguin Books, 1982).

Council on Environmental Quality. *Environmental Quality* (Washington, DC: U.S. Government Printing Office, 1980).

MacArthur, R. H. *Geographical Ecology* (New York: Harper and Row, 1972).

Miller, G. T., Jr. *Living in the Environment,* 3rd ed. (Belmont, CA: Wadsworth Publishing Co., Inc., 1982).

Van Lier, I. H. *Acid Rain and International Law* (Toronto: Bunsel Environmental Consultants, 1981).

APPENDIX A

CEQ GUIDELINES
FOR ENVIRONMENTAL
IMPACT STATEMENT
40 CFR 1502 et seq.

1502.24   Methodology and scientific accuracy.
1502.25   Environmental review and consultation requirements.

AUTHORITY: NEPA, the Environmental Quality Improvement Act of 1970, as amended (42 U.S.C. 4371 et seq.), Sec. 309 of the Clean Air Act, as amended (42 U.S.C. 7609), and Executive Order 11514 (Mar. 5, 1970, as amended by Executive Order 11991, May 24, 1977).

SOURCE: 43 FR 55994, Nov. 29, 1978, unless otherwise noted.

§ 1502.1   Purpose.

The primary purpose of an environmental impact statement is to serve as an action-forcing device to insure that the policies and goals defined in the Act are infused into the ongoing programs and actions of the Federal Government. It shall provide full and fair discussion of significant environmental impacts and shall inform decisionmakers and the public of the reasonable alternatives which would avoid or minimize adverse impacts or enhance the quality of the human environment. Agencies shall focus on significant environmental issues and alternatives and shall reduce paperwork and the accumulation of extraneous background data. Statements shall be concise, clear, and to the point, and shall be supported by evidence that the agency has made the necessary environmental analyses. An environmental impact statement is more than a disclosure document. It shall be used by Federal officials in conjunction with other relevant material to plan actions and make decisions.

§ 1502.2   Implementation.

To achieve the purposes set forth in § 1502.1 agencies shall prepare environmental impact statements in the following manner:

(a) Environmental impact statements shall be analytic rather than encyclopedic.

(b) Impacts shall be discussed in proportion to their significance. There shall be only brief discussion of other than significant issues. As in a finding of no significant impact, there should be only enough discussion to show why more study is not warranted.

(c) Environmental impact statements shall be kept concise and shall be no longer than absolutely necessary to comply with NEPA and with these regulations. Length should vary first with potential environmental problems and then with project size.

(d) Environmental impact statements shall state how alternatives considered in it and decisions based on it will or will not achieve the requirements of sections 101 and 102(1) of the act and other environmental laws and policies.

(e) The range of alternatives discussed in environmental impact statements shall encompass those to be considered by the ultimate agency decisionmaker.

(f) Agencies shall not commit resources prejudicing selection of alternatives before making a final decision (§ 1506.1).

(g) Environmental impact statements shall serve as the means of assessing the environmental impact of proposed agency actions, rather than justifying decisions already made.

§ 1502.3   Statutory requirements for statements.

As required by sec. 102(2)(C) of NEPA environmental impact statements (§ 1508.11) are to be included in every recommendation or report.
On proposals (§ 1508.23).
For legislation and (§ 1508.17).
Other major federal actions (§ 1508.18).
Significantly (§ 1508.27).
Affecting (§§ 1508.3, 1508.8).
The quality of the human environment (§ 1508.14).

§ 1502.4   Major Federal actions requiring the preparation of environmental impact statements.

(a) Agencies shall make sure the proposal which is the subject of an environmental impact statement is properly defined. Agencies shall use the criteria for scope (§ 1508.25) to determine which proposal(s) shall be the subject of a particular statement. Proposals or parts of proposals which are related to each other closely enough to be, in effect, a single course of action shall be evaluated in a single impact statement.

(b) Environmental impact statements may be prepared, and are sometimes required, for broad Federal actions such as the adoption of new agency programs or regulations (§ 1508.18). Agencies shall prepare statements on broad actions so that they are relevant to policy and are timed to coincide with meaningful points in agency planning and decisionmaking.

(c) When preparing statements on broad actions (including proposals by more than one agency), agencies may find it useful to evaluate the proposal(s) in one of the following ways:

(1) Geographically, including actions occurring in the same general location, such as body of water, region, or metropolitan area.

(2) Generically, including actions which have relevant similarities, such as common timing, impacts, alternatives, methods of implementation, media, or subject matter.

(3) By stage of technological development including federal or fed-

erally assisted research, development or demonstration programs for new technologies which, if applied, could significantly affect the quality of the human environment. Statements shall be prepared on such programs and shall be available before the program has reached a stage of investment or commitment to implementation likely to determine subsequent development or restrict later alternatives.

(d) Agencies shall as appropriate employ scoping (§ 1501.7), tiering (§ 1502.20), and other methods listed in §§ 1500.4 and 1500.5 to relate broad and narrow actions and to avoid duplication and delay.

§ 1502.5   Timing.

An agency shall commence preparation of an environmental impact statement as close as possible to the time the agency is developing or is presented with a proposal (§ 1508.23) so that preparation can be completed in time for the final statement to be included in any recommendation or report on the proposal. The statement shall be prepared early enough so that it can serve practically as an important contribution to the decisionmaking process and will not be used to rationalize or justify decisions already made (§§ 1500.2(c), 1501.2, and 1502.2). For instance:

(a) For projects directly undertaken by Federal agencies the environmental impact statement shall be prepared at the feasibility analysis (go-no go) stage and may be supplemented at a later stage if necessary.

(b) For applications to the agency appropriate environmental assessments or statements shall be commenced no later than immediately after the application is received. Federal agencies are encouraged to begin preparation of such assessments or statements earlier, preferably jointly with applicable State or local agencies.

(c) For adjudication, the final environmental impact statement shall normally precede the final staff recommendation and that portion of the public hearing related to the impact study. In appropriate circumstances the statement may follow preliminary hearings designed to gather information for use in the statements.

(d) For informal rulemaking the draft environmental impact statement shall normally accompany the proposed rule.

§ 1502.6   Interdisciplinary preparation.

Environmental impact statements shall be prepared using an interdisciplinary approach which will insure the integrated use of the natural and social sciences and the environmental design arts (section 102(2)(A) of the Act). The disciplines of the preparers shall be appropriate to the scope and issues identified in the scoping process (§ 1501.7).

§ 1502.7   Page limits.

The text of final environmental impact statements (e.g., paragraphs (d) through (g) of § 1502.10) shall normally be less than 150 pages and for proposals of unusual scope or complexity shall normally be less than 300 pages.

§ 1502.8   Writing.

Environmental impact statements shall be written in plain language and may use appropriate graphics so that decisionmakers and the public can readily understand them. Agencies should employ writers of clear prose or editors to write, review, or edit statements, which will be based upon the analysis and supporting data from the natural and social sciences and the environmental design arts.

§1502.9   Draft, final, and supplemental statements.

Except for proposals for legislation as provided in § 1506.8 environmental impact statements shall be prepared in two stages and may be supplemented.

(a) Draft environmental impact statements shall be prepared in accordance with the scope decided upon in the scoping process. The lead agency shall work with the cooperating agencies and shall obtain comments as required in Part 1503 of this chapter. The draft statement must fulfill and satisfy to the fullest extent possible the requirements established for final statements in section 102(2)(C) of the Act. If a draft statement is so inadequate as to preclude meaningful analysis, the agency shall prepare and circulate a revised draft of the appropriate portion. The agency shall make every effort to disclose and discuss at appropriate points in the draft statement all major points of view on the environmental impacts of the alternatives including the proposed action.

(b) Final environmental impact statements shall respond to comments as required in Part 1503 of this chapter. The agency shall discuss at appropriate points in the final statement any responsible opposing view which was not adequately discussed in the draft statement and shall indicate the agency's response to the issues raised.

(c) Agencies:

(1) Shall prepare supplements to either draft or final environmental impact statements if:

(i) The agency makes substantial changes in the proposed action that are relevant to environmental concerns; or

(ii) There are significant new circumstances or information relevant to environmental concerns and bearing on the proposed action or its impacts.

(2) May also prepare supplements when the agency determines that the purposes of the Act will be furthered by doing so.

(3) Shall adopt procedures for introducing a supplement into its formal administrative record, if such a record exists.

(4) Shall prepare, circulate, and file a supplement to a statement in the same fashion (exclusive of scoping) as a draft and final statement unless alternative procedures are approved by the Council.

§ 1502.10   Recommended format.

Agencies shall use a format for environmental impact statements which will encourage good analysis and clear presentation of the alternatives including the proposed action. The following standard format for environmental impact statements should be followed unless the agency determines that there is a compelling reason to do otherwise:

(a) Cover sheet.

(b) Summary.

(c) Table of contents.

(d) Purpose of and need for action.

(e) Alternatives including proposed action (secs. 102(2)(C)(iii) and 102(2)(E) of the Act).

(f) Affected environment.

(g) Environmental consequences (especially sections 102(2)(C) (i), (ii), (iv), and (v) of the Act).

(h) List of preparers.

(i) List of Agencies, Organizations, and persons to whom copies of the statement are sent.

(j) Index.

(k) Appendices (if any).

If a different format is used, it shall include paragraphs (a), (b), (c), (h), (i), and (j), of this section and shall include the substance of paragraphs (d), (e), (f), (g), and (k) of this section, as further described in §§ 1502.11 –1502.18, in any appropriate format.

§ 1502.11   Cover sheet.

The cover sheet shall not exceed one page. It shall include:

(a) A list of the responsible agencies including the lead agency and any cooperating agencies.

(b) The title of the proposed action that is the subject of the statement (and if appropriate the titles of related cooperating agency actions), together with the State(s) and county(ies) (or other jurisdiction if applicable) where the action is located.

(c) The name, address, and telephone number of the person at the agency who can supply further information.

(d) A designation of the statement as a draft, final, or draft or final supplement.

(e) A one paragraph abstract of the statement.

(f) The date by which comments must be received (computed in cooperation with EPA under § 1506.10).

The information required by this section may be entered on Standard Form 424 (in items 4, 6, 7, 10, and 18).

§ 1502.12 Summary.

Each environmental impact statement shall contain a summary which adequately and accurately summarizes the statement. The summary shall stress the major conclusions, areas of controversy (including issues raised by agencies and the public), and the issues to be resolved (including the choice among alternatives). The summary will normally not exceed 15 pages.

§ 1502.13 Purpose and need.

The statement shall briefly specify the underlying purpose and need to which the agency is responding in proposing the alternatives including the proposed action.

§ 1502.14 Alternatives including the proposed action.

This section is the heart of the environmental impact statement. Based on the information and analysis presented in the sections on the Affected Environment (§ 1502.15) and the Environmental Consequences (§ 1502.16), it should present the environmental impacts of the proposal and the alternatives in comparative form, thus sharply defining the issues and providing a clear basis for choice among options by the decision-maker and the public. In this section agencies shall:

(a) Rigorously explore and objectively evaluate all reasonable alternatives, and for alternatives which were eliminated from detailed study, briefly discuss the reasons for their having been eliminated.

(b) Devote substantial treatment to each alternative considered in detail including the proposed action so that reviewers may evaluate their comparative merits.

(c) Include reasonable alternatives not within the jurisdiction of the lead agency.

(d) Include the alternative of no action.

(e) Identify the agency's preferred alternative or alternatives, if one or more exists, in the draft statement and identify such alternative in the final statement unless another law prohibits the expression of such a preference.

(f) Include appropriate mitigation measures not already included in the proposed action or alternatives.

§ 1502.15   Affected environment.

The environmental impact statement shall succinctly describe the environment of the area(s) to be affected or created by the alternatives under consideration. The descriptions shall be no longer than is necessary to understand the effects of the alternatives. Data and analyses in a statement shall be commensurate with the importance of the impact, with less important material summarized, consolidated, or simply referenced. Agencies shall avoid useless bulk in statements and shall concentrate effort and attention on important issues. Verbose descriptions of the affected environment are themselves no measure of the adequacy of an environmental impact statement.

§ 1502.16   Environmental consequences.

This section forms the scientific and analytic basis for the comparisons under § 1502.14. It shall consolidate the discussions of those elements required by secs. 102(2)(C) (i), (ii), (iv), and (v) of NEPA which are within the scope of the statement and as much of sec. 102(2)(C)(iii) as is necessary to support the comparisons. The discussion will include the environmental impacts of the alternatives including the proposed action, any adverse environmental effects which cannot be avoided should the proposal be implemented, the relationship between short-term uses of man's environment and the maintenance and enhancement of long-term productivity, and any irreversible or irretrievable commitments of resources which would be involved in the proposal should it be implemented. This section should not duplicate discussions in § 1502.14. It shall include discussions of:

(a) Direct effects and their significance (§ 1508.8).

(b) Indirect effects and their significance (§ 1508.8).

(c) Possible conflicts between the proposed action and the objectives of Federal, regional, State, and local (and in the case of a reservation, Indian tribe) land use plans, policies and controls for the area concerned. (See § 1506.2(d).)

(d) The environmental effects of alternatives including the proposed action. The comparisons under § 1502.14 will be based on this discussion.

(e) Energy requirements and conservation potential of various alternatives and mitigation measures.

(f) Natural and depletable resource requirements and conservation potential of various alternatives and mitigation measures.

(g) Urban quality, historic and cultural resources, and the design of the built environment, including the reuse and conservation potential of various alternatives and mitigation measures.

(h) Means to mitigate adverse environmental impacts (if not fully covered under § 1502.14(f)).

[43 FR 55994, Nov. 29, 1978; 44 FR 873, Jan. 3, 1979]

§ 1502.17   List of preparers.

The environmental impact statement shall list the names, together with their qualifications (expertise, experience, professional disciplines), of the persons who were primarily responsible for preparing the environmental impact statement or significant background papers, including basic components of the statement (§§ 1502.6 and 1502.8). Where possible the persons who are responsible for a particular analysis, including analyses in background papers, shall be identified. Normally the list will not exceed two pages.

§ 1502.18 Appendix.

If an agency prepares an appendix to an environmental impact statement the appendix shall:

(a) Consist of material prepared in connection with an environmental impact statement (as distinct from material which is not so prepared and which is incorporated by reference (§ 1502.21)).

(b) Normally consist of material which substantiates any analysis fundamental to the impact statement.

(c) Normally be analytic and relevant to the decision to be made.

(d) Be circulated with the environmental impact statement or be readily available on request.

§ 1502.19   Circulation of the environmental impact statement.

Agencies shall circulate the entire draft and final environmental impact statements except for certain appendices as provided in § 1502.18(d) and unchanged statements as provided in § 1503.4(c). However, if the statement is unusually long, the agency may circulate the summary instead, except that the entire statement shall be furnished to:

(a) Any Federal agency which has jurisdiction by law or special expertise with respect to any environmental impact involved and any appropriate Federal, State or local agency authorized to develop and enforce environmental standards.

(b) The applicant, if any.

(c) Any person, organization, or agency requesting the entire environmental impact statement.

(d) In the case of a final environmental impact statement any person, organization, or agency which submitted substantive comments on the draft.

If the agency circulates the summary and thereafter receives a timely request for the entire statement and for additional time to comment, the time for that requestor only shall be extended by at least 15 days beyond the minimum period.

§ 1502.20   Tiering.

Agencies are encouraged to tier their environmental impact statements to eliminate repetitive discussions of the same issues and to focus on the actual issues ripe for decision at each level of environmental review (§ 1508.28). Whenever a broad environmental impact statement has been prepared (such as a program or policy statement) and a subsequent statement or environmental assessment is then prepared on an action included within the entire program or policy (such as a site specific action) the subsequent statement or environmental assessment need only summarize the issues discussed in the broader statement and incorporate discussions from the broader statement by reference and shall concentrate on the issues specific to the subsequent action. The subsequent document shall state where the earlier document is available. Tiering may also be appropriate for different stages of actions. (Sec. 1508.28).

§ 1502.21   Incorporation by reference.

Agencies shall incorporate material into an environmental impact statement by reference when the effect will be to cut down on bulk without impeding agency and public review of the action. The incorporated material shall be cited in the statement and its content briefly described. No material may be incorporated by reference unless it is reasonably available for inspection by potentially interested persons within the time allowed for comment. Material based on proprietary data which is itself not available for review and comment shall not be incorporated by reference.

§ 1502.22   Incomplete or unavailable information.

When an agency is evaluating significant adverse effects on the human environment in an environmental impact statement and there are gaps in relevant information or scientific uncertainty, the agency shall always make clear that such information is lacking or that uncertainty exists.

(a) If the information relevant to adverse impacts is essential to a reasoned choice among alternatives and is not known and the overall costs of obtaining it are not exorbitant, the agency shall include the information in the environmental impact statement.

(b) If (1) the information relevant to adverse impacts is essential to a reasoned choice among alternatives and is not known and the overall costs of obtaining it are exorbitant or (2) the information relevant to adverse impacts is important to the decision and the means to obtain it are not known (e.g., the means for obtaining it are beyond the state of the art) the agency shall weigh the need for the action against the risk and severity of possible adverse impacts were the action to proceed in the face of uncertainty. If the agency proceeds, it shall include a worst case analysis and an indication of the probability or improbability of its occurrence.

§1502.23   Cost-benefit analysis.

If a cost-benefit analysis relevant to the choice among environmentally different alternatives is being considered for the proposed action, it shall be incorporated by reference or appended to the statement as an aid in evaluating the environmental consequences. To assess the adequacy of compliance with sec. 102(2)(B) of the Act the statement shall, when a cost-benefit analysis is prepared, discuss the relationship between that analysis and any analyses of unquantified environmental impacts, values, and amenities. For purposes of complying with the Act, the weighing of the merits and drawbacks of the various alternatives need not be displayed in a monetary cost-benefit analysis and should not be when there are important qualitative considerations. In any event, an environmental impact statement should at least indicate those considerations, including factors not related to environmental quality, which are likely to be relevant and important to a decision.

§1502.24   Methodology and scientific accuracy.

Agencies shall insure the professional integrity, including scientific integrity, of the discussions and analyses in environmental impact statements. They shall identify any methodologies used and shall make explicit reference by footnote to the scientific and other sources relied upon for conclusions in the statement. An agency may place discussion of methodology in an appendix.

§ 1502.25   Environmental review and consultation requirements.

(a) To the fullest extent possible agencies shall prepare draft environmental impact statements concurrently with and integrated with environmental impact analyses and related surveys and studies required by the Fish and Wildlife Coordination Act (16 U.S.C. 661 et seq.), the National Historical Preservation Act of 1966 (16 U.S.C. 470 et seq.), the Endangered Species Act of 1973 (16 U.S.C. 1531 et seq.), and other environmental review laws and executive orders.

(b) The draft environmental impact statement shall list all Federal permits, licenses, and other entitlements which must be obtained in implementing the proposal. If it is uncertain whether a Federal permit, license, or other entitlement is necessary, the draft environmental impact statement shall so indicate.

APPENDIX B

TABLE OF CONTENTS AND SUMMARY AND CONCLUSIONS FOR FINAL ENVIRONMENTAL STATEMENT ON THE BISON BASIN PROJECT*

CONTENTS

---

*Licensing of a uranium mine and recovery plant in Fremont County, Wyoming. United States Nuclear Regulatory Commission, April 1981.

255

SUMMARY AND CONCLUSIONS

This Final Environmental Statement (FES) was prepared under the direction of the staff of the U.S. Nuclear Regulatory Commission (NRC) and issued by the Commission's Office of Nuclear Material Safety and Safeguards.

1. This action is administrative.

2. After an assessment of concerns, alternatives, and the addition of license conditions as discussed below, the proposed action is the issuance of a combined Source and Byproduct Material License to Ogle Petroleum, Inc., which, on August 10, 1979, applied to the NRC for an NRC Source Material License to construct and operate in Fremont County, Wyoming, an in situ leach uranium mine and recovery plant designed to produce 4.54×10^5 kg (1.0×10^6 lb) of U_3O_8 at a rate of about 1.8×10^5 kg/year (4.0×10^5 lb/year).

The total project site area consists of about 308 ha (761 acres) located approximately 80 km by air (50 miles) south of Riverton and about 48 km by air (30 miles) southwest of Jeffrey City, Wyoming.

The applicant proposes to mine, in situ, uranium ore contained in the Laney member of the Green River formation, using sodium carbonate/bicarbonate solution and an oxidizing agent injected and recovered through a complex of well patterns. Each well pattern will consist of six injection wells surrounding a central production well. Each production well will be pumped at a rate between 34 to 45 liters/min (9 to 12 gpm), and enough patterns will be operated to supply up to 4550 liters/min (1200 gpm) of uranium-containing solution to an onsite extraction and concentrating plant producing the final product (U_3O_8). About 16 ha (40 acres) are proposed for actual mining. A total of 5.4 ha (13.5 acres) will be excavated for building and equipment foundations and for evaporation ponds. An additional 17 ha (43 acres) will undergo surface disturbance during well-field development and operation.

The applicant proposes to restore the groundwater system to its former potential use (and as close to baselines as reasonably achievable) after mining is complete by recycling mined formation water through a reverse osmosis cleanup system and back into the formation until acceptable water quality has been reached. The above-ground solid wastes produced by the mining process are defined as byproduct material by the Uranium Mill Tailings Radiation Control Act; they will be removed to a licensed disposal site.

3. Concerns receiving special attention are listed in detail in Section 1.5, Results of the Scoping Process. These concerns include issues for which analysis and assessment were necessary. The major categories of concern were:

    a. the effect of the mining operation on both availability and quality of groundwater;

    b. the impact of the mining operation, roads, fences, and employee activities on wildlife, recreational activities, and archaeological and paleontological resources;

    c. the management of waste disposal facilities during operation, with particular emphasis on the evaporation ponds, groundwater restoration, final disposal of project wastes, and surface reclamation;

    d. the definition of the geology of the ore body to ensure that it is adequately confined above and below, by rock layers of low permeability with continuous properties that will prevent vertical movement;

    e. the details of well completion, testing, and operating and monitoring procedures, to prevent or detect excursions; and

    f. the socioeconomic effects of the project.

4. Including the proposed action, the following alternatives were considered:

    a. Alternative of no licensing action: If a source material license was not issued, the applicant could open pit or deep mine the ore body and have the ore processed at an existing mill. The staff considers these alternatives neither economically viable nor in the public interest.

    b. Alternative energy sources: Fossil and nuclear fuels were compared; and solar, geothermal, synthetic fuels, and energy conservation were considered. The staff conclusion is that effective implementation of all these options will not preclude the need for additional uranium production.

c. Alternatives if uranium ore is mined and refined on the site: The staff considered the following:

- mining alternatives,
- processing alternatives,
- mining and milling waste disposal alternatives,
- uranium extraction facility siting alternatives,
- alternative of processing in an existing mill, and
- alternatives specific to in situ leaching, including alternative lixiviants and oxidants, and alternative aquifer restoration methods.

The staff evaluated the applicant's proposed operation in relationship to the above alternatives. Staff conclusions were as follows:

a. Conventional mining and milling are not economically viable for recovering uranium from this ore body at present or in the foreseeable future, as discussed in Sect. 2.3.3.

b. Based on all of the hydrogeologic data presented to date on the project site, the geological and hydrological conditions appear to meet the criteria for in situ leaching, as specified in Sect. 2.3.3.2, including vertical confinement of the fluid to the ore zone by lithologic zones of low permeability. Acquisition of additional hydrogeological data in units 2, 3, and 4 is required prior to authorized well-field expansion into each unit.

c. The applicant has provided aquifer restoration data from the pilot project indicating the ore-bearing aquifer can be restored to a condition of potential use equal to or better than its present condition as established by baseline measurements.

d. The applicant's proposed operation will result in less solid wastes for disposal than any other alternative.

e. The applicant's proposed operation will minimize groundwater usage.

The staff concurs with the applicant's choice of in situ leaching to extract uranium at this site.

5. From the analysis and evaluations made in this Statement, it is proposed that the Source Material License contain at least the following conditions:

a. The applicant shall implement the monitoring programs described in Sect. 4.4, including the associated reporting requirements.

b. The residual above-ground solid radioactive wastes from solution mining activities shall be finally disposed of off-site at a licensed disposal facility as described in Sect. 4.6.3.

c. Prior to use in conducting mining operations, the applicant shall verify well integrity by conducting packer tests in accordance with a test procedure which shall be approved by the NRC, by license amendment. During mining operations, well-head injection pressures shall be monitored and shall not exceed the pressures to which the individual wells were previously tested. Individual well-head injection pressure shall in no case exceed 0.63 psi per foot of well depth.

d. The applicant shall not use any lixiviant other than sodium bicarbonate/carbonate, and shall not use any oxidant other than oxygen and/or hydrogen peroxide, without prior NRC review and approval by license amendment.

e. The applicant shall conduct two additional aquifer pump tests in mining unit 1, to demonstrate confinement of the ore zone aquifer, as described in Section 3.6.2.2. The applicant shall submit reports on these tests for NRC review, and shall obtain NRC approval by license amendment prior to mining in unit 1.

f. The applicant shall not initiate construction of any evaporation ponds until the NRC has reviewed, and approved by license amendment, complete engineering, design, and construction plan specifications and details for all embankments, leak detection systems, and liners.

g. The applicant shall obtain NRC approval, by license amendment, of a quality assurance program to assure the validity of all environmental sample analysis, in accordance with the recommendations and criteria contained in U.S. NRC Regulatory Guide 4.15, prior to mining.

h. The applicant shall implement a groundwater restoration program on mined-out well field areas, which shall include restoration of all mining-affected groundwater, in accordance with the general plan described in Sect. 2.3.10.3 and the criteria discussed in Sect. 4.3.1. Active restoration of each mined-out well field unit shall commence as mining begins in another unit, or as soon thereafter as practicable, and in no case shall commence later than six months following the cessation of mining. Restoration shall be performed without the injection into groundwater of any chemicals to assist in restoration, unless otherwise authorized by the NRC by license amendment.

i. The applicant shall submit complete design and performance specifications for the reverse osmosis water purification system(s) to be used during groundwater restoration activities, for NRC review and approval of use by license amendment.

j. The applicant shall not mine in other than mining units 1 and 2 until the ability to achieve restoration in mining unit 1 has been favorably determined, and the NRC has concurred with such determination by license amendment.

k. The applicant shall obtain NRC approval, by license amendment, for the specific number and location of all monitoring and restoration sampling wells for mining unit 2 and subsequent mining units, prior to well drilling.

l. The applicant shall provide additional hydrogeologic information as specified in Sects. 3.6.2.3, 3.7.1.3, and 4.2, for NRC review and approval, by license amendment, prior to mining beyond mining unit 1.

m. The applicant shall immediately notify the NRC, by telephone and telegraph, of any failure of any evaporation pond, pipeline, or any other fluid or material conduit or storage facility which results in the release of radioactive materials to unrestricted or restricted areas, and/or of any unusual conditions which if not corrected could lead to such a failure. Such notification shall be followed, within seven days, by submittal of a written report detailing the conditions leading to the failure or potential failure, corrective actions taken, and results obtained.

n. The applicant shall establish a program that shall include written procedures and instructions to control all process activities and all environmental monitoring and control programs.

o. Before engaging in any activity not evaluated by the NRC staff, the applicant shall prepare and record an environmental evaluation of such activity. When the evaluation indicates that such activity may result in a significant adverse environmental impact that was not evaluated or that is significantly greater than that evaluated in this Environmental Statement, the applicant shall provide a written evaluation of such activities and obtain prior approval of NRC.

p. If unexpected harmful effects or evidence of irreversible damage not otherwise identified in this statement are detected during construction or operations, the applicant shall provide to NRC an acceptable analysis of the problem and a plan of action to eliminate or significantly reduce the harmful effects or damage.

q. Prior to disturbing any land, including topsoil removal, outside the area previously surveyed as indicated in Attachment 1 of Ogle's July 14, 1978, submittal to the NRC (Docket No. 40-8693), including site decommissioning, the licensee shall have an archaecological survey of the areas performed and shall submit the results to the NRC for review. The licensee shall not proceed with any land disturbance until the NRC has evaluated the report and given the applicant approval to proceed.

r. The applicant shall notify the NRC and the Wyoming State Archaeologist when any artifacts of earlier culture are encountered during site preparations or operations. Further activity in the immediate area shall be deferred until a determination of their significance by the NRC is completed. Mitigating measures, if needed to preserve them, shall be proposed by the licensee.

s. The applicant shall provide surety that funds will be available for aquifer restoration, surface reclamation, decommissioning, and final waste disposal, and shall obtain NRC approval thereof, by license amendment, prior to commencing mining operations.

6. With these specific license conditions, and conformity with other local, state, and federal regulations, the expected environmental consequences are the following:

a. Total suspended particulates (mostly wind erosion and dust) would not likely exceed State or Federal standards and would not be expected to harm living plants, animals, or humans.

b. The project site and all surrounding land are used for grazing. Wildlife at the site includes antelope, sage grouse, rabbits, and coyotes. Evaporation ponds and building sites will occupy fewer than 5.4 ha (13.5 acres), and areas fenced to exclude wildlife and livestock cover a 5-ha (12-acre) area. This amount of land use for five years will have an insignificant effect on land use. Well-field development, operation, and restoration on an additional 17 ha

(43 acres) will also have no appreciable effect on land use. All disturbed areas will be reclaimed after project termination to original use condition or better.

c.   The total use of groundwater from the Laney member of the Green River formation is estimated to be about 2.96×10^5 m^3 (240 acre-ft) over the five-year project lifetime. Groundwater in the mining zone will temporarily be degraded during operation of the well fields. Restoration is required to return this water to the condition consistent with premining potential use or better. Total groundwater use will not affect local or regional supplies.

Surface water may be temporarily affected by increased sediment loading. Impacts on surface water quality will be minor during construction and operation of the project. The single exception would be from accidental failure of an evaporation pond embankment. These embankments will be constructed to the engineering standards of NRC Regulatory Guide 3.11, and total failure is not considered credible.

d.   There will be a temporary loss of sagebrush and cushion plant communities. No unique plant communities or endangered plant species will be affected. No endangered or threatened animal species are involved. Wildlife mortality from vehicle collisions should be minimal because of the unrestricted visibility. The scarcity of aquatic life in the intermittent playas and drainage channels near the site preclude significant impacts for aquatic biota. Because no liquid effluents will be discharged during normal operation, significant impacts on aquatic biota are possible only under unlikely accident scenarios.

e.   The radiation dose to the nearest members of the general public will be small in comparison to natural background as shown in the table below.

f.   The proposed project will not produce any significant socioeconomic impact on the local area because of the small number of employees.

g.   The staff opinion is that any potential accident postulated for this project will not result in significant permanent damage to the environment.

7.   The position of the NRC is as follows:

Solution mining (in situ leaching) of uranium is a developing technology. Uncertainties regarding environmental impacts, particularly with respect to groundwater contamination and the effectiveness of groundwater restoration techniques, have been recognized. The applicant has provided initial evidence that groundwater restoration can be achieved from the pilot-scale test program (Sect. 4.3.2). Furthermore, the scope of the proposed project is sufficiently limited in size to enable continued development of solution mining technology without significant environmental risk.

The position of the NRC is that after weighing the environmental, economic, technical, and other benefits of the Bison Basin solution mining project against environmental and other costs and considering available alternatives, the action called for under the National Environmental Policy Act of 1969 (NEPA) and 10 CFR Part 51 is the issuance of a combined Source and Byproduct Material License to the applicant, subject to at least the conditions presented above.

Dose Commitments to Individuals from Radioactive Releases from the Bison Basin Project

Location	Exposure Pathway	Dose (millirems)[a]			
		Total Body	Bone	Lung	Bronchial Epithelium[b]
Nearest residence	Inhalation	1.9E-2[c]	1.8E-2	1.2	1.7
(11 km ENE)	Immersion in air	8.8E-3	1.0E-2	8.4E-3	
	Ground surface	2.8E-3	3.3E-3	2.9E-3	
	Total	3.1E-2	3.1E-2	1.2	
Sweetwater Station	Inhalation	5.0E-3	4.5E-3	3.1E-1	3.1E-1
(30 km NNE)	Immersion in air	3.3E-3	3.8E-3	3.1E-3	
	Ground surface	1.0E-3	1.1E-3	1.0E-3	
	Total	9.3E-3	9.4E-3	3.1E-1	
Natural background	Total	1.44E+2	1.2E+2	1.8E+2	5.0E+2[d]

[a]1 millirem = 0.01 millisievert.
[b]Doses to the bronchial epithelium result from the inhalation of short-lived radioactive daughters of ^{222}Rn.
[c]Read as 1.9×10^{-2}.
[d]Dose from ^{222}Rn.

APPENDIX C

STATUTE AND REGULATIONS FOR MOTOR CARRIER NOISE EMISSION STANDARDS. STATUTE: NOISE CONTROL ACT 42 U.S.C.S. § 4917 REGULATIONS: 40 CFR, PART 202

§ 4917. Motor carrier noise emission standards

(a) Regulations; standards; consultation with Secretary of Transportation.

(1) Within nine months after the date of enactment of this Act [enacted Oct. 27, 1972], the Administrator shall publish proposed noise emission regulations for motor carriers engaged in interstate commerce. Such proposed regulations shall include noise emission standards setting such limits on noise emissions resulting from operation of motor carriers engaged in interstate commerce which reflect the degree of noise reduction achievable through the application of the best available technology, taking into account the cost of compliance. These regulations shall be in addition to any regulations that may be proposed under section 6 of this Act [42 USCS § 4905].

(2) Within ninety days after the publication of such regulations as may be proposed under paragraph (1) of this subsection, and subject to the provisions of section 16 of this Act [42 USCS § 4915], the Administrator shall promulgate final regulations. Such regulations may be revised from time to time, in accordance with this subsection.

(3) Any standard or regulation, or revision thereof, proposed under this subsection shall be promulgated only after consultation with the Secretary of Transportation in order to assure appropriate consideration for safety and technological availability.

(4) Any regulation or revision thereof promulgated under this sub-section shall take effect after such period as the Administrator finds necessary, after consultation with the Secretary of Transportation, to permit the development and application of the requisite technology, giving appropriate consideration to the cost of compliance within such period.

(b) Regulations to insure compliance with noise emission standards. The Secretary of Transportation, after consultation with the Administrator shall promulgate regulations to insure compliance with all standards promulgated by the Administrator under this section. The Secretary of Transportation shall carry out such regulations through the use of his powers and duties of enforcement and inspection authorized by the Interstate Commerce Act and the Department of Transportation Act. Regulations promulgated under this section shall be subject to the pro-visions of sections 10, 11, 12, and 16 of this Act [42 USCS §§ 4909–4911, 4915].

(c) State and local standards and controls. (1) Subject to paragraph (2) of this subsection but notwithstanding any other provision of this Act, after the effective date of a regulation under this section appli-cable to noise emissions resulting from the operation of any motor carrier engaged in interstate commerce, no State or political sub-division thereof may adopt or enforce any standard applicable to the same operation of such motor carrier, unless such standard is identi-cal to a standard applicable to noise emissions resulting from such operation prescribed by any regulation under this section.

(2) Nothing in this section shall diminish or enhance the rights of any State or political subdivision thereof to establish and enforce stan-dards of controls on levels of environmental noise, or to control, license, regulate, or restrict the use, operation, or movement of any product if the Administrator, after consultation with the Secretary of Transportation, determines that such standard, control, license, regulation, or restriction is necessitated by special local conditions and is not in conflict with regulations promulgated under this section.

(d) Definitions. For purposes of this section, the term "motor carrier" includes a common carrier by motor vehicle, a contract carrier by motor vehicle, and a private carrier of property by motor vehicle as those terms are defined by paragraphs (14), (15), and (17) of section 203(a) of the Interstate Commerce Act (49 U.S.C. 303(a)).
(Oct. 27, 1972, P. L. 92-574, § 18, 86 Stat. 1249.)

Title 40 — Protection of Environment

PART 202 — MOTOR CARRIERS ENGAGED IN INTERSTATE COMMERCE

Subpart A — General Provisions

Sec.
202.10   Definitions.
202.11   Effective date.
202.12   Applicability.

Subpart B — Interstate Motor Carrier Operations Standards

202.20   Standards for highway operations.
202.21   Standard for operation under stationary test.
202.22   Visual exhaust system inspection.
202.23   Visual tire inspection.

AUTHORITY: Section 18, 36 Stat. 1249, 42 U.S.C. 4917(a).

SOURCE: 39 FR 38215, Oct 29, 1974, unless otherwise noted.

Subpart A — General Provisions

§ 202.10   Definitions.

As used in this part, all terms not defined herein shall have the meaning given them in the Act:

(a) "Act" means the Noise Control Act of 1972 (Pub.L. 92-574, 86 Stat. 1234)

(b) "Common carrier by motor vehicle" means any person who holds himself out to the general public to engage in the transportation by motor vehicle in interstate or foreign commerce of passengers or property or any class or classes thereof for compensation, whether over regular or irregular routes.

(c) "Contract carrier by motor vehicle" means any person who engages in transportation by motor vehicle of passengers or property in interstate or foreign commerce for compensation (other than transportation referred to in paragraph (b) of this section) under continuing contracts with one person or a limited number of persons either (1) for the furnishing of transportation services through the assignment of motor vehicles for a continuing period of time to the exclusive use of each person served or (2) for the furnishing of transportation services designed to meet the distinct need of each individual customer.

(d) "Cutout or by-pass or similar devices" means devices which vary the exhaust system gas flow so as to discharge the exhaust gas and acoustic energy to the atmosphere without passing through the entire length of the exhaust system, including all exhaust system sound attenuation components.

(e) "dB(A)" means the standard abbreviation for A-weighted sound level in decibels.

(f) "Exhaust system" means the system comprised of a combination of components which provides for enclosed flow of exhaust gas from engine parts to the atmosphere.

(g) "Fast meter response" means that the fast dynamic response of the sound level meter shall be used. The fast dynamic response shall comply with the meter dynamic characteristics in paragraph 5.3 of the American National Standard Specification for Sound Level Meters, ANSI S1. 4-1971. This publication is available from the American National Standards Institute, Inc., 1430 Broadway, New York, New York 10018.

(h) "Gross Vehicle Weight Rating" (GVWR) means the value specified by the manufacturer as the loaded weight of a single vehicle.

(i) "Gross Combination Weight Rating" (GCWR) means the value specified by the manufacturer as the loaded weight of a combination vehicle.

(j) "Highway" means the streets, roads, and public ways in any State.

(k) "Interstate commerce" means the commerce between any place in a State and any place in another State or between places in the same State through another State, whether such commerce moves wholly by motor vehicle or partly by motor vehicle and partly by rail, express, water or air. This definition of "interstate commerce" for purposes of these regulations is the same as the definition of "interstate commerce" in section 203(a) of the Interstate Commerce Act. [49 U.S.C. Section 303(a)]

(l) "Motor carrier" means a common carrier by motor vehicle, a contract carrier by motor vehicle, or a private carrier of property by motor vehicle as those terms are defined by paragraphs (14), (15), and (17) of section 203(a) of the Interstate Commerce Act [49 U.S.C. 303(a)].

(m) "Motor vehicle" means any vehicle, machine, tractor, trailer, or semitrailer propelled or drawn by mechanical power and used upon the highways in the transportation of passengers or property, or any combination thereof, but does not include any vehicle, locomotive, or car operated exclusively on a rail or rails.

(n) "Muffler" means a device for abating the sound of escaping gases of an internal combustion engine.

(o) "Open site" means an area that is essentially free of large sound-reflecting objects, such as barriers, walls, board fences, signboards, parked vehicles, bridges, or buildings.

(p) "Private carrier of property by motor vehicle" means any person not included in terms "common carrier by motor vehicle" or "contract carrier by motor vehicle", who or which transports in interstate or foreign commerce by motor vehicle property of which such person is the owner, lessee, or bailee, when such transportation is for sale, lease, rent or bailment, or in furtherance of any commercial enterprise.

(q) "Sound level" means the quantity in decibels measured by a sound level meter satisfying the requirements of American National Standards Specification for Sound Level Meters S1.4-1971. This publication is available from the American National Standards Institute, Inc., 1430 Broadway, New York, New York 10018. Sound level is the frequency-weighted sound pressure level obtained with the standardized dynamic characteristic "fast" or "slow" and weighting A, B, or C; unless indicated otherwise, the A-weighting is understood.

§ 202.11 Effective date.

The provisions of Subpart B shall become effective October 15, 1975.

§202.12 Applicability.

(a) The provisions of Subpart B apply to all motor carriers engaged in interstate commerce.

(b) The provisions of Subpart B apply only to those motor vehicles of such motor carriers which have a gross vehicle weight rating or gross combination weight rating in excess of 10,000 pounds, and only when such motor vehicles are operating under the conditions specified in Subpart B.

(c) Except as provided in paragraphs (d) and (e) of this section, the provisions of Subpart B apply to the total sound produced by such motor vehicles when operating under such conditions, including the sound produced by auxiliary equipment mounted on such motor vehicles.

(d) The provisions of Subpart B do not apply to auxiliary equipment which is normally operated only when the transporting vehicle is stationary or is moving at a speed of 5 miles per hour or less. Examples of such equipment include, but are not limited to, cranes, asphalt spreaders, ditch diggers, liquid or slurry pumps, air compressors, welders, and trash compactors.

(e) The provisions of Subpart B do not apply to warning devices, such as horns and sirens; or to emergency equipment and vehicles such as fire engines, ambulances, police vans, and rescue vans, when responding to emergency calls; or to snow plows when in operation.

Subpart B—Interstate Motor Carrier Operations Standards

§ 202.20   Standards for highway operations.

No motor carrier subject to these regulations shall operate any motor vehicle of a type to which this regulation is applicable which at any time or under any condition of highway trade, load, acceleration or deceleration generates a sound level in excess of 86dB(A) measured on an open site with fast meter response at 50 feet from the centerline of lane of travel on highways with speed limits of 35 MPH or less; or 90 dB(A) measured on an open site with fast meter response at 50 feet from the centerline of lane of travel on highways with speed limits of more than 35 MPH.

§ 202.21   Standard for operation under stationary test.

No motor carrier subject to these regulations shall operate any motor vehicle of a type to which this regulation is applicable which generates a sound level in excess of 88 dB(A) measured on an open site with fast meter response at 50 feet from the longitudinal centerline of the vehicle, when its engine is accelerated from idle to wide open throttle to governed speed with the vehicle stationary, transmission in neutral, and clutch engaged. This § 202.21 shall not apply to any vehicle which is not equipped with an engine speed governor.

§ 202.22   Visual exhaust system inspection.

No motor carrier subject to these regulations shall operate any motor vehicle of a type to which this regulation is applicable unless the exhaust system of such vehicle is (a) free from defects which affect sound reduction; (b) equipped with a muffler or other noise dissipative device; and (c) not equipped with any cut-out, bypass, or similar device.

§ 202.23   Visual tire inspection.

No motor carrier subject to these regulations shall at any time operate any motor vehicle of a type to which this regulation is applicable on a tire or tires having a tread pattern which as originally manufactured, or as newly retreaded, is composed primarily of cavities in the tread (excluding sipes and local chunking) which are not vented by grooves to the tire shoulder or circumferentially to each other around the tire. This § 202.23

shall not apply to any motor vehicle which is demonstrated by the motor carrier which operates it to be in compliance with the noise emission standard specified for operations on highways with speed limits of more than 35 MPH in § 202.20 of this Subpart B, if the demonstration is conducted at the highway speed limit in effect at the inspection location, or, if speed is unlimited, the demonstration is conducted at a speed of 65 MPH.

PORTIONS OF A DISCHARGE PERMIT
FORM FOR WATER POLLUTANTS

Permit No. _____
File No. _____

AGENCY OF ENVIRONMENTAL CONSERVATION
 NPDES Permits Section State Office Bldg.
 MONTPELIER, VERMONT 05602

Application Number: _____

Name of Applicant: _____

_____

Expiration Date: _____

DISCHARGE PERMIT

In reference to the above application for a permit to discharge in compliance with the provisions of the Vermont Water Pollution Control Act as amended (hereinafter referred to as the "Act"), _____

_____

(hereinafter referred to as the "permittee") is authorized by the Secretary, Agency of Environmental Conservation, Montpelier, Vermont, to discharge from _____

_____

to _____
in accordance with the following general and special conditions:

I. SPECIAL CONDITIONS

A. *Effluent Limits*

1. Until _____, the permittee is authorized to discharge
   from_____
   to the _____
   an effluent whose characteristics shall not exceed the values listed
   below.

Effluent Characteristic	kg/day (lbs/day) Monthly Average	Weekly Average	Maximum Day	(specify units) Monthly Average	Weekly Average	Maximum Day
Flow, cu. M/day (MGD)	**	**	**	(1)	**	**
Biochemical Oxygen Demand, 5-day, 20°C						
Total Suspended Solids						
Settleable Solids						
Total Coliform Bacteria						

(1)   Annual Average

2. From _____ until _____, the permittee
   is authorized to discharge from _____
   to the _____
   an effluent whose characteristics shall not exceed the values listed
   below.

Effluent Characteristic	kg/day (lbs/day) Monthly Average	Weekly Average	Maximum Day	(specify units) Monthly Average	Weekly Average	Maximum Day
Flow, cu. M/day (MGD)	**	**	**	(1)	**	**
Biochemical Oxygen Demand, 5-day, 20°C						
Total Suspended Solids						
Settleable Solids						
Total Coliform Bacteria						

(1)   Annual Average

   a. The pH of the effluent shall not be less than 6.0 nor greater than 8.5
at any time.

b. The chlorine residual shall not be greater than 4.0 MG/L. The total chlorine residual of the effluent shall not result in any demonstrable harm to aquatic life or violate any water quality standard which has been or may be promulgated. Upon promulgation of any such standard, this permit shall be reviewed or amended in accordance with such standard, and the permittee shall be so notified.

c. The effluent shall contain neither a visible oil sheen, foam, nor floating solids at any time.

d. The discharge shall not cause visible discoloration of the receiving waters.

e. The discharge shall not cause a violation of the water quality standards of the receiving waters.

f. The monthly average concentrations of BOD and total suspended solids in the discharge shall not exceed 15 percent of the monthly average concentrations of BOD and total suspended solids in the influent into the permittee's wastewater treatment facilities. For the purposes of determining whether the permittee is in compliance with this condition, samples from the discharge and the influent shall be taken with appropriate allowance for detention times.

g. When the effluent discharged for a period of 90 consecutive days exceeds 80 percent of the permitted flow limitation, the permittee shall submit to the permitting authority projected loadings and a program for maintaining satisfactory treatment levels consistent with approved water quality management plans.

h. Maintenance activities or emergencies which cause reductions of effluent quality below effluent limits as specified herein shall be considered a violation of the conditions of the permit, unless the permittee shall immediately apply for an emergency pollution permit under the provisions of 10 VSA Chapter 47, Subchapter 1, Section 1265 (f). Application shall be made to the Secretary of the Environmental Conservation Agency, State Office Building, Montpelier, Vermont 05602.

i. Any action on the part of the Agency of Environmental Conservation in reviewing, commenting upon or approving plans and specifications for the construction of wastewater treatment facilities shall not relieve the permittee from its responsibility to achieve effluent limitations set forth in this permit and shall not constitute a waiver of, or act of estoppel against any remedy available to the Agency, the State of Vermont or the federal government for failure to meet any requirement set forth in this permit or imposed by state or federal law.

II. GENERAL CONDITIONS

A. All discharges authorized herein shall be consistent with the terms and conditions of this permit. The discharge of any pollutant more frequently than, or at a level in excess of, that identified and authorized by this permit shall constitute a violation of the terms and conditions of this permit. Such a violation may result in the imposition of civil and/or criminal penalties as provided for in Section 1274 and 1275 of the Act. Facility modifications, additions and/or expansions that increase the plant capacity must be reported to the permitting authority and this permit then modified or reissued to reflect such changes. The permittee shall provide notice to the Secretary of the following:
    1. any new introduction of pollutants into the treatment works from a source which would be a new source as defined in Section 306 of the Federal Water Pollution Control Act if such source were discharging pollutants;
    2. except as to such categories and classes of point sources or discharges specified by the Secretary, any new introduction of pollutants into the treatment works from a source which would be subject to Section 301 of the Federal Water Pollution Control Act if such source were discharging pollutants, and
    3. any substantial change in volume or character of pollutants being introduced into the treatment works by a source introducing pollutants into such works at the time of issuance of the permit.
    The notice shall include:
    1. the quality and quantity of the discharge to be introduced into the system, and
    2. the anticipated impact of such change in the quality or quantity of the effluent to be discharged from the permitted facility.
B. After notice and opportunity for a hearing, this permit may be modified, suspended, or revoked in whole or in part during its term for cause including, but not limited to, the following:
    1. violation of any terms or conditions of this permit;
    2. obtaining this permit by misrepresentation or failure to disclose fully all relevant facts; or
    3. a change in any condition that requires either a temporary or permanent reduction or elimination of the permitted discharge.

INDEX